INDIA BOOKVARSITY
LOTUS CHOICES
Editor: Mahendra Kulasrestha

India in China

The Gift of Buddha

By
Samuel Beal

**Tallest Buddha Statue in the World
Sechuan, China.**

A positive
chapter of
world history

Dedicated to
Ming Ti
and
Kablai Khan

Lotus
PRESS

4735/22, Prakash Deep Building,
Ansari Road, Darya Ganj,
New Delhi-110002

INDIA IN CHINA

THE GIFT OF BUDDHA

Authored and Translated from the Chinese by SAMUEL BEAL

The story of the spread of India's Buddhism in China, and the unusual pilgrimages of Fa Hian and Huen Tsang in search of scriptures to India

Sources: **(1) Buddhism in China,**
by Rev. S. Beal, Society for Promoting
Christian Knowledge, London, 1884;
(2) Travels of Fah-Hian and Sung-Yun,
Tr. by Samuel Beal, Trubner and Co.,
London, 1869;
(3) The Life of Hiuen-Tsiang,
by Shaman Hwui Li, Tr. by Samuel Beal,
Kegan Paul, Trench, Trubner and Co. London, 1911.

INDIA IN CHINA: The Gift of Buddha

New First Edition—2012
ISBN: 978-81-8382-291-6(H/B)

Published by:
Lotus Press Publishers & Distributors
Unit No. 220, Second Floor, 4735/22, Prakash Deep Building,
Ansari Road, Darya Ganj, New Delhi-10002
Ph.: 011-23280047, 32903912 • Mob.: 098118-38000
E-mail: lotus_press@sify.com

Printed at: **Concept Imprint,** Delhi

Buddha from Java

Other Works
in the Buddha Pitaka Series
by the same publisher

— • —

The Golden Book of Buddhism

The Life of Lord Buddha: Asvaghosa's Buddha Charita

The Discourses of Lord Buddha
Sutta Nipata

The Last Days of Lord Buddha
Mahaparinibbana Sutta

The Dhammapada

The Lotus Sutra
Saddharma Pundarika

India in China: The Gift of Buddha
Buddhism in China,
FaHian and Huen Tsang

Editorspeak

THE GLORY OF BUDDHA

India and China—or China and India, if the numbers of people living there are regarded as the deciding factor of their importance—have been and still are the most significant countries, nations, cultures, of the planet known as the Earth. Together, they constitute, more or less, one third, a very large segment of the total population of the world. They are also the oldest in terms of history—and almost neighbours on the largest continent, Asia, or Eurasia, to be more exact. Though, of late, since the Mao-planned Chinese attack on India in 1962, there has been a strongly antagonistic feeling between each other, both the countries have been friendly and cooperative, nay, it has been a relation of, if we may say so, a relation of teacher and disciple since the start of the Christian era, India being the former and China the latter; chiefly because of the import of Lord Buddha's great religion by China—I'm not calling it 'export' for the simple reason that India did not, of her own intent, take it to China as a missionary project, but **it was purposefully invited by China to work in that country;** and her highly motivated seekers kept walking, mostly on foot, to India, one after the other, in search of the true tenets of the religion. It was in fact the details of this perilous journey of one such pioneer, Fa Hian, which in modern times, brought this relatively unusual chapter of world history to light, resulting in further studies after studies by Western scholars, exploring other aspects of the subject in greater and the required detail.

India's Buddhism in China—which further spread from the latter to Mongolia, Korea and Japan—is a most interesting and enlightening subject for the students of history and religion, and to the believers in humanism and the fast spreading idea of globalisation—one world, one culture—in modern times, suffering from the horrors of religion-generated terrorism. **A Buddhism revised and regenerated in modern terms is perhaps the answer to present-day problems;** it has space for atheists also because it does not believe in the existence of God. Compassion being the central message of Buddhism, it also is supportive of the century's mighty phenomenon of Social Work and NGOs—and there are reports that in Taiwan Buddhist groups are organising such projects in a rather big way.

Returning to our subject, I have tried to collect in the present book the major outlines of the spread of Buddhism in China from perhaps the only work on the subject, adding to it the work of the two most famous Chinese pilgrims, Fa Hian and Huen Tsang, both of which are available in book form. It is interesting to note that Fa Hian, when asked to write down his story, refused to do so, because he feared that it might encourage others to follow his example, which he thought was quite hazardous and should not be promoted; and though Huen Tsang did pen his journey to the west, the complete story of his life and travels was written by another monk, which is being presented in this book. His party was attacked by robbers quite a few times, and in India he was caught by them to be sacrificed at the altar of Devi Durga. It was a drama of unimaginable proportions, but he was somehow saved, and not only that, the perpetrators were converted to Buddhism.

Buddhism in India has been a phenomenon of high value—I would say, real value, to understand which one must deliberate the views of the (Hindu) Swami Vivekananda—and **I regard it as the greatest mistake of the mainline Hindu religious culture, to have rejected it after a period**—for which Sankaracharya has been held responsible. (Though, ironically, he has been widely regarded as a 'Prachchhana Buddha'—a Buddhist in disguise—which seems to be correct because of the philosophical bent and pattern on which he organised his cult.) I am also of the view that had Vivekananda lived longer—he passed away without completing forty—he would have done this.

Since Buddhism is non-existent in our country in the present times, we find it hard to imagine how strong it had been all over in earlier times; for almost 1700 years it was the chief religion of India. And as Swami Vivekananda has noted, its first 500 years were devoted to Dharma, the second 500 to idols, and the third 500 to Tantra.

Buddhism did not develop a temple-culture like the Hindus, it had Stupas, which when not in use, scattered in dust, leaving formless mounds. Many of these are now being discovered; as I write this I have a report that one has been found in the Kistna district of Andhra Pradesh, which already has four scattered stupas. The report goes: 'A hemispherical Buddhist stupa dating back to 6th and 7th century was by chance unearthed...following sighting of a large brick in the vicinity of Munjuluru village... The 10-metre main stupa is now in a dilapidaled state...is built of bricks made of husk measuring 23 cm width, 7cm height and 28cm length—a typical Buddhist construction material of that period. One of the *avaka* pillars, which is in octagonal shape, was perched on a square base.' (*The Hindu*, 19 Sept. 2011)

The wonderful caves of Ajanta are proofs of the religion's spread upto those regions and beyond; and the museum of Maldives contain statues of Buddha found in the isles.

As an admiring student of Buddhism, I used to think that the spread of Buddhism in the eastern parts of Asia would have played a positive role in softening the violent temperament of those peoples, who were fond of riding on horses, attacking and killing all and sundry, drinking blood, etc., etc. Even the religions of China in olden times welcomed the killing of prisoners and people of other countries in their precincts by their kings. While going through these books I was pleased to find that **the famous Mongol king Kublai Khan, whose reign was spread upto China, deliberately**

used this religion as a state policy to change the behaviour pattern of his people.

Let me here relate my own observations in Japan, another Buddhist country of note. While there, I was amazed to find that their Samurai culture, another segment of hardy fighters, were vegetarians—in fact the whole Japanese nation was vegetarian—much more than we Hindus are in India—till a particular date: when in the nineteenth century their Mikado-king travelled to Tokyo from Kyoto, to live there permanently and started eating meat (because he thought—like Gandhiji did at a later date—that by doing so he will acquire the qualities of the Europeans.) The books of those times relate that following their Mikado's example, all Japanese males started eating meat almost immediately, though the females strongly resented the change, and separated their kitchens by hanging curtains etc. around them.

Which other religion has done this, or even given it a thought? Even Hindu religion, or parts of it, had it at a later stage. Now Veganism is breaking new ground, though very slowly, in the West and it would do well to associate itself with Buddhism in this matter.

Talking of eating norms and cuisine, the Chinese are perhaps the lowest on the scale; they eat anything and everything, including snakes. I read in a work published two hundred year ago, that—as the British writer describes it: the person he was talking to saw an insect moving over his cloth and he immediately put it into his mouth. The surprised onlooker mentioned it to another British friend of his, and he remarked that it was nothing new for him. Another striking example of the Chinese eating human flesh even in the 20th century is their famous writer Lu Hsun's story entitled. 'A Madman's Diary'—in which he severely criticises this habit. Perhaps it is now time that the Chinese changed themselves.

Cultures are strange materials and the habit of taking every part of it as sacrosanct, is the foremost fault of their peoples. No one even in times we call modern is willing to accept his culture's criticism. Arthur Koestler a few decades earlier, did quite courageously try to start this new trend by writing *The Lotus and the Robot*—but the trail ended with him. If we are serious about One World and Globalisation, we will have to shed this habit for ever.

Every culture has its strong as well as weak points, and I'm surprised at the genius of China in the solidity of their basic thinking: like, their inclusion of Wood and Metal in their counting of the five life-elements—the others being air, water and earth. (In comparison, the five Hindu elements have the vague sky and horizon.) Their chief sage Confucius, similarly, propounded the philosophy of good government and general morality. In India—as also in other countries—there is nothing like it.

I'm inspired to know more about the Chinese culture, but, unfortunately, the language/script is the great barrier. Someone has discribed it as another Chinese wall, which not only prohibits entry, but also curtails dissemination. In the view of several historians the Japanese acceptance of Chinese script was a great mistake, from which they will always suffer. I've found that the Japanese have difficulty in reading their materials though they have added two more scripts, Hiragana and Katakana, to the Chinese Kanji.

China accepted Buddhism so willingly because their genius could not provide a good religion. Confucianism was no religion, and Tao was too magical. But the spread of Buddhism was not easy; it was proscribed by several rulers and the monasteries were burnt. Yet it prevailed and flourished and was thoroughly Chinaised. Lots and lots of Buddhist materials were translated and retranslated and several new sects were born in the course of its spread. All of it is a delightfully interesting fact, stranger than fiction. The Communist ideology and rule tried for some time to eliminate religion but things are now fast changing.

Lord Buddha—or Sakya-muni, as he is called in China—has been India's rather unusual gift to that country, which did help in bringing both the countries together in various other ways. The Communist intervention in China—which did not help that country in any big way; and had ultimately to be thrown out by one of themselves, after a convolutionary and so called Cultural Revolution and the ridiculous farce of the Gang of Four—has resulted in some ludicrous acrimony; it seems to have also changed the essential Confucian moralistic character of China—but we still hope and believe that the great Lord Buddha will give a second visit to China, bringing both the countries together once again, in right earnest, serving the cause of Bahujana Hitaya, Bahujana Sukhaya—for the absolute growth of not only many, but all and everybody. Amen!

Translatorspeak

THE MORAL BASE

Buddhism, which had arisen in India (500-600 B.C.) under the form of a reaction against the material worship and the intolerant claims of the Brahmins in time (260 B.C.)became the adopted religion of China. Missionaries, proceeding from the various centres of religious influence, carried the knowledge of their doctrines and discipline north and south—until, from Balkh to Sri Lanka and from Pattala on the Indus to Tamluc on the Hugli, the vast territory was leavened by their teaching.

During this period, there was occurring an equally important movement in the eastern portions of Central Asia. This vast territory, that portion of it commonly known as Chinese Tartary, had been long occupied by conflicting races of people, who, from early times, descended from the northern steppes of Mongolia and the country watered by the Amur and its branches, towards the more tempting territory bordering on China.

During the Chow dynasty, which ruled the empire from 112 to 250 B.C., China was divided into a number of petty states or nations—at one time amounting to 125, and at another to 41—each of which was governed by its own prince, who paid but a limited obedience to the monarchs of the reigning dynasty. In knowledge of this disunion, the empire was repeatedly attacked by the migratory bands of northern barbarians, who hovered on its frontier, until Che Hwang ti, the first universal monarch of the world—as he boasted—250 B.C., built the Great Wall to repel further aggression, and burnt all the books and records he could find in the country, to obliterate the recollection of any one event or person before himself.

The Yuchi were the most formidable of these Tartar hordes. Just before 200 B.C. they had been defeated and driven from their territories by Mothe, chief of the Hiungnu (Huns), who finally extended his conquests from the frontier provinces of China on the east, to the Volga on the west. The increasing power of the prince alarmed the Chinese. The victorious career of the Hiungnu continued unchcked during the following half century. In 139 B.C. the Emperor Woo-ti of the Han dynasty, wishing to humble the power of the Hiungnu, sent an embassy to the Great Yuchi to obtain assistance from them against their common enemy. The Chinese ambassador, Chang-kian, however, was captured, and only after ten years' imprisonment managed to effect his escape.

It was during this war with the Hiungnu that Hou Kiuping, the **Chinese general, first saw a golden statue of Buddha, to which the King of Hieou-to (Kartchou?) paid worship,** and which accurately corresponded with the reports of Chang-Kian respecting the worship of Feou-to (Buddha) in Thian (India). This statue was taken and brought to the emperor in 121 A.D., and was the origin of the statues of Buddha, that were afterwards in use. Thus, while the missionary zeal of the Buddhist church had spread their doctrines to the borders of the great country of the conflicting tribes, the warlike spirit of the Chinese, under the Han dynasty, had caused their arms to extend to the same point, and **the knowledge of Buddha and of his doctrine was carried back to the seat of government as a seed ready to germinate in due season.** The events on the Indian frontier which followed this first intercourse of the two civilisations were rapid and most interesting.

The Emperor Wu-ti' al though at first unsuccessful, was yet in the end able to check and humble the power of the Hiungnu; and his successor, Chaou-Ti, signally defeated them. In 60 B.C. they became subject to the Chinese Empire. It was in the fourth year of the reign of Ming Ti (62 A.D.), the second emperor of the Eastern Han dynasty, that **a remarkable vision appeared to him by night. He saw a**

golden image, 19 feet high resplendent as gold, and its head surrounded by a halo as bright as the sun, approach his palace and finally enter it. This dream was interpreted by the Confucian Literati to refer to Buddha.

Another account states that "that golden spirit, speaking to the Emperor, said, 'Buddha bids you send to the west countries to search for him, with a view to obtain books and images.' On which the Emperor despatched an embassy that returned and entered Loyang in company with a white horse, carrying the books and images—on which occasion the Temple of the White Horse was founded." The account further states that "these books still remain, and are reverenced and worshipped; and from the cover, in which they are wrapped, often proceeds a miraculous shining light."

Ming Ti immediately dispatched a mission to the country of the Great Yuchi and also to Central India. After eleven years his messengers returned. **They were accompanied by the Indian Kasyapa Matanga who translated the Sutra of 42 Sections, and died at Loyang.** He was soon followed by Tsu-fah-lan, who worked conjointly with him in the task of translation. They had together brought five Buddhist works from India—amongst which was the Dasabhumi Sutra, and the Lalita Vistara (Fo-pen-hing-king). These were translated by imperial order, and their date may be fixed at about 76 A.D.

In 150 A.D., An-shi-kau, a priest of An-sih, a country in Eastern Persia, is noticed in the annals as an excellent translator. About 170 A.D., Chi-tsin, a priest of the Yuchi, produced a translation of the Nirvana Sutra. Sun-k'iuen, prince of Wu, who received at his court (226 A.D.) a Roman merchant, treated with equal regard an Indian priest who translated for him some of the books of Buddha. About 250 A.D. we find Chi-Meng, residing at Kao Tch'ang (Tourfan), translating the Seng-ki-liuh (Rules of the Priesthood), which he is said to have obtained at Hwa-chi, i.e., Kusumapura or Pataliputra (Patna). Shortly after this (260 A.D.), we read of a Sraman called Fa-hou (Dharmaraksha) reaching China and living under the dynasty of the Western Tsin. Subsequently, he traversed the Western countries in every direction, and gained a knowledge of the dialects of 36 kingdoms. On his return he brought with him a large number of Buddhist and Brahmin works, which he presented to the imperial court. He finally took up his residence at Loyang, and, from the year 265 A.D. to 308 A.D., translated, with the help of many Sramans, 165 Buddhist books. About 300 A.D., a foreign priest named Chi-kung-ming translated the Wei-ma, Vimalakirti Sutra, and the Fa-hwa, Saddharma Pundarika. **Shortly after him (335 A.D.) the prince of the Chau kingdom (Pei-chi-li, and Shan-si) first permitted his subjects to take Buddhist monastic vows.** He was influenced to do this by an Indian named Bouddhasinha (Fo-to-ching). Hitherto natives of India had been allowed to build temples in the large cities, but now, for the first time, the people of the country were permitted to become Sramans; and, as a final proof of the rapid growth of the religion, we find that **at Loyang alone there had been erected (350 A.D.) 42 pagodas,** from three to nine stories high, richly painted and formed after Indian models.

It was at this time that Fa Hian lived. He was apparently a native of Tchang'an, or, at any rate, a resident there. He was grieved to observe the imperfect rules of discipline of the monks in that city—the translations of Buddhist books as yet known in China were, in fact, to a great extent, erroneous. For this reason the Emperor Yao-hing (397-415) had **sent an army to Koutche to bring back a learned Indian priest, Kumarajiva, who might supply correct versions of the chief books known in the country.** More than 800 priests were called to assist, and the king himself, an ardent disciple of the new faith, was present at the conference, while the Prince Yao-wang and the Count Yao-seng helped to transcribe the sheets of the new translations. While this task was proceeding, Fa Hian was travelling through India in search of original copies of works not yet known to his countrymen.

During the early period of the Sun and Wei dynasties, the Buddhist religion in China was persecuted, and image-making and building of temples forbidden. It was made a capital crime to construct idols of earth or brass, or to worship foreign divinities.

In 451 A.D., there was a relaxation of these severe rules. An edict was issued permitting one Buddhist temple in each city, and 40 or 50 of the inhabitants to become priests. The rapid progress of Buddhism excited much opposition from the Literati and followers of Lao-tsu. The latter affirmed that Sakya Buddha was but an incarnation of their own master, who had died in 517 A.D., shortly after which date, it was said Buddha was born.

Buddhism, rapidly prevailed in the Wei kingdom. In the year 467 A.D. **the prince of that kingdom caused an image of Buddha to be constructed, 50 feet high. Five tons of brass and 6 cwt. of gold were used in its composition.** This prince resigned his throne five years afterwards and became a monk. About this time, also, Ming Ti, the sixth of the Sung emperors, erected a magnificent Buddhist temple, for which he was severely rebuked by the Literati.

At the beginning of the sixth century the number of Indians in China was upwards of 3,000. **The Buddhist temples had multiplied to 13,000. The prince of the Wei country discoursed publicly on the Sacred Books.** The adverse government of the Liang, established in the South, was also eminently favourable to foreign priests. **The first emperor of the dynasty (502-550 A.D.) three times assumed Buddhist vow and expounded the Sutras to his assembled courtiers.** In the 26th year of his reign, he entered the T'ung-Tae monastery in Nanking.

Bodhidharma, the 28th Buddhist Patriarch, having grown old in Southern India, reached Canton by sea (526 A.D.). His arrival in China is an important epoch in its religious history. Hitherto the form of Buddhist doctrine most prevalent there was that which taught the practice of Morality to be the means of deliverance. But now the mysticism which had developed itself gradually in India was imported full-blown into China. **"Do nothing," was the creed of Bodhidharma; for in doing nothing, and abstracting the mind from every**

object, we arrive at a state of entire self-absorption; lust is suppressed and bliss attained. Bodhidharma, after a while, left Canton and the Liang kingdom, and came to Loyang, the Wei capital. **Here he sat with his face to a wall for nine years. The people called him the Wall-gazing Brahmin.** Bodhidharma's example was not without effect. We read of one enthusiastic disciple arguing thus: "Bodhisattva formerly broke off his bone, poured out his marrow, shed his blood, gave himself to the famishing tiger cubs—what can I do?" Accordingly, while snow was falling, he exposed himself to it, till it had risen above his knees. The Patriarch, observing him, asked what he hoped to gain by such conduct. "I only desire," he said, "that Mercy may open a path to save the whole race of men." The Patriarch replied that his suffering could not be compared with that of Bodhisattva. Stung with the answer, the disciple took a knife and severed his arm and placed it before his master. On this he was satisfied, and highly commended him, and subsequently appointed him his successor in China. Bodhidharma died of old age, and was buried in the Hiungh mountains, between Honan and Shansi.

We may gather from the records of the Sui dynasty (beginning 589 A.D.) that Buddhism was yet subject to persecution. The first of these emperors, Kaou-tsu, issued an edict, giving full toleration to the sect. Towards the close of his reign, he prohibited the destruction or disfigurement of images used in religious worship. **There were now 1950 distinct Buddhist works, translated into Chinese.**

It was in the reign of the second emperor of Tang dynasty, Tae-Tsung, that the celebrated Buddhist traveller, HuenTsang, set out for India (629 A.D.). Tae-Tsung was still reigning when Huen Tsang returned, and the pilgrim was summoned to the court at Loyang, to answer for his conduct in leaving his country and undertaking so perilous a journey without the imperial permission. His apology consisted in the result of his undertaking, which is thus detailed: "twenty-two horses carrying 657 Buddhist works; 115 grains of relics; a gold statue of Buddha 3 ft 3 in. high with a transparent pedestal; a second, 3 ft. 5 in. high; and many others of silver and sandalwood."

The emperor, after listening to the traveller's account of what he had seen, commanded him to write a history of the Western countries, and the work called the Si-yu-ki was the result. After this Huen Tsang lived for nineteen years, and passed nearly the whole of that time in translating. He completed 740 works in 1335 books. We are casually informed that the number of monasteries in China at this time was 3,716; at the request of Huen Tsang, the Emperor issued an edict that five new monks should be received in each of these, thus swelling the number by some 18,000 persons.

Kublai Khan (She Tsu), the first Mongol emperor (1280 A.D.) was strongly attached to Buddhism. The Confucian temples were converted to Buddhist uses, and Taoism was openly persecuted. In the reign of the second emperor of this dynasty, Ching Tsung (1295 A.D.), we read of 3,000 taels of gold being set apart to provide materials for writing Buddhist books in gilt letters, and other expenses for this religion on an equally extravagant scale. **The aim of Kublai, in his preference for Buddhism, was a politic one. Having become sovereign of a wild and extensive country, with an intractable and quarrelsome population, in order to give his native deserts a civilized appearance, and to soften down the natural roughness of his people and unite them in a compact body, he resolved to adopt the Chinese model of government and to put the people under a Public Instructor. To this latter office he appointed a Buddhist monk,** whose orders were to be received with the same respect as imperial proclamations, and who was only second to the Chief Civil Mandarin in privileges and rank. **It was in this way the mild character of the Buddhist religion gradually leavened the mass of the Mongolian people and produced amongst them some degree of order and love of peace.**

Towards the end of the thirteenth century a census of the Buddhist temples and monks in China was taken by imperial command. Of the former there were reported 42,318; of the latter, 213,148. Three years after at the close of Kublai's reign, a priest came from Tibet to be appointed National Instructor; the Emperor regretting that he could not converse with him, ordered Kalutanasi, a Mongolian, to learn the Tibetan language from him. This task was accomplished in a year, and the complete translation of the Buddhist Sutras and Shastras from Tibetan and Sanskrit into Mongolian (written in the Ouigur characters), was presented to Kublai in the year of his death, 1294 A.D. He ordered the whole to be cut in blocks and distributed it among the kings and great chiefs of his nation.

Chinese pilgrims still visited India. In 965 A.D. a Buddhist priest, Tai-yuen, returned from a journey to the Western countries with relics and Sanskrit copies of Buddhist books written on palm leaves, in forty volumes. **The next year, 157 Chinese priests set out together, with the Emperor's permission, to visit India and obtain books.** Early in the Yuen dynasty, a priest named Tau-wu was excited, by reading the account of Fa Hian, to try his fortune in a similar way—a contingency that Fa Hian himself appears to have foreseen and wished to prevent. He passed the Sandy Desert, through the kingdoms of Kui-tsi and Sha-la to Kipin. He there learned the original language of Buddhist books; and turning westward, proceeded through the country of the Getae into India. He returned by sea to Canton. This is the last record, however, of any such pilgrimage.

Buddhism in China has exhibited a vitality which has enabled it to survive persecution and triumph over obstacles. This may be attributed to three circumstances:

1. The character of this religion. The system of Confucius, highly moral and truthful within its province, cannot be considered as a religious system in the true meaning of the phrase. Its scope does not extend beyond the present life. It

does not profess to speak of man's future destiny, or the consequences of death. Buddhism, therefore, supplied a need felt by the people, when it brought to their notice the subject of a future life—its rewards and punishments and the possible destiny of the soul, in arriving at the Supreme good, known as Nirvana.

2. Buddhism in China owes its success, and continuance also, to the character of the Chinese people. Their tendency is to approve of that which is moral. This national preference results, no doubt, from the teaching of Confucius. Hence the doctrine of Buddha, founded on a rigid morality, recommended itself to their notice. The corrupt Sakti worship, which found its way into the northern schools of Buddhism in India, and developed itself still further in Tibet, would not be tolerated by the better classes of the Chinese. In the Lama temples near Peking may be found traces of this impure symbolism; but it is confined to them. The great majority of monastic establishments throughout China, however ignorant the priests may be, are at least free from any taint of this sort. It is contrary, in fact to the genius of the people. On this account, Buddhism in China has retained something of its natural vigour, and is still, however imperfectly so, a living witness in favour of virtue and purity of life.

3. A third reason for this may be found in the absence of the scholastic element in Chinese Buddhism. Even if the priests were inclined to scholasticism, the fact of their religion being a foreign one, and the language of its books unknown to them, would forbid the indulgence of such a taste. Not that the Chinese are incapable of appreciating subtle scholastic enquiries. On the contrary, there is no Buddhist Sutra so popular among them as the Ling-yeh-king (Surangama Sutra), and this is perhaps the most scholastic of all the later productions of Mahayana system. They appreciate, however, the subtleties of the book without enlarging upon them. Their commentators confine themselves to a bare explanation of terms, and indulge in no original speculation.

In India, the fate of a monastery, nay, of many together, often depended on the ability of a favourite champion of the faith to defend a thesis or maintain a point in dialectics, against every opponent. But in China no such necessity could occur. The question between the Literati and the priests was not one of logic, but of morals, and of fact. What was the right motive to a virtuous life? Is there a Heaven for the good or a Hell for the bad? These were the questions raised, the answers to which, in the very nature of the case, come within the province of dogma rather than scholasticism.

Contents

I. Buddhism in China

II. They Walked to India

The Adventurous Seekers of the First World Religion

KWAN-YIN or AVALOKITESVARA

108 m. tall statue at Hainan island in South China

First Sermon at Sarnath, Ajanta

1

Buddha Everywhere

To understand the position which Buddhism holds in China, it must be borne in mind that **its influence depends not so much on its recognised authority as on the tone which it has given to the religious thought of the people.** Although it was formerly patronised by the emperors and the court, it is now, when I write this book (1860), proscribed. Yet in the presence of this, its influence is everywhere felt, and it undoubtedly affects the whole religious condition of the empire. Hence it is not erroneous to include in the number of professed Buddhists throughout the Eastern world the great proportion of the Chinese people, who, if not professed disciples, are at least implicit believers in the leading fact, of this religion and conform themselves to its teaching in daily life.

The result of the co-existence of the three religious systems, Confucianism, Taoism and Buddhism, for so many years has been, indeed, to obliterate the distinctive features of each separately. The worship of Pu-sah, in the houses of the rich and poor, is hardly recognised as Buddhist in its origin; and, indeed, the very term Pu-sah, which is the Chinese form of Bodhisattava, is explained in the ordinary language as of native origin, and signifying "universal benevolence," whilst the objects of Buddhist worship, such as the "Goddess of Mercy" and the "Queen of Heaven," have been placed among the number of their genii, and, in the case of the former, at least, attributed to their own country. Hence, again, the images of their Bodhisattvas, or Pu-sahs, are to be found in the houses of the people and the officers of government, who would otherwise strongly object to be called Buddhists.

At the capture of Canton, in 1858, a large golden image of Kwan-yin (Avalokitesvara) was found in a shrine in an inner room of the Yamen of Yeh Ming-shin, the governor of the province. The same official had, about two years before the loss of the city, written to the emperor to state that on one occasion, at a critical juncture, while engaged in exterminating a band of roving plunderes, "a large figure in white had been seen beckoning to the army from the sky." This was Kwan-yin; the soldiers were inspired with courage, and won an easy victory over the enemy. We are not surprised to find that one of the largest temples in the city of Canton dedicated to Kwan-yin, "who came flying from heaven" to defend the town from the first attack of the English, was mainly restored by the exertions of the chief officers of the neighbourhood, and regarded as the source of security to the inhabitants at the time of the second siege of the city. In this way we may understand how the Buddhist religion has affected the entire population of the country, and, although not supported or countenanced by the Government, is yet secretly respected even by the highest functionaries of the state.

So much, then, as to the general influence of this religion in explanation of the statement often made, that the Chinese are Buddhists. Independently of this general conformity, however, there is a large proportion of the population professedly Buddhist. What this number may be we have no means of ascertaining, but in every town and village, so far as we know, there are found some; and, in many cases, a Buddhist temple or temples may be seen, with numerous worshippers, so that China undoubtedly contributes to the total of Buddhists throughout the world a large proportion.

Notwithstanding our improved acquaintance with the country, however, it is discouraging to find that our actual knowledge of the Buddhist community there is very limited. The monasteries are visited, but there is little information given about the condition of the priests, or their mode of teaching, or the character of their distinctive doctrine, so that for the purpose of this we shall have to depend on the books which embody the doctrine more than the actual working of the system or the mode of enforcing the doctrine on its adherents.

And in this respect we have an abundant supply of materials; in every large monastery is to be found a collection of books published and printed at the royal mandate, composing what is called the "threefold treasure," or the Tripitaka. In these books we find translations of Indian and other works, and native commentaries relating to the teaching of the various schools of the religion. Besides this, there is a large circulation amongst the people of tracts and treatises relating to the more popular forms of worship and belief, so that the materials, as we said, abundant for a knowledge of the system as it is taught in their books, and as this is the surest guide in all cases where practices may vary according to circumstances, we shall rely principally on it in our further inquiry on the subject.

Classification of Books

Buddhist literature is ordinarily classified under two great heads or divisions, northern and southern. This partition is unknown to the Buddhists themselves, but it is a convenient one. In the first place, it was supposed to denote the division of the books under the two heads, Pali and Sanskrit. The former represented the southern literature, the latter the northern. This, however, is not found to be the case, for the books taken to China were certainly not all of them in Sanskrit, but rather composed in various dialects, and it is well known that many of the Tibetan works have been translated from Pali. Moreover, it is stated that Pali texts to this day are to be found in Japan, and if further search were made in the neighbourhood of Loyang, in China, there is good reason to believe similar texts might be found there. The division, then, of Buddhism into the so-called northern and southern schools does not depend on the sharp distinction alluded to, but rather denotes the differences between the primitive and the mixed, or developed system, as known respectively from the Pali Scriptures in the south, and the mixed books, Sanskrit, Pali, and other Prakrits, in the north.

There is another division which is constantly referred to in Buddhist literature which is equally useful, but yet unknown, at least, to the southern school; this is the classification known as the Great and the Little Vehicle, Mahayana and Hinayana. We find this division referred to in the northern books of a late date; but being unknown in southern canonical books, we conclude it came into use after those books were written, and the separation between the northern and southern school of thought was completed. The Little Vehicle may be said to represent the teaching of the early Buddhists. It is called "little," or "imperfect" (hina), because it affords means of salvation of "the few" only, i.e., those within the limits of the community; whereas the great or complete, vehicle, means of conveyance, over the sea of sorrow, or the world holds out the assurance of safety or deliverance to all.

The formula in the first instance is, "all those that are to be saved, are saved"; in the second, "all that are not saved, shall be saved," by the bequeathed law or doctrine preached in the world. We cannot venture to define exhaustively the further differences between these two systems. It may be accepted as generally true, that the early school knew nothing of the distinctions that arose at a later period and caused the classification we are speaking about. But yet, it was well recognised by the Buddhists themselves, when the developed system was shaped by the writers of Sastras and others, who lived principally in North India towards the close of the first century B.C., and later; and therefore, we meet with the terms "Little" and "Great Vehicle" constantly in the travels of the Chinese Pilgrims Huen Tsang and Fa Hian and in the controversial works of the scholastic period of Buddhist history.

The great and fundamental division of the system, however, occured about one hundred years after the death of its founder. In order to make this point as clear as possible, it will be necessary to allude briefly to the early history of the system, leaving a more particular account of it, as we find it in the later books, for subsequent notice.

The date of Buddha's death has been variously computed from data which may, for the present, be confined to the southern records, as occurring between 543 B.C. and 412 B.C. One hundred years after his Nirvana, a schism arose in the Sangha, resulting from neglect of discipline among some Bhikshus living at Vaisali, a town not far to the north of Patna. The lay members of the community in this place had been induced by the Bhikshus to give them money, which was divided at stated periods among the disciples. This liberty of possessing money was in contradiction to the rules of the order. A leading member of the brotherhood, named Yasa, protested against this violation of discipline, and in consequence was expelled from the community by an act of the brotherhood of Vaisali. In consequence of this, he brought before the notice of the leading brethren (Sthaviras) resident in other places ten faults or sins which had crept in among the Vaisali priests, and, having settled the questions as to their non-legality, a council was summoned, under the presidency of Revata, to stamp the offences with its disapprobation, and root out the offenders from the society.

This was the cause of the great schism from which the minor division that afterwards occurred must be traced.

The practices of the Vaisali brethren were condemned, and the purity of the rules of the order vindicated. Whether the sacred books were written at this time, or not, we cannot know positively, but in any case it is very probable that they were recited in the convocation with a view to establish the primitive discipline; they were then handed down in that form in the school that represented the orthodox party of the council. This party was called "the followers of the Sthaviras" or "elders." The other section of the community, headed by the Vaisali party of priests, formed their own body, and were called the Mahasanghikas, or "great congregation." In these two bodies was kept the knowledge of the early tenets of Buddhism, according to their determination at this time.

Undoubtedly, the more reliable form is that preserved in the Sthavira school; the tenets of the "great congregation" were adapted to the looser discipline and less accurate knowledge of the Vaisali priests. It may be stated broadly, that the Pali Scripture embody the doctrine of the Sthaviras or elders from the teaching of popular party, known as the Mahasanghikas.

We know little about the history of Buddhism previous to the meeting of this council. The common account is that an earlier assembly had been held near Rajagriha, shortly after Buddha's death, in which the canon of the sacred writings had been fixed, and the place where, and occasion on which each discourse had been delivered, or each rule enacted, precisely laid down. This first council called that of the 500 is not, as now stated, historical. We may; however, suppose that there was some agreement between the leading members of the order, as to their rules of discipline and doctrines, on the decease of the master. But, beyond the light afforded us at the opening of the period belonging to the council at Vaisali, we know nothing of the events of the hundred years that had elapsed between these two points.

We gather, from the account given us of the errors of the priests, that each town had its own customs, and that the community was bound together, at this time at least, by no well-understood discipline. Leading members of the order had fixed their abodes at spots of their own selection, and to them resorted, on emergency, teachers or learners to have their doubts settled, whilst they themselves were attended by a body of disciples who followed them where they went and received from them daily instruction. Thus we find Revata in the company of a select body of followers when Yasa came to consult him on the Vaisali heresy, and the older teachers who came with Revata to the council must have brought with them their attendants or disciples, who thus swelled the number of the assembly to its traditional complement of 700. This being the first historical event in the Buddhist history, it was thought better to state so much, at least, respecting it.

2

Buddhist Literature

We must briefly allude to the character of the materials from which our knowledge of northern Buddhism is derived. For this end we will mention the three great groups of books which have been discovered and partly examined during the last half century. These are (1) the Sanskrit works found in Nepal; (2) the Tibetan books, generally styled the Ka-gyur or Kan-gyur; and (3) the Chinese San-tsong, or Tripitaka.

With regard to the Sanskrit works of Nepal, which are genereally supposed to have been the origin of the "northern" translations, the discovery of these is due to Brian Houghton Hodgson. This gentleman, in 1820, was appointed assistant to the English Resident at Kathmandu, the chief town of Nepal. He afterwards became himself the Resident, and his career in that office extended from A.D. 1833 to the close of 1843. Altogether, his sojourn in Nepal lasted through a period of twenty-one years. During this period he devoted himself to earnest inquiries to the physical character of the country in which he lived, and the condition and religion of the people. Before his time our knowledge of Buddhism was of the thinnest character possible.

Even Dr. Marshman, who lived in India and was in every way so ripe a scholar, in his Chinese grammar, published at Serampore (1824), could give no better account of Buddha than that his worship was probably connected with the Egyptian Apis. And on every hand we find theories of the most grotesque kind started to explain the origin and nature of this mysterious religion. Hodgson, however, took up the matter at first hand, and with his native Buddha teacher by his side, drew up a scheme of the religion as accepted in Nepal, which, when published in the "Transactions" of the Royal Asiatic Society, completely upset the theories which had higtherto been prevalent on the subject, and shed a new light on the matter. Quoting from the pages of Dr. Rajendra Lal Mitra's "The Sanskrit Buddhist Literature of Nepal," Calcutta, 1882, "Hodgson's researches into religion are limited to that form of it which prevails in Nepal—the Buddhism of Sakya Sinha, as it developed itself in that Alpine region on its expulsion from Hindustan,—but he has done more on that subject than any other European writer. Before his time, all that was known of Buddhism was crude, vague, and shadowy, derived from secondary and by no means reliable sources. It is he who established the subject on a sound philosophic basis. Altogether, he wrote eighteen papers on the subject, and they are replete with the most varied and instructive information. Much has been done since, but no one can even now write on Buddhism with any accuracy who has not thoroughly studied Hodgson's essays."

Without alluding further to the work done by Hodgson, we will state the result of his investigations as briefly as possible. He found, then, that in the valley of Nepal there was a collection of Sanskrit Buddhist books, which, before his time, were perfectly unknown. Quoting again from Dr. Mitra: "His discovery has entirely revolutionised the history of Buddhism as it was known to Europeans in the early part of this century. The total number of books discovered is not stated, but it is believed that the works when carefully arranged and indexed will amount to about two hundred.

Copies of these works to the total number of 381 bundles have been distributed so as to render them accessible to European scholars.

"Of these 85 bundles, comprising 44 separate works, were presented to the Asiatic Society of Bengal; 85 to the Royal Asiatic Society of London; 30 to the India Office Library; 7 to the Bodleian Library, Oxford; and 174 to the Societe Asiatique in Paris, or to M. Burnouf personally. This last collection is now deposited in the Bibliotheque Nationale of France." The character of these works was first noticed by Hodgson, in his "Essays," since published separately—"Essays on the Languages, Literature, and Religion of Nepal and Tibet". He was thus not only the discoverer of these ancient and authentic records, but also the first intelligent exponent of their nature and value, both in their ritualistic and philosophical aspects.

The outcome of this discovery was shown first of all in the enthusiasm it excited in France on the subject. Hodgson entered at once into the arena as a controversialist, especially with Abel Remusat, who appeared to question some of the deductions drawn from Hodgson's examination of the Nepalese books. But this soon passed by, and the more solid result of the discovery was shown in the publication of two works by M. Eugene Burnouf: first, the "Introduction to the History of Indian Buddhism," in 1844; and secondly, "The Lotus of the Good Law," translated from the Sanskrit, in 1852. These two works remain the foundation of our knowledge of Northern Buddhism. They were the first books published in Europe claiming to exhibit the system in its real character, and they are still the best authority upon the questions.

M. Burnouf gracefully dedicated the second of these works to Hodgson, as the founder of the true study of Buddhism. Speaking generally, the points established by the discovery of these works are: (1) That Buddhist books were written at an early date in Sanskrit; (2) that the works so written were not translations but original compositions, for they are not known in the south; and (3) that they contain a system of expanded doctrine, alien in many points from the spirit of early Buddhism, and principally of a philosophic or mystic character.

It would be impossible in a work like this to enter on an examination of the doctrine of this school of Buddhism. For those who wish to do so, however, Hodgson's own "Essays" are still the best guide, supplemented by the researches of M. Burnouf.

Secondly, with respect to the Tibetan books—these also were discovered, in the first instance, by Hodgson. They are not, strictly speaking, books, but xylographs, being inscribed on wooden boards or splints. These works, or at least the Kagyur, or Kangyur, include no less than 100 volumes, arranged under the three heads of Dulva, Do, and Sherchin, whence their common name De-not-sum, or, in Sanskrit, Tripitaka—"the three repositories, or baskets." The name Kagyur means "translations of commandments," and the works are avowed to be translations of texts existing between the seventh and thirteenth centuries, in Magadha, the language of Magadhi. But, although Hodgson procured on his own account, and as it appears, independently, copies of these works, our knowledge of their contents is due to the singular zeal and devotion of a simple Hungarian student, Alexander Csoma Korosi (so he signed himself in English, the word Korosi being an adjectival form, signifying "of Koros").

He was the son of a military family of Egerpatak, in the Transylvanian circle of Hungary. After having been educated for the Church, and having studied at Gottingen under Gottfried Eickhorn, he made up his mind to devote his life to the study of Eastern languages. So he set forth from Bucharest on the Ist of January, 1820, without friends or money, travelling on foot or by water on a raft till he reached Baghdad. Thence he pushed on to Teheran, where he spent four months. In March, 1821, he again started with a caravan, travelling as an American, and, after a stay of six months in Khorasan, arrived in the middle of November at Bukhara. There he intended to pass the winter, but alarmed by the reported approach of a numerous Russian army, he travelled with a caravan to Kabul, where he arrived early in 1822. At the end of a fortnight he again set out, and, coming to Lahore, obtained permission to visit Kashmir; thence he travelled on to Ladakh, where he finally settled with Moorcroft, who lent him the "Alphabetum Tibetanum," published at Rome in 1762, and compiled by Father Antonio Agostino Georgi.

The perusal of this book determined him to study Tibetan. Accordingly, in 1824, we find him sojourning at Zanskar in the province of Ladakh working with a Lama. After this he arrived at Sabathu, in India. Thence he travelled again into Western Tibet, where he continued till 1831: in the autumn of this year he was at Simla, "dressed in a coarse blue cloth loose gown, extending to his heels, and a small cloth cap of the same material. He wore a grizzly beard, shunned the society of Europeans, and passed his whole time in study. In May, 1832, he went to Calcutta, where he was met with great kindness from many scholars, especially Professor H. H. Wilson and James Princep. Here he resided during many years, and published his two principal works, the "Eassy towards a Dictionary, Tibetan and English," and "A Grammar of the Tibetan Language."

Finally, in 1842, he left Calcutta with a view to find his way to Lhasa; but, arriving at Darjeelling, in Nepal, he was attacked by fever, and on the 6th of April in that year he died, a victim, as Professor Max Muller has said, "to his heroic devotion to the study of ancient languages and religions."

We have thought it only due to the memory of this singularly devoted student to say this much as to his career. With respect to his work on the Tibetan Buddhist books, we may find all information necessary for the purpose of this outline in the first part of the XXth volume of "Asiatic Researches." Speaking of the great compilation of Tibetan sacred books, A. Csoma says:—'These books contain the doctrine of Shakya Buddha, and were compiled at three different times and in three different places in India. First, immediately after the death of Shakya; afterwards, in the time of Ashoka, 110 years after the decease of Shakya Buddha; and, lastly, in the time of Kanishka, a king in the north of India, upwards of 400 years from Shakya. These works were imported into Tibet, and translated there between the seventh and thirteenth century of our era, but mostly in the ninth.'

Without attempting to explain the number or character of these works, we may state, as a general conclusion, that they were not translated solely from Sanskrit, but from various Prakrits, and especially Pali, that they differ from the works of Nepal, in as much as they assume the form of threefold collection, Tripitaka, known in the south, and include many of the same books. One marked feature, with reference to these books, is that the whole of the Vinaya, or code of discipline, is found among them, whereas these are absent in the Nepalese collection,— the latter, in fact, being almost exclusively made up of scholastic or philosophical treatises of a comparatively late date. Since the time of Csoma, many labourers have worked in the same field of Tibetan literature, but we need not name these; sufficient to know that the Buddhist books of Tibet are in the main derived from the same sources as those found in China, about which we now come to speak.

It had been long known, principally through the papers written by Dr. Edkins in the "Shanghai Almanac," that the Buddhist Tripitaka was to be found in the great monasteries of China. But no attempt was made to procure these books in England, until the interest aroused by the discoveries already made in Nepal and Tibet excited some curiosity on the point. This was greatly increased by the publication of the translation from the Chinese of the travels of one of the Chinese Buddhist pilgrims who visited India in the beginning of the fifth century of our era, by M. Abel Remusat, in 1836. Here for the first time, it was found that there were books in China relating to India in the early period of the Christian era, which might throw a flood of light on its history.

This interest was greatly increased when M. Stas Julien published, in 1858, his concluding volume relating to the life and travels of another pilgrim from China, called Huen Tsang. It may safely be said that these books created a new opinion in Europe with reference to Chinese literature and to some extent with reference to the Chinese people. **It was hard to believe that such enthusiasm and devotion could have been found in natives of that country as are so eminently conspicuous in the character of these pilgrims.** Besides this, the history and chronology of India were illustrated in a remarkable degree by their memoirs, insomuch that it has been said by one able to judge, Bishop Bigandet, in his 'Life of Gautama' (1868) that the voyages of two Chinese travellers, undertaken in the fifth and seventh centuries of our era, have done more to elucidate the history and geography of India than all that has hitherto been found in the Sanskrit and Pali books of that and the neighbouring countries. This interest in Chinese Buddhism having been aroused, several students entered the field, and have contributed to our further knowledge of the subject. But it was felt that until we had the very books before us which form the sacred writings of Buddhism in China, we should not be able to arrive at any final judgment on the question.

The present writer was fortunate enough to be the means of procuring these works as they now stand on the shelves of the India Office Library. He had been led to a consideration of the question of Buddhism in China during a temporary residence in that country and in Japan in the years 1854-9. The number of monasteries in such a little Japanese town as Hakodate in Yezo and the remarkable character of the discipline and services followed in these establishments, first drew his serious attention to the subject. It was plain to him that no real work could be done among the people by missions until the system of their belief was understood, and the system could not be fairly understood until we had their books.

Accordingly, application was made through the India Office to our minister at Peking to urge the Chinese Government to allow either the purchase of the Tripitaka, as it is known in that country, or to procure the books as a free gift. But these attempts were unsuccessful, owing to the strained relationship existing at that time between the Chinese government and the Western powers. On the occasion of the Japanese ambassador, Iwakura-Tomomi, visiting this country, the same request was made to him. The Japanese, it was known, had adopted Buddhism from China, through Korea, and the books they possessed had all come to them from this direction. The ambassador at once acceded to the request, and on his return to Tokyo ordered the whole collection of the books, known as The Sacred Teaching of the Three Treasures, printed during the great Ming dynasty in China, to be forwarded to this country.

With respect to these books, which form the basis of the Buddhist religion both in China and Japan, I will quote from the opening pages of the Catalogue which was prepared for the India Office. "This collection was published by order of the Emperor of China Wan-lieh towards the end of the sixteenth century. It was reproduced, in Japan, in the sixth year of the Nengo (year-period) Im-po, i.e., A.D. 1679, and afterwards issued with imperial preface in the period Ten-wa, A.D. 1681-3. As first received at the India Office, the collection was contained in seven large boxes, carefully packed in lead, with padding of dry rushes and grass. The entire series of books was arranged in 103 cases or covers; in each case there were, on an average, twenty volumes, so that the entire number of volumes is more than 2,000. Placed one above the other, the books in the collection would reach to a height of about 110 feet." This is according to Beal's catalogue of the Buddhist Tripitaka as known in China and Japan.

This body of literature represents the entire series of sacred books taken during successive years from India to China and there translated, as well as the works of native Chinese priests, with commentaries, catalogues, and indexes. Here, then, is the ground. work of our knowledge of the Buddhist religion in China and Japan. They contain valuable materials for a knowledge of Buddhism in all its periods of expansion or development, from the simple creed taught in the first instance by its founder down to the subtle and fine drawn doctrine of the latest period of scholastic development.

As a brief summary, sufficient for present purposes, we will quote from the Catalogue already referred to. First of all, it may be well to state that the term Tripitaka, or, in Chinese, San-tsong, means the three treasures or baskets. The last term may possibly allude to the mode of preserving the palm leaves on which the sacred texts were written, in baskets, or cases of basket-work. The three divisions of the texts, corresponding to the three baskets, are known as the Vinaya, or code of discipline; the Sutras, or discourses delivered by Buddha; and the Abhidharma, or metaphysics. These terms-so explained are elastic. The Vinaya sometimes contains sermons, and the Sutras are often discourses on points of discipline, whilst the one and the other frequently assume a metaphysical character; so that the definition can only be regarded as a general one. In the Chinese collection each of these sections is fully represented.

So far as we can ascertain, the Vinaya division—called by the name of Agama, as well as Vinaya—includes the books known in the southern school, and many more. There is, in fact, a Vinaya section belonging to the Great Vehicle—Mahayana, or expanded form of Buddhist doctrine—as well as the Little Vehicle. These are given in the Catalogue, and are included in five covers or *han*. The Vinaya of the lesser development, on the other hand, is included in forty-eight covers or *han*. It is amongst these that we may expect to find many of the books known to us by translations from the Pali. With respect to the Sutra and Abhidharma divisions, there are some already ascertained to be translations from primitive works known in the southern school; the majority are of a late date, that is, later than the time when the southern canon was finally adjusted, and therefore not found therein.

The Southern Canon

The inquiry as to the identity of the southern and northern books, is of such interest and importance that we may perhaps dwell on it a little longer. One thing is certain, that the southern canon surpasses any other collection of Buddhist books in point of arrangement and perspicuity. It is, in fact, on the face of it, a primitive arrangement. The northern collection, on the other hand, especially in China and Japan, is a miscellaneous and haphazard assortment of books, classified according to the will of the scholars who had charge of the work, with very little reference either to precedent or authority. As the question involved is as to the identity of fundamental belief, it is well to mark the agreements as we find them.

Vinaya Texts

First then with respect to discipline, or the constitution of the order. There is in the north and south agreement on this point. The Pratimoksha, or, in the Pali, Patimokkha, is a primitive work; it is the oldest, and in many respects the most important material of the Vinaya literature, according to Sacred Books of the East, vol.13. Now, this work has been translated as well from Chinese as from Pali, and the result shows almost an identity of character and contents. By an oversight on the part of the learned translators of the Pali text, the translation from the Chinese is not even referred to. They say: The text, as it lies before us, stands so well against all proofs, whether we compare its different parts one with another, or with the little that is yet known of its northern counterparts, that we are justified in regarding these Pali books as in fact the authentic mirror of the old Magadhi text, as fixed in the central schools of the most ancient Buddhist church.

And then they add, in a note in reference to the northern school: "How little this is [i.e., our knowledge of what the northern school teaches] is apparent from the fact that Burnouf, who had studied all those books that were then accessible, did not even find the words *parajika* and *samghadisesa* (two terms occurring in the Patimokkha)," and then they proceed: "Of the Chinese we have only the brief notices of M. Remusat and of S. Beal (in H. Oldenberg's 'Introduction to the Vinaya'). The last scholar also mentions several Vinaya works (of the contents of which, however, nothing further is known) in his Catalogue of Chinese Buddhist Works now in the India Office Library." But, as a matter of fact, the Pratimoksha had been translated by the present writer from the Chinese language so far back as the year 1859, and had been printed in a special manner side by side with Gogerly's translation from the Pali to show the close agreement of the two versions. Spence Hardy prefaced the paper with some remarks as to the importance of the fact thus established, that the Buddhism of China and of SriLanka were, so far as this goes, in complete accord. By a comparison of the two versions, we find that the number of the rules laid down slightly varies: in the Pali they are 227, in the Chinese, 250; but the division into sections or classes of faults requiring a different degree of penance is the same throughout.

These sections are eight in number, and are classed in both schools in the following order:-

	PALI	CHINESE
1.	Parajika (four)	Po-lo-i (four)
2.	Samghadisesa (thirteen)	Sang-kia-poshish (thirteen)
3.	Aniyata (two)	Wu-teng (two)
4.	Nissaggiya Pachittiya (thirty)	Ni-sa-chi-po-ye-to (thirty)
5.	Pachittiya (ninety-two)	Po-ye-to (ninety)
6.	Paridesamya (four)	Po-lo-ti-ti-che-ni-(four)
7.	Sekhiya (seventy-five)	Chung-hioh (one hundred)
8.	Adhikarana-samalha (seven)	Mih-tsan (seven)

The order of the rules in the above comparative list is the same, and the number, under each head, varies but slightly. Under the fifth section the number in the Pali is ninety-two, in the Chinese it is ninety. On referring to the two versions, we find that the difference arises from the absence in the Chinese of rules four and five. Whether the omission was accidental or the original from which the Chinese was translated defective, or whether the two rules have crept into the Pali version or been introduced by a particular school, we cannot decide. The absolute agreement in other points makes the divergence of less importance.

As to the difference in number under the seventh head, this is found by inspection to result from the introduction of a number of rules (twenty-five) relating to reverence or decorum to be observed when near a pagoda or stupa. These rules occur in the Chinese version from sixty to eighty-four, and are wanting in the Pali. This difference is easily accounted for. The reverence for stupas, and the merit of building and repairing them, was a comparatively late feature introduced after the great builder Asoka had lived and died. We do not find these rules in the Pali, therefore, because, presumably, the Pali version was prepared from a code of rules in existence before the time of this king. But the Chinese version was made at a later date, and probably from an original drawn up in India after Asoka's time, so that the reverence for sacred spots and buildings, which was so marked a feature in the later discipline of the order, had taken shape and found a place in the code at the time of the preparation of the version of the Pratimoksha, from which tbe Chinese was translated.

This explanation is so far probable and satisfactory as it agrees with all the conditions of tbe question; for, first, it is highly probable that the Pali copy is as old as Asoka's time, if not older; while, on the other hand, the reverence for sacred buildings did undoubtedly result from the zeal displayed by that monarch, who, according to the popular account, erected in one day throughout Jambudwipa 84,000 of these sacred towers. Then, again, the love of the Chinese people for these pagodas, as proved by their universal presence in the country, would naturally excite in them a desire to perpetuate a reverence for them by the adoption of such rules as they found laid down in the copy of the Pratimoksha brought to their country. With reference to the other rules, there is an exact agreement between the two schools, and the identity of the code in both cases, therefore, seems to be established.

But it is not only in point of arrangement and number, but also in respect to ritual and matter that this agreement is seen. The theory was, that there should be a general assembly of the Sangha, or congregation, twice during each month—at the new moon and full moon—and that then, after certain preliminary inquiries, there should be a repetition of the rules in the order laid down, according to their character and, after each section of rules had been repeated, that any brother who had offended in either of the particulars named should confess his fault and accept the penance allotted. If there were no offenders, then they all remained silent, and the officiating brother declared the assembly to be pure.

Now, this is absolutely the same discipline observed in China as in Sri Lanka. To show this, I will adduce a few instances. There is an introduction in each case, not literally the same but in strict agreement. In the Chinese, the assembly is convened on the sacred day, i.e., the fifteenth day of the half month,—the words are: "In this fifteenth day [or fourteenth according to the number of days in the month] of the white division, or, the dark division, of the month let the assembly [chapter] listen attentively whilst the precepts [rules] are distinctly recited." The Pali is: "Today is the sacred day [of the full or new moon] the fifteenth day of the half month. If it be convenient to the chapter, let the chapter hold uposatha, let it repeat the Patimokkha." The Chinese goes on:" I desire to repeat the Pratimoksha,—if any brothers have transgressed let them repent, if no brothers have transgressed let them stand silent,—thus it shall be known ye are guiltless!"

The Pali has: "Whosoever has incurred a fault, let him declare it! If no fault has been incurred, it is meet to keep silence! Now, venerable sirs! it is by your silence I shall know whether ye are pure!" Both versions then go on to speak of the guilt of deception or lying [i.e., not confessing]. The Chinese says: "Buddha has declared that prevarication effectually prevents our religious advancement. That brother, therefore, who is conscious of transgression, and desires absolution, ought at once to declare his fault, and after proper penance he shall have quiet." The Pali says: "Venerable sirs! the uttering of a deliberate lie has been declared by the blessed one to be a condition hurtful to spiritual progress. Therefore, a fault, if there be one, should be declared by that Bhikshu [brother] who remembers it, and desires to be cleansed therefrom. For a fault, when declared, shall be light to him."

And so the introduction in each case continues, in parallel sections, not absolutely and literally the same (and this would be impossible in translations from languages so different as Pali and Chinese), but sufficiently alike to show that the originals were founded on one code of discipline, established at an early period, in the primitive Buddhist church.

But this will be yet more clear if we compare together a few rules drawn from both versions of this interesting work. For this purpose we will select some of the first rules coming under the heading Sekhiya Dhamma. These rules refer to decorum on the part of the Bhikshus in their intercourse with the world, or, as it is explained in the Pali rules, regarding matters connected with discipline. The observance of decorum in walking, sitting, and speaking, is regarded as most important by the Buddhists; and in the books there is frequent allusion made to the effect produced on observers by the dignified walk or attitude of the Bhikshus on their daily rounds when begging their food. It is no matter of surprise, therefore, that rules such as these should be found in their code of moral discipline.

The first Sekhiya rule, according to the Pali, is this: "I will put my under-garment all round me, that is, so as to cover the body from the navel to the knee (in the Pali *parimandalam*)." The Chinese version is simply, "I will adjust my inner robe properly," which is explained in the note to mean just what the Pali signifies. The second rule is, in the Pali, "I will put on my robe all around me," that is, the outer robe, or *sanghati*, for the Buddhist monk was allowed three robes (in Pali *ticivaram*), the *antaravasika*, the *uttarasanghati*, and the *sanghati*—of these the last was the outer one. The Chinese version gives the second rule thus: "I will adjust properly the outward robes." The third rule from the Pali is: "Properly clad will I go amidst the houses"; from the Chinese: "Not with disordered robes will I enter the houses of laymen." The fourth rule, again, in both versions forbids a priest to sit down in a layman's house with disordered robes; and although the order of the rules following under this section is not the same in both, there is such agreement as to make it evident that both codes were drawn from a common source.

But the agreement between the books of China and the Pali canonical works may be traced further than this. The rules for the ordination of novices and admission to full order are identical in both cases. The service of ordination is generally conducted on an Uposatha (Chinese u-po) day, i,e., one of the days when the Pratimoksha is recited, or one of the alternate seventh days between the new and full moon, and vice versa. The order for this service (Upasampada-kammavaka) has been detailed by F. Spiegel, in his translation of the 'Kammavakya,' or ordination book, of the Buddhists. It is also found, though not as a service, but in its primitive shape, as a code of directions in the Mahavagga, of the Vinaya Pitaka, of the southern (Pali) school. On comparison, the service as laid down in the Chinese version of the Vinaya, according to the Dharmagupta school, is found to correspond closely with the Pali.

The order is this: first, the boundary within which the robes may be kept and the service of ordination conducted is determined. Then the Upadhyaya (Chinese, Hoshang), spiritual director, presents the candidate for ordination. He is questioned as to his age, permission of parents, freedom from disease, debt, or other impediments. He then shows his begging-dish and vestments, and retires. Being again summoned, request having been made for his ordination in the meantime, the questions as to age (he must be above 20 years of age), absence of disease, freedom from debt, and permission of parents, are again repeated in the presence of the assembled chapter, and, being answered satisfactorily, the several vows are taken one by one, after being clearly recited, and the promise is made by the candidate to keep them absolutely.

These vows are: 1. I will not kill any living thing (*panitapata veramani*). 2. I will not steal (*adinnadana veramani*) . 3. I will not commit any unclean action (adultery or even marriage) (*Abrahma chariya veramani*). 4. I will not lie (*musavada veramani*). 5. I will not drink wine or any intoxicating drinking (*suramereyya majjapamadathana*). 6. I will not eat at unseasonable hours (*vikalabhojana veramani*). 7. I wIll not take part in singing, dancing, musical, or theatrical performances, not witness them of listen to them (*natchchagita vadita visukadassana veramani*) 8. I will not decorate myself with flowers, nor anoint my body with perfumes. 9. I will not occupy an elevated or broad couch. 10. I will not possess, or own, or acquire, coined or uncoined money or jewels.

These are the vows taken at full ordination, and the questions, ceremonies, and sequence of service observed and explained in Chinese ritual according to the Vinaya of the Dharmagupta school, appears to be identical with that given in the 'Kammavakya' by Spiegel, and translated from the Pali. Moreover, the order observed in the Mahavagga, as we have it translated by Dr. Rhys Davids, corresponds closely, though not entirely, with that of the Vinaya according to the Mahasanghika school in the Chinese version; for in both works we have, first of all, a brief history of Buddha after his enlightenment, followed by rules or sections (Khandhakas) relating to various matters of discipline, and the first of these is the ordination of Novices and Bhikshus.

When the Chinese Vinaya has been fully examined and translated, the agreement between the two versions of this portion of the Buddhist Tripitaka will be capable of determination. It would be out of the question to enter on any detailed comparison here, we are satisfied to know that there is such an agreement as to show, beyond doubt, that the Buddhist ritual in China, so far as this part of it is concerned, is derived from the same sources, and probably the same books, as those to which the southern school is indebted for theirs.

The Sutras

It seems necessary to settle this inquiry, however, as to the agreement or non-agreement of the northern and southern books, as it has been discussed hitherto from one side only: I shall, therefore, proceed to make some remarks concerning the second great division of the three treasures, or the sacred books, which is the Sutra Pitaka. The Sutras were, in the first instance, supposed to be discourses or sermons delivered by Buddha himself. When Ananda, the personal attendant and a relative of Buddha, was called upon in the first convocation to recite these discourses with a view to their being accepted as canonical, he began as follows:— "On a certain time, in a certain place [naming it], I heard thus." This formula, I heard thus, became typical of the Sutra collection of discourses; but the corruption of later times led to the invention of numberless books professing to be sermons of Buddha, and beginning in the accepted way, which could never have been recited by him, nor by any of his early followers.

Thus we have a book known as the Amitabha Sutra, which deals with the fabulous paradise of the west, an invention probably of medieval Buddhism, after the beginning of the Christian era. In this Sutra there is the customary formula:- "Thus have I heard. On a certain occasion, Buddha was residing etc.," and in the Chinese commentary it is said: "Thus have I heard," that is, Ananda heard Buddha recite the words. Now this is clearly fictitious; but in the earlier or primitive books the formula in question may really have stamped the discourse with authority. For these early Sutras or sermons we must look to the Pali version; and if we find similar sermons in the northern collection, we may assume that on further search the correspondence will be found more complete.

Now there are various Sutras already translated from the Pali which are found also in a Chinese form, somewhat changed perhaps, but agreeing to an extent that shows they were translated from a text derived from, or existing collaterally with, the southern version of the sacred books as now known in Sri Lanka. I will name some of these primitive Sutras as they are found in Chinese, corresponding with others of the same name in Pali. First of all, let us take a sermon known as the Brahmajala Sutta, in Pali. The text of this discourse has been published by M. P. Grimblot, and translated by the Rev. D. Gogerly, Wesleyan missionary in Sri Lanka. He says, in his preface: "The first reason why I have made the selection of the first sermon in the series of discourses attributed to Gotama Buddha is, that a comparison may be instituted between the sacred books of the Buddhists, as they exist in Sri Lanka and as they exist in Nepal."

This comparison has never yet been made, because, so far as it is at present known, this primitive Sutra has not been found among the Nepalese books: it is not, at least, in the list given by Dr. Rajendralal Mitra in his examination of the Nepalese Buddhist literature. But in the Chinese Tripitaka, two works bearing the name Brahmajala have been discovered. The first is a book of a late date and purely fictitious: it relates to the conduct of the Bodhisattva, and has nothing in common except the name with the southern Sutra as translated by Gogerly. But there is another work in the Tripitaka in China, called "Fan-kong-luh shih 'rh kien," that is, "The sixty-two heretical views contained in the Brahmajala Sutra," which on examination turns out to be a version of the same text as we have before us in M. Grimblot's book.

We can only compare a few passages. The Chinese begins thus:—"Thus have I heard, Buddha was passing through the Kuru country with his great disciples, 1,250 in all; at this time the Paribbajaka (taou jin) Suppiya (Su-pi), accompanied by his attendant, Brahmadatta

Manava, followed Buddha and the Bhikshus along the road, at which time Suppiya and his followers reviled Buddha and his doctrine, and the priesthood; whilst his disciple, Brahmadatta Manava, praised Buddha, and his law and the priesthood. And thus the master and his disciple continued disputing as they followed Buddha and his disciples along the road. At length Buddha, leaving the Kuru country, came to the kingdom ot Sravasti, and there rested in the Jetavana Vihara. At this time, all the Bhikshus being assembled in the preaching-hall called Kia-li-Io, they said, 'It is wonderful, it is unprecedented, etc.' "

And then the Sutra following on the same lines as the Pali, shows how Buddha entered the hall where the priests were and exhibits in succession the character of the sixty-two heretical views held respecting the existence of soul, that is, a personal self, residing in the senses.

Now, the opening of the Pali Sutra is this:—"Thus I have heard. At one time Bhagavan entered the high road between Rajagaha and Nalanda, attended by about 500 of his principal priests. The Paribbajako Suppiyo also entered the high road between Rajagaha and Nalanda, accompanied by his attendant pupil, the youth Brahmadatta: at which time the Paribbajako Suppiyo spake in many respects against Buddha spake against his doctrines, and spake against the priesthood; while the youth, Brahmadatta, the attendant pupil of the Paribbajako Suppiyo, in many respects spake in favour of Buddha, spake in favour of his doctrines, and spake in favour of his priesthood; thus both the preceptor and pupil, engaged in the disputation which had arisen between them, continued following Buddha and the priests. At length Bhagavan, accompanied by his priests, entered a royal residence at Amballatthika to pass the night," etc. The Pali Sutta then goes on to relate how Buddha, entering the hall where the priests were assembled, questioned them as to the subject of their conversation, and from their answer takes occasion to exhibit his doctrine in reference to the non-existence of soul, just as we find him doing in the Chinese version of the Sutra.

It is plain, as well from their agreements as from the slight differences that occur throughout, that these discourses are derived from one source, not the original, but from versions made from the original; and from one of these versions the Chinese translation was prepared. It will be an advantage when the entire Chinese Sutra is before us in an English form; but there are difficulties in the way, which must be removed before that can be the case. But, from a perusal of the Chinese text, and a comparison with the English version from the Pali, it is plain the two Sutras are one and the same: and what is true in this case is also so in others.

There is, for example, the well-known Sutra found in the southern canon, and called the "Mahaparinibbana Sutra," or "The Book of the Great Decease," a translation of which into English is found in the Sacred Books of the East. In his introduction, Dr. Rhys Davids speaks of some Chinese works bearing the same name as that of the Sutta he translates. All he states is very true: there are in the Chinese collection, several books called Mahaparinirvana Sutras and they are quite unlike the Pali Sutta of that name. This only shows that in years following the redaction of the early canon there were forgeries in the Buddhist society, as there have been in other cases. But there is one Chinese book to which Dr. Davids refers which, on examination, turns out to be a version of the southern work, or, rather, a version of a collateral text existing in some part of India, and derived from the same source as the Pali, which agrees in a remarkable way with the southern Sutta. It is called " Fo-pan-ni-pan-king," i.e., the Parinirvana of Buddha.

It was translated into Chinese by a priest called Pih-fa-tsu, who was devoted to the study of the sacred books, and was in the habit of reciting daily eight or nine thousand words. This last statement, and it frequently occurs in relation to other priests, shows us how these texts of the Buddhists were preserved, especially in the case of travelling priests, who would, instead of carrying books with them, recite by word of mouth the texts they had committed to memory. This priest, who came to China about A.D. 300, translated the Sutra in question; and, on examination, it is found that out of 324 sections in the Pali there are only 46 wanting in the Chinese, and if from these 46 we deduct those sections which have evidently been interpolated in the Pali, from section 21 to section 42, we find that there are only 25 sections found in the Chinese version which do not occur in the southern work. These books, therefore, represent the original; and we are sure that the book Pih-fa-tsu brought to China, was a copy of, or a parallel text, with the Pali Sutta now translated into English.

This argument might be followed up by reference to several other Sutras, such as the Dhammachakka-pavattana Sutta; the Sigalovada Sutta the Dhammapada, and others, but it cannot be pursued further in this place. Sufficient has been said on the point to show that, as regards this section of the sacred books, the Buddhism of China is one in origin with that of the southern Buddhism of Sri Lanka.

Abhidharma

With respect to the third portion of the threefold collection or Tripitaka, which is known as the Abhidharma or metaphysics, so little is known by translation either from the north or south, that no comparison can be instituted. But from what we do know, it would appear that the northern school possesses a collection of works under this head, unknown elsewhere. I refer to the books called Prajna Paramita, which are named by Hodgson as taking a conspicuous place in the Nepalese collection, and which occupy a similar place in China. The wearisome length to which these treatises run; and the constant repetition of the same idea, or verbal formula, will prevent anyone from translating them; but from what we know of them, it is plain they cannot belong to the early school or have formed a part of the original collection of books. Their aim is to prove that all around us, i.e., all phenomenal existence, is empty or unreal that the thing is only a name, and therefore cannot be treated as a reality. Whether there lies behind this complete negation the inference of a reality or positive existence that admits of no name because of its actual existence is a question not to be discussed, since there are no data before us but, in any case, the teaching of the treatises classed under this name of Prajna Paramita that is, transcendental wisdom, is negative in its aim, and would appear to be the despair of reason in the search after the Infinite Being of God.

These works are unknown in the south. They represent the Abhidharma class of books in Nepal, they occupy a similar place in the Chinese collection but they are evidently late compilations, and can claim no consideration in the examination of the genuine division of the sacred books. Referring to the books named by Dr. Rhys Davids under the head of Abhidhamma, according to the southern school, there is no corresponding list, so far as is known, in the Chinese Tripitaka. It is probable that when translated we may recognise some ot them under different names in the Chinese collection; but, as far as our knowledge goes at present, there is here no correspondence; but in fact, beyond the Prajna Paramita books, there is a large collection of Chinese works classed as Abhidharma, confessedly of a late origin. These are treatises, sastras, written by men of distinction in the Buddhist community during various periods and for different aims and purposes.

Now, all these, though classed as Abhidharma, are interpolations or intrusions into the primitive canon. They represent the scholastic period of the development of Buddhism, and can claim no original, or what we should call, canonical authority, they are, therefore, not known elsewhere. They have been preserved principally under the form of Chinese translations, and they contain valuable data for the study of the system as a whole, but they have no authority as being *Tathagatena vutto*, i.e., spoken by Buddha. Nevertheless, they are valuable works for a history of Buddhism, and the study of these books will become a necessity when we come to a searching investigation of the whole question.

Referring to the list of books in the Chinese Tripitaka, it will be seen that there are 173 volumes (*han*) of Abhidharma works in that collection: seventy-three belonging to the Little Vehicle and fifty to the Great Vehicle; this will show at least the important place which they occupy in the north. With respect to their contents, they may be said to be controversial in their character, taking generally a text from the canon and dilating upon it to prove a point in connexion with the belief of the writer or composer. Thus, in a work by Nagarjuna, called the Sastra of one Sloka, he takes a verse from an ancient and authentic book, and deduces from it a conclusion agreeable to his own views, as in this case for instance, that there is no such thing as self-nature. So also in another Sastra by the same writer, the Pranyamula Sastra Tika, he labours to prove that Nirvana is neither a positive condition of enjoyment, nor yet, on the other hand, the absence of existence:

> *"That which is not striven or not obtained.*
>
> *" That which does not admit of limitation as to time, nor yet can be spoken of as ' eternal,'*
>
> *"That which has no beginning, and does not come to an end,*
>
> *"This is what is called Nirvana."*

And so the discourse proceeds through a succession of antithetical verses to show that Nirvana, while it is not capable of definition, still exists. Now, all this is peculiar to the north, it is the development of the early teaching of the system, and in that aspect it is valuable.

There is one other aspect in which to regard the Buddhism of China and compare it with that of the southern school—I mean as to external ritual; but here our knowledge is imperfect. We only know that, in general, the life of the Bhikshus in both cases is alike. The robes, vows, and discipline are in their main features identical only in the point of worship, or what might be called liturgical service, do they differ. The objects of reverence in the north have been introduced at a later period, and especially in reference to Kwan-yin and Amitabha—and these form the chief portion of the northern cults—they are entirely unknown in Sri Lanka. We shall be called to consider these differences further on, but meanwhile the agreement in discipline and religious life is sufficient to settle the point as to the origin. The Chinese Buddhists derived their knowledge on these points from the same sources as the Buddhists of the south, and the two schools, so far, are but offshoots of one primitive stock. We have dwelt on this point at some length, because it was essential, to show that **the Buddhism of which we speak is, in fact, not Chinese Buddhism but the Buddhism of India in China.**

This will be plainer still from a brief notice of the historical connection which can be traced between China and India previous to and after the introduction of Buddhism into the former country.

3

Buddha Comes to China—71 A.D.

There is reason to believe that, from an early date, the tribes bordering on the north and west of the Chinese empire had moved in the direction of India and Western Asia, and, as they were able, had taken possession of the best and richest portion of the countries they invaded. The great Scythian invasion of Asia in the seventh century B.C. may have had its origin in the Far East, caused by the pressure of nomadic tribes on the borders of the settled districts of Central Asia, and resulting in a general displacement, the Cimmerans being driven before the Scythian invaders, while they, on their part, were probably pressed on the east by restless tribes who sought larger pastures or richer settlements.

However this may be, we find that a tribe of the Yue-chi, or White Huns, had moved away from the Chinese frontier so early as the second century B.C., and, according to Chinese accounts, had taken possession of the north-west provinces of India. Ma-twan-lin, the Chinese historian, tells us that at this time, i.e., in the time of the emperor Wu-Ti (B.C. 126), all these kingdoms of north-west India, belonged to the Yue-chi. It was at this period that Wu-Ti, having broken the power of the Hiung-nu, i.e., the Kara-Nirus, sent an ambassador, called Chang-kien, to try and open communication with these Yue-chi who were occupying the territory now called Tokharistan, whilst some of them had crossed the Indian frontier and penetrated as far as the valley of the Ganges, where they occupied some chief towns and were known as the Samvijjis or "united Yue-chis."

They had established, in fact, a republican form of government in the very centre of Indian civilisation, and were destined to act an important part in the history of Buddhism and its diffusion through the north. The adventures of the ambassador, Chang-k'ien, are very remarkable, and as it was at this time that the first authentic communication of China with India took place, we will dwell on the point. The ambassador, Chang-k'ien, on his outward journey from China on his way to the Yue-chi, was captured by the Turks, i.e., the Hiung-nu! or Kara-nirus, who had driven the Yue-chi from the Chinese western frontier. He was held in captivity by them for ten years. Having at length escaped, he determined to carry out his mission to the Yue-chi, who dwelt to the north of the Oxus, where they had settled, after defeating the Tokhari, whom they had driven southward towards the Indian frontier.

After travelling westward he came to Tawan, a country, according to our latest Kingsmill authority, situated near Yarkand, to the east of the Pamir plateau. Here he tried to engage the inhabitants to enter into a league with the Chinese against the Hiung-nu or Turks—they were, in fact, the nomadic tribes who had wandered from the banks of the Selenga river to the north of the Gobi desert—, but without success. Thence he still went western till he came to the country of the Yue-chi, but was unsuccessful with them also, for although they hated the Turks who had driven them out of Kansu (Western China), still they feared them too much to enter into an alliance with so distant a power as China for offensive operations against them.

Chang-k'ien then proceeded southwards to the country of Tahia (i.e., of the To-Khari) intending to return to China through Tibet. Here he was again held in captivity for more than a year, but at length he once more escaped, and returned to China B.C. 126, after an absence of thirteen years. It was when Chang-k'ien was in Tahia that he had observed some Chinese goods and inquired how they came there. He then found out that they had come from the province of Sze-chuen, by way of India. No doubt this was an old trade-route from China, through Kamarupa, the western part of Assam, towards the Ganges, and thence either to the central or northern provinces. Huen Tsang, one of the Chinese pilgrims, when in the province of Kamarupa inquired as to the distance, and he found that a journey of two months was required "before reaching the country of Chou," i.e., Sze-chuen. Chang-k'ien, therefore, advised the emperor to try to open the route for trade and military expeditions by this road towards Tawan, as he had heard that the people of this last country had already entered into alliance with Tokharia and Parthia. The emperor was pleased, and accordingly directed Chang-k'ien to despatch expeditions from Sze-chuen along the four roads leading outwards from that province towards the west.

Two of these expeditions, those by the northern and southern routes, were stopped and defeated by the barbarians. They heard, however, of a country to the westward called Tin-yue (India), where elephant-carriages were used, and the people of which carried on a clandestine trade with China. Chang-k'ien, therefore, determined to try to communicate with India by opening a road in the direction of the south-west. This route would have passed through the territory of the "I", or western barbarians. Much money was spent in the attempt, but it was unsuccessful and finally given up. Chang-k'ien, however, affirmed that it was possible by this route to reach Tokharia, and a second time he tried negotiations with the "I"; but, being called away to conduct a force against the Riung-nu, the undertaking appears to have failed.

Without following the history of Chang-k'ien further, we can see, from what has been stated, the importance of events now happening with respect to China and its communications with the west—for these occurrences ultimately led to an embassy from China to Parthia, probably during the reign of Mrithridates II., B.C. 124, and to subsequent relationships between these two empires. We read, that when the Chinese envoy arrived in Parthia the king despatched a general with 20,000 horsemen to meet him on the eastern frontier, from which to the capital was about 1,000 li. On the way they passed some ten cities; the inhabitants were all of the same race, and very numerous. On the return of the mission, he sent envoys with it that they might see the extent and power of China. He sent with them eggs and the great bird of the country, and a curiously deformed man from Samarkand.

Here we have a striking illustration of the kind of presents sent by Pandion (Porus), who reigned over some part of Western India, and might himself have been an Indo-Scyth, to Augustus. Among these gifts were a partridge larger than a vulture, large vipers and snakes, a tortoise-shell three cubits in length, and a deformed man without arms (a Hermes) who shot arrows with his feet. These ambassadors were seen at Antioch by Nicolas of Damascus, who says there were only three who survived, and that they had a letter written in Greek on prepared skin, written by Porus, who said that he ruled over 600 kings, but that he valued much the friendship of Caesar, and that he was ready in any way to open communications with him; and then Strabo adds, with reference to the deformed man, "whom we also have seen," giving reality to the narrative.

Let us remember that the ascetic who burnt himself at Athens also accompanied this embassy, over whom was raised the tomb with the inscription, "Here lies the Indian

Sramanacharya [one who leads the life of a Sraman, i.e., an ascetic] from Bargoza [Baroch], who, according to the custom of his native country, put an end to his life." It has been well supposed that it was this very inscription which prompted the memorable words of St. Paul: "Though I give my body to be burned and have not charity, it profiteth me nothing." All this, taken in connection with the incidents occurring about the same time between China and the Indo-Scyths and Parthia, tends to show that a communication was being opened between the east and west which, if properly employed, might have led to a still closer acquaintance and ultimate friendship.

China Hears of Buddha

In any case, it seems that it was by this acquaintance with the west that China first heard of Buddha and his doctrine. For Chang-k'ien reported to the emperor that "he had been told that in India they worshipped a divine person, Feou-to [Buddha]"; and another general, Hu Kiu-ping, saw at Hiu-to a small district in the Pamir "a golden image of the same person, which the king of that country adored." **This is the first authentic record concerning the knowledge of Buddha in China.** There are other statements made, indeed, in various books, with the view to make this knowledge date from an earlier period. For example, in a work written by Fa-lin, called the "Po-tse-lun," the writer brings a mass of evidence to show that **Buddhist books were known in China before the time of the emperor She hwang-ti (B.C. 221).** It was this monarch who built the great wall to check the incursions of the wandering tribes that threatened the empire; he also burnt the sacred books of Confucius, and assumed the title of the "first" emperor.

The writer, Fa-lin, states that amongst the books burnt were the Buddhist Scriptures; but of this there is no proof, and, in fact, it is doubtful whether the Buddhist doctrine was at this time collected in a written form even in India, and there is no account of any translation made in China from any Indian original. We must regard this story as untrustworthy, and as part of the method followed by the contending sects in China who desired to claim priority in point of time for their religious founder.

There is another story, also found in the pages of Fa-lin, equally improbable, relating to Li-fang, who is described as an Indian priest who came with seventeen companions to China in the reign of She-hwang-ti, and introduced the sacred writings of the Buddhist faith there. The emperor, it is said, shut them up in prison. During the night six men of supernatural character came and opened the prison doors and brought them out. On this, the emperor paid them reverence. But, as Mayers observes, "the legend appears to have no historical basis." There are other notices equally fabulous to be found in Chinese books. We can, however, only accept as historical the circumstances above related in connection with the emperor Wu-ti, of the Han dynasty (B.C. 140-86), and the negotiations carried on by Chang-k'ien with the western tribes especially with Mithridates II., king of Parthia, and with the Yue-chi, through which a knowledge of Buddha and his golden statue was brought to the ears of the court and the Chinese people.

At best we know little respecting the commotions of China and the restless tribes on its frontiers during the period to which we have referred. Until the pages of the Chinese historian, Sze-ma T'sien, have been carefully translated, and compared with statements found in Strabo and other historical works, our acquaintance with these events will remain imperfect. But yet, for a general outline, we know enough, and for convenience's sake it may be thus summed up:—The tribes of nomads who threatened the western and north-western portions of China at the time of She-hwang-ti, 221 B.C., were turned, by the erection of the great wall, to seek an opening for their warlike tastes elsewhere. A portion of these tribes, called by the Chinese,

Yue-chi, had been driven away from the western province of Kansu by a horde of new invaders called Hiung-nu. These last were Turks, and became a terror to the empire: the energy and ability of the emperor Wu-ti (140-86 B.C.) broke their power; but the consequence of the pressure they exercised on the Yue-chi, who are described as fair-complexioned men pink and white, and as being famous horsemen, and accustomed to dress in bright-coloured garments, caused them to encroach on the Tokhari, who had just broken up the Greek Bactrian kingdom. They drove out the Sikas, or Sus, from the borders of the Pamir and its eastern slopes, and settled there.

But in their early migration a portion of them, the Little Yue-chi, Ephthalitae or White Huns, had already entered Tibet, and penetrated into North India and the Panjab. We find them at Vaisali and other towns bordering on the Ganges valley at an early date, probably as early as the middle of the second century B.C.; the others remained stationary on the north bank of the Oxus. Gradually they separated into lesser tribes and pushed further west, where, in all probability, they became known as Goths.

The remaining portions finally coalesced, after the dismemberment of the Hiung-nu confederation by the Chinese, and a few years before the Christian era they marched in a body, led by the chief of the Gushan horde, to invade India and the entire Indian frontier. This was accomplished, and at the time of Kanishka, who reigned at, or shortly after, the beginning of our era, the whole of North India and the portions of Central Asia between Parthia and China were brought under their power. It is this Kanishka who became a Buddhist, and who built the vast towers and Topes (stupas) which still remain in a ruined state, but yet monuments of his energy and zeal, throughout portions of Afghanistan and Kashmir. Thus it was the northern tribes of barbarians, as we call them, are seen to play a conspicuous part in the history of the early dissemination of the Buddhist doctrine, for it was through them that the first knowledge of Buddha reached China; and it is, as we shall now proceed to show, principally through them, and their zeal in spreading the knowledge of their books, that the system of Buddhism came eventually to be patronised and established in that empire.

The Dream of Ming-Ti

It was in the reign of the Chinese emperor Ming-ti—who came to the throne A.D. 58, and reigned until A.D. 76—that Buddhism was definitely introduced into the empire. The capital at this time was at Loyang; and it was here that for many years afterwards the great Buddhist centre of work lay. The Emperor Ming-ti had probably heard of the progress of Buddhism among the tribes bordering on China and India; and if, so early as the reign of Wu-ti, **a golden image of the Indian saint had been set up in one of the Chinese possessions,** we may suppose with reason that the worship had spread in the interval, and some reports respecting the religion of Buddha come to the ears of the Chinese people.

The emperor, at any rate, is said to have had a dream in the third year of his reign (A.D. 61) in which he saw a golden figure fiying from heaven and hovering over his palace. Its head was surrounded by a glory equal to that of the sun and moon. Being moved by his dream to inquire about its meaning, one of his ministers, Fu-yih, told him that he had heard there was a divine person born in the west, called Buddha, and that probably his dream was connected with that circumstance. This clearly shows that Fu-yih had received some intelligence about this religion, and we might venture to think that he himself had a partial belief in the truth of what he had learned.

But, at any rate, **the emperor was induced, on hearing the minister's report, to send a mission to India in search of correct tidings about this mysterious personage.** We are told in the annals that the mission, numbering in all eighteen men, arrived in India and came as far as the country of the Yue-chi. It is probable that the district referred to under this name was the country of the Vajjis, who were in all probability an offshoot of the northern tribe of the Yue-chi, or White Huns, of whom we have already spoken. We are told by Sze-ma, that the languages spoken throughout the district where these tribes of northern people lived, from Tawan, about Yarkand, as far west as Parthia, differed but slightly and were mutually intelligible. It would be easy, therefore, for the Chinese mission to proceed through these territories and pursue their inquiries respecting Buddha; and the special occurrences of the period would make their mission still more practicable, for at this time, probably, Kanishka was rising in power and his hordes preparing to invade India.

They actually advanced as far as Magadha, south of the Ganges, and carried off from that country some of the sacred relics which were treasured there, as well as the persons of some eminent Buddhist teachers. At such a time, therefore, as this, the Chinese embassy penetrated to India and arrived among these Yue-chi. Here they collected books and pictures and relics, and, accompanied by two priests of the religion, they returned homewards and arrived at the capital, Loyang, A.D. 67. The emperor appears to have lent a ready ear to the instruction of the foreigners, and **in the end caused a temple to be built in which the books and relics might be stored.** The temple was called after the name of the "white horse" on which the books, etc., had ueen brought from the west. Such is the account given of the introduction of Buddhism into China; there is nothing improbable in the narrative, so far as the outline is concerned; and it is accepted on every hand by the Chinese themselves.

But, as in most cases, there is much incredible matter added to the story—as for instance, with regard to the controversy between the Taoist priests and the new missionaries or envoys from India. In this account, we are assured that miracles were wrought to convince the emperor and people of the superior claims of the Buddhist religion; and it is added, the Taoist priests, abashed at their defeat, fell dead in the presence of the assembled multitudes. Leaving these stories out of the account, we seem to have before us a simple narrative of an event probable in itself, of the introduction into China of books and teachers related to a foreign religion, now gathering notice throughout the east, and which had already spread to the confines of the empire. When we remember, too, that Kanishka and his followers had embraced this creed, and that it had probably found its way into Parthia,—all this taken into connection with the story of the emperor's dream, makes it likely that we have in the foregoing record an historical fact, that Buddhism found its way from India to China in 71 A.D.

4

Sakya-Muni in China, Not Gautama

The two Indian priests who accompanied the Chinese mission on its return to China were called Matanga and Gobharana (Chinese: Chu-fa-lan). They brought with them some books, and these they translated into Chinese. One of the books was 'A Life of Buddha,' in five chapters,—it is to this book we will now allude.

There is no life of Buddha known as a distinct work in the southern canon. But in China we find several such works. We shall consider some of them hereafter; for the present, there is one point that calls for notice, the origin of the family to which Buddha belonged. The general name by which Buddha is known in the books is Sakya-Muni, or, the monk of the family of Sakya. This name is not so common in southern accounts. Professor Childers makes the following remarks:—"The Sakyas formed a great clan or people engaged in agriculture, among whom probably a very few families were princely. Their territory appears to have been of some extent. Sakya-Muni, the Sakya sage, or philosopher, is given as an epithet of Gautama (i.e., Buddha). But I enter my protest against the continental custom of speaking of Gautama Buddha as Sakya-Muni, which is a mere epithet. Gautama is the name by which he is universally known and addressed.

Perhaps nothing could show more clearly the difference that exists in the two schools of Buddhism than this remark. The northern tribes adopted the term Sakya as the right name of Buddha, probably because it is related to the name of a tribe akin to themselves. The Sakya play an important part in the history of central Asia. We shall show that the Buddhism of the north was certainly framed and fashioned during its development by legends and doctrines derived from outside influences; so that it seems likely the very name of Sakya was applied as a distinctive name to Buddha, because it brought him and his teaching more closely into connection with the current of northern traditions.

The title of Gautama, on the contrary, which is essentially Indian, "borrowed by the Sakyas" (after their settlement in India) "from one of the ancient Vedic bard-families," is almost unknown in the Chinese books. It does occur undoubtedly, but compared with the name of Sakya (which name, indeed, forms the title of the Buddhist community in China) very seldom, and never as a distinctive title for Buddha after his enlightenment. M. Burnouf has the following remark as to the origin of the name Gautama. "He, i.e., Sakya-Muni, retained in one of the names which he bore, a trace of the connection, essentially religious, which attached his family to the Brahmin caste. He called himself the Sramana Gautama, or the Gautamite ascetic, without doubt because Gautama was the name of the sacerdotal family of ihe military race of the Sakyas, who, in the quality of Kshatriyas, had neither ancestor nor tutelary saint after the manner of the Brahmins, but who were able to take, as the law of India allows, the name of the ancient sage to whose race their spiritual director belonged." In a note to this passage the same writer adds: "The origin of this title—or Gautama, or the Gautamas—remains unknown, and the explanation I have offered is, after all, only a conjecture."

This account of the matter appears very probable, as we know from other sources that, according to a well understood custom, the Rajas (i.e., kings of the Kshatriya caste) were considered members of the gotras of their purohitas, and called themselves after the latter. And so Oldenberg states of the three Buddhas preceding the present age, who belonged to the Kshatriya caste, "The gotta [gotra] is mentioned as sometlling existing as a matter of course: they are all Kondannas." This gotra name, then, of Gautama was probably adopted by the Sakyas because it was that of the purohita, or court teacher, adopted first by them after their settlement in the district of Kapila, where we find them at the opening of their history as a settled people. But this would recommend the name especially to Indian converts. They would adopt it naturally, and apply it to Buddha as his correct title; not so, however, among the northern, non-Indian people; they would hold to the name which they considered to be derived from one of their own tribes or clans, and this, in fact, would greatly account for their early adoption of the teaching of the Sakya saint, and explain the hold it took almost at once on the northern tribes of invaders.

There is an incident in the life of Buddha written by Asvaghosha, about the beginning of the first century, which will illustrate the point before us. Buddha had just attained what he called "enlightenment," and therefore was now a Tathagata, or inspired prophet. He is going to seek some ascetics who had remained with him during his penance, but had left him when he broke his fast. They are described as speaking thus together, when they saw him approach— Seeing from far Tathagata approaching, sitting together and conversing, thus they spake: "This Gautama, defiled by worldly indulgence, leaving the practice of austerities, now comes again to find us here; let us be careful not to rise in salutation, nor let us greet him when he comes, nor offer him the customary refreshments; because he has broken his first vow, he has no claim to hospitality.'

Having spoken thus, and so agreed, each kept his seat, resolved and fixed. And now Tathagata slowly approached, when, lo! these men, unconsciously against their vow, rose and invited him to take a seat: offering to take his robe and alms bowl; they begged to be allowed to wash his feet, and asked him what he more required; thus in everything attentive they honoured him and offered all to him as teacher. They did not cease, however, to address him still as Gautama, after his family. Then spake the lord to them, **'Call me not after my familiar name, for it is a rude and careless way of speaking... call me, therefore, Buddha.'** Here we see the familiar name of Gautama is forbidden, and consequently it is seldom met with in the books found in China; but he is still called Sakya and Sakya-Muni; and those who take the vows are frequently distinguished by the name, as distinctly religious, as for instance, Fa-hian, the pilgrim, is known as Shih Fa-hian, i.e., the Buddhist priest Fa-hian.

The origin of the term Sakya is referred by the early writers to a story related of one of the ancestors of the family. Ikshvaku Virudhaka, who reigned at Potala, on the Indus, had banished his four eldest sons from his kingdom, and afterwards, on inquiry, finding that they had established a powerful kingdom elsewhere and were reigning in prosperity, is said to have exclaimed, "They are able! they are able!" which, put into a Sanskrit form, was converted into this name Sakya, from the root *sak*, "to be able." This is probably an invention; there may be a verbal root, indeed, found in other languages of the form here named, signifying "ability" or "power," and it is possible that the Sakyas were a race remarkable for their strength, and had derived their name from this characteristic, but there is no proof of it, and for the present we must be content to consider the Sakyas as an old family found in

North India of an exclusive and proud character, derived probably from an immigrant branch of the great Saka race that from early times, according to Strabo, occupied the frontier land along the borders of all India.

This may be gathered from a consideration of the circumstances mixed up with the Buddhist legend as it comes to us in the north. Whilst, on the one hand, there is no Brahmin or native Indian family known by the name of Sakya, on the other, there are several circumstances which tend to show that these people were allied to a northern, non-Indian race. They were a chivalrous, exclusive, and proud people. Their own legend connects them with a tribe or family settled at an early period at the mouth of the Indus; and, when they are found at Kapilavastu, it is still as emigrant settlers who had sought this spot so as to continue as distinct people, and, for the purpose of preserving their pure descent, intermarrying amongst themselves, brother with sister. But we may go further than this: the Sakyas appear to have had the character not only of a distinct race or tribe; but a degree of sanctity or holiness is attached to them as a race.

There is a curious story told by the Chinese pilgrim Huen Tsang, respecting them which may be given as an illustration of this. He tells us that he saw, among many other remains, in the country of Kapilavastu, i.e., the country over which the Sakyas ruled, four little towers, or stupas, and he goes on thus—"This is the place where four Sakya youths withstood an army. When first Prasenajita became king of Kosala he sought an alliance by marriage with the Sakya race. The Sakyas despised him as not being of their family, and so they gave him as his wife the daughter of a slave whom they largely endowed, but this they did to deceive him.

"The king made this girl his principal queen, and she bore him a son in due time, whom they called Virudhaka. This prince, when he grew up, desiring to complete his education, purposed to go to the country of his maternal uncle, i.e., to the king of the Sakyas, for this end. Having arrived at the south part of the city of Kapilavastu, he there saw a new preaching-hall, and there he stopped his chariot. The Sakyas, hearing of his arrival, went out and drove him away, saying: 'How dare you, base-born fellow! occupy this abode, a hall built by the Sakyas, intended for a preaching-hall for Buddha?' So then, after Virudhaka had succeeded to the throne, he longed to revenge the insult he had received. Raising an army, therefore, he occupied the country with his troops, who took possession of the fields and devastated the crops. Now, it happened that four men of the Sakyas were engaged in ploughing between the water courses in a particular field; seeing the soldiers approach, they opposed their progress, and eventually drove them off.

"After this, they entered the town and told what they had done. Then their clansmen, considering that their tribe was one in which a succession of holy kings had appeared, and in which the sacred king of religion had now been born (i.e., Buddha), and that now these four men, not withstanding this, had dared to act revengefully and cruelly, and to slay and kill, without patiently enduring wrong, and so had brought disgrace on their name, drove them from their home. Being thus banished, they went to the north of the Snowy Mountains, and became each one of them king of a different country. One ruled over the country of Bamian; another over Udyana; another over Himatala; and another over Sambi [Kausambi?]. Here they have reigned without interruption, transmitting their kingly authority from generation to generation."

To this account, M. Stas. Julien, the first translator of Huen Tsang, appends the following note—"It seems strange that these noble champions should be driven from their town and exiled by their parents because they resisted the troops of the destroyer of the great Sakya family." And so it does appear strange; but the story confirms the supposition, which is in keeping with the entire Sakya legend, that these people had traditions among them relating to the sanctity of their tribe and the appearance of a great saint among them, which explains a great deal of the Buddhist expanded history." With respect to the foregoing extract, the circumstance of the banishment of the Sakyas is also found in the southern records, but the cause of it does not appear to be named. "When Buddha yet lived—so says the Atthakatha, i.e., the commentaries on the sacred books, belonging to the Uttaraviharo priests in Sri Lanka—driven by the misfortunes produced by the war of Prince Vidudhabo [Virudhaka], certain members of the Sakya line, retreating to Himavanto, discovered a delightful and beautiful location, well watered, and situated in the midst of a forest of lofty bo and other trees. Influenced by the desire of settling there, they founded a town at a place where several great roads met, surrounded by a durable rampart, having gates of defence therein, etc.

"Moreover, that city having a row of buildings covered with tiles, which were arranged in the pattern of the plumage of a peacock's neck, and as it resounded with the notes of flocks of 'konchos' and 'mayuros' [pea-fowls], from this circumstance, these Sakya lords of this town and their children and descendants were renowned throughout Jambudwipa by the title of Moriya. From that time the dynasty has been called the Moriyan dynasty." This is probably without authority, but the record of the early dispersion of members of the Sakya family in the region of the Himavanto is, to all appearance, a reliable one, as it is preserved in the south as well as the north. No doubt, then, these Sakya youths not only settled in these districts because they found members of allied tribes already there, but, having established themselves there, they would perpetuate the traditions of their own tribe and preserve the knowledge of the coming of a great teacher amongst their people. We do not wonder, therefore, to find the doctrine and discipline of Buddha so readily accepted at a subsequent period in these regions and by these tribes.

There is a curious confirmation of this idea of sacredness attached to the Sakya tribe to be drawn from a remark found in Josephus. Before referring to it, however, it will be necessary to premise that the Sakya family were known also as Ikshvakus, or the "sugar-cane" family. This name was derived from the old king who reigned at Potala, on the Indus, who was called Ikshvaku Virudhaka. Doubtless, he inherited the name from his ancestors, or the clan to which he belonged. That the Sakyas were known as Ikshvakus (Pali, Okkakas) is evident from all the records: "The son of Kalaranjanaka was Asoka, whose successor was the first Okkaka king." (Spence Hardy) And the last of this race was Amba or Okkaka III, from whose direct line descended the father of Buddha.

The peculiar character for holiness or sanctity attaching to this family is to be gathered from various notices found scattered through the different lives of Buddha. For instance, we are told in the southern records, that when the four sons of the Okkaka king, after their banishment from Potala, consulted together as to their future home, they said, "We have so large a retinue that there is no city in Jambudwipa which could withstand us; but if we were to seize on any kingdom by force it would be unjust and contrary to the principles of the Okkaka race, it would be inconsistent in us to take that which belongs to another, we will therefore erect for ourselves a city and reign in righteousness." Again, the Chinese version of the Buddha-charita, or Life of Buddha, by Asvaghosha (dating, from the beginning of the "first century, A.D., begins in this way—"Descended from the Ikshvaku family, pure in mind, of unspotted virtue, reverenced by all, was Suddhodana, the father of Buddha." And in other passages the Ikshvakus are spoken of as distinguished for their purity and piety of life.

It is curious to find in Josephus a passagc which seems to refer to this "sugar-cane" family of India. It occurs in the fourth book 'Against Apion' Ch. 22. The author is showing that the most eminent of the Greeks were acquainted with the Jewish nation. He says:—"For Clearchus, who as the scholar of Aristotle, and inferior to no one of the Peripatetics whomsoever, in his first book concerning sleep, says that Aristotle, his master, related what follows of a Jew, and sets down Aristotle's own discourse with him. The account is this as written down by him. 'Now, for a great part of what this Jew said, it would be too long to recite it; but what includes in it both wonder and philosophy, it may not be amiss to discourse of. Now, that I may be plain with thee, Hyperochides, I shall herein seem to thee to relate wonders, and what will resemble dreams themselves.' Hereupon Hyperochides answered modestly, and said, 'For that very reason it is that all of us are very desirous of hearing what thou art going to say.' Then replied Aristotle: 'For this cause it will be the best way to imitate that rule of the rhetoricians which requires us first to give an account of the man and of what nation he was, that so we may not contradict our master's directions.' Then said Hyperochides: 'Go on, if it please thee.' 'This man,' then said Aristotle, 'was by birth a Jew, and came from Coele-Syria; **these Jews are derived from the Indian philosophers; they are named, by the Indians, Calami, and by the Syrians, Judaei, and took their name from the country they inhabit.'"**

And then Josephus goes on to say that "Aristotle discoursed particularly of the great and wonderful fortitude of this Jew in his diet and continent way of living." We cannot doubt that the word used by Aristotle, "Calmi," is a translation of the Indian "Ikshvakus," or the "sugar-cane" people. He speaks of them as philosophers, which is natural enough; but he compares them with the Jews because of their purity and continency of life. There seems here to be a covert reference to the family from whom the Buddhists sprang, and perhaps to the Buddhists themselves, known as Ikshvakus.

It is true, that there were other families in India belonging to these Ikshakuidae besides the race of the Sakyas. The kings of Ayodhya were of this family and, according to Oldenberg, the later ages trace back the royal race of Eastern Hindustan to Ikshvaku; but this does not stand in the way of the unanimous tradition found in the Buddhist books with reference to the pure descent of the founder of their religion, that—"he belonged to the holy family of the Okkakas, in which there had been a succession of sacred kings, known as Chakravartins." These Ikshvakus were, from an early date, settled at Potala, and thence established themselves as a royal race at Ayodhya, and afterwards at Kapilavastu.

If, then in agreement with our supposition, **the Sakyas were an immigrant tribe settled in India, and related to the Sakas, and if they were described as peculiar for their "just laws and righteous conduct,"** do we find anything corresponding with this description among the Sakas themselves? We know little of them, but yet there are not wanting some references on this point which seem to sustain the argument. In the seventh book of Strabo's "Geography" there is some discussion in reference to the character of the Getae, amongst whom Zamolxis, the teacher of Pythagoras, was esteemed as a god. These nomads were remarkable for their justice. And he connects them with the blameless Aethiopians of Homer, who were, in fact, Scythians. And then he proceeds to say that Aeschylus also speaks of the Scythians as a just race and so he connects them with the Sacae or Sakas, quoting Choerilus. And so Homer, speaking of the Aethiopians, calls them "blameless."

Were these Aethiopians a branch of the Sakas? There is, in Chinese, a well-known tribe of the Yue-chi, called

Ye-tha, and the situation which Homer gives his eastern people, close to the flowings of ocean, would correspond with the mountains of Gandhara, the "earth-holding mountains" of the Buddhist cosmogony. But, in any case, it would seem, from what has been said, that there was a belief prevalent from earliest times that a tribe of nomads, corresponding with the Sacao, or Sakas, were renowned for their justice and purity of life, and that the same character is given to the Ikshvakus, or Sakyas, found as settlers in India, from whom the founder of Buddhism, the lion of the Sakya tribe, sprang.

These remarks have been made with a view to clear the way for a conclusion to which the legend of Buddha seems to lead us. It will be seen that in the northern story of his life and teaching there are found fragments of early traditions which have been preserved in their integrity and completeness in the Jewish records. The argument, therefore, which the presence of such fragmentary allusion seems to suggest is this: that the Sakya race, and perhaps other allied families or tribes, had preserved amongst them some broken knowledge derived from earliest times, and that this knowledge took shape in a distorted form in the legend of their founder. Many allusions seem to express what is called a "felt want" in their system. And as the knowledge of Buddha's teaching spread further and further north, so the system he had framed adapted and adopted these fragments of truth, until we have before us the entire legend as it is known now among northern nations. What this legendary story is we shall next proceed to inquire, only premising this much—that it is the result of a succession of increments added on to one simple historical narrative, which narrative is found in the earliest records of the southern Pali school.

The Legend of Sakya Buddha

It is plain that, so far as our argument is concerned, it does not matter whether the legend of Buddha's life as known in China be derived from the authentic books belonging to the southern canon or not. The legend took shape, and it must have derived its parts from either (1) the original story, or (2) from traditions known among the people where it gathered its present form. As we have it in China, it is a perfect whole. The Buddha descended from heaven, and he was incarnated miraculously; born in a royal line, he was impelled by a sense of the misery of the world to seek enlightenment in order to save the world; he was enlightened and became a teacher, gathered disciples around him, converted those that were to be saved, and died at the end of a long life, surrounded by his followers; and, finally, after his death, was honoured and worshipped, being still present in the world in the form of a bequeathed system of law.

Now we find that a great portion of this is unknown in the south or rather in the early books of the Pali school. We are told by Oldenberg in his 'Life of Buddha' that "no biography of Buddha has come down to us from ancient times, from the age of the Pali texts, and we can safely say that no such biography was in existence then." But, at any rate, so early as the beginning of our era, a life of Buddha in seven chapters was brought to China, and that this contained the full legendary story as it is now commonly known is evident from extracts found in works at present extant, especially the "Shin Shing taou," by Wong puh. Beside this, however, is the Buddha by Asvaghosha, known as the "Buddha-Charita Kavya," which was undoubtedly written in the early part of the first century, and must have been founded on a legendary history in common circulation before it was put in a poetical form by that writer. We are brought to the conclusion, therefore, that between the period of the collection of Pali books, which may perhaps be placed about 350 B.C., and the first century B.C., the legend as known in the north was framed, and so familiarly known that it was put into a poetical form by Asvaghosha, who flourished either just before or just after the Christian era.

It has been said that the particulars of the legend are derived from nature-myths, and that these myths are to be found hidden in Indian texts. But the fault of this theory seems to lie here, that the legend of Buddha is not framed after any Indian model, but is to be found worked out, so to speak, among northern nations who were ignorant of, or indifferent to, any of the pedantic stories of the Brahmins. In the southern and primitive records, the terms of the legend are wanting. **According to Oldenberg, Buddha is not born of a royal family; he is not tempted before his enlightenment; he works no miracles; and he is not a universal saviour.** Whence come these ideas in the legend of the north? for we must repeat, the legend is known nowhere else in its completeness but in northern records or southern adaptations from northern records. It seems far fetched to suppose that the northern tribes had recourse to the figurative and obscure readings of the Brahmins and the epics of India, and there can be no proof brought to show that the traditions found elsewhere were known amongst the tribes who adopted Buddhism, except in the shape of a common inheritance. It is for the champion of the nature-myth theory to prove that the common folk-lore of the northern people was based on nature-myths only, and not on .a common tradition. We have already indicated that such traditions might have existed among the holy or pious families of the far east, and from them have passed into the history of Buddha, the great sage of the Sakya race.

5

Asvaghosha's Life of Buddha

Asvaghosha was the eleventh patriarch, as it is called, of the Buddhist order. He was born in Middle India, of a Brahmin family, and brought up in that faith; but, having been converted to Buddhism, he became an opponent of his old creed, and laboured earnestly to show its insufficiency. He was a poet and musician. It is said the early hymns of the Buddhists were chiefly written by him. He was taken from Magadha, in Middle India, to the north, by Kanishka, and it is probable he there wrote the life of Sakya Buddha to which we are about to refer.

In fixing the date of Asvaghosha, we have several notices to guide us, but the most satisfactory clue is the agreement in all the records that he was a contemporary of Kanishka. This monarch was an Indo-Scyth, who had come (circ. A.D. 70) to be the ruler of all North India, and probably of a great portion of Central Asia. There is no certainty as to the exact date of his reign, but it is now made probable that he was the founder of the Saka era, or samvat, or that this era dates from his death. This would make him flourish in the middle of the first century A.D., and, therefore, Asvaghosha would probably be living from the early part of this century till towards the close of it. He would thus be contemporary with the rise and establishment of the Christian religion in Western Asia.

At any rate, it is sufficiently clear that Asvaghosha, in writing a life of Buddha, derived his material from India and its neighbourhood, and that we have in his book a purely independent composition. We do not know whether the life of Buddha taken to China in A.D. 72 was in any way derived from this work of Asvaghosha, or whether he derived his material from this work; but it is likely that the envoys sent by Ming ti would hear of the writings of the patriarch of the Northern Buddhists, and it is possible that the book they took back with them was connected either as the original form of it, or as a digesty with the "Buddha Charita Kavya."

The poem is in five kiouen, or chapters, divided into 28 sections (vargas). It embraces 2,310 slokas, or verses, of four lines each. Thus, in the Chinese version there are 9,240 lines. The outline of the biography, or the poetical romance, is this: The miraculous conception of Buddha by the descent of a spirit on his mother, Maya. She was pure in mind as the water-lily, and strong and calm in her purpose as the earth. When the time for her delivery approached, she begged the king to allow her to visit a favourite garden called Lumbinl, and to wander therein, amid its fountains and its flowers and fruit-trees. Resting on a beautiful couch, religiously observing the rules of pure discipline, her son was miraculously born, constrained by great pity, come to deliver the world—on the eighth day of the fourth month—a season of serene and agreeable character. Without causing his mother pain, he came forth from her right side, sparkling with light, as when the sun rises from the east.

He deliberately stood upright and took seven steps, planting his foot evenly on the ground as he went, and then looking to the four quarters, he spake thus: "Now only am I born this once for the purpose of saving all the world." Forthwith from heaven there fell two streams of pure water upon his head, and causing refreshment to his body. Meanwhile, the devas in space raised in responsive harmony their heavenly songs, whilst he is carried on a jewelled couch back to the palace. Then the soothsayers cast his horoscope, "this most excellently endowed child will bring deliverance to the entire world, none but a heavenly teacher has a body such as this; or, if he be induced to continue in the world—that is, as a secular person—then he will become a universal monarch, mighty in his righteous government, ruling the world, uniting all other kings under his sway."

Then another well-known seer, called Asita, comes to the palace, and, taking the child in his arms, predicts his greatness as a teacher and sage. "This son of thine," he said, addressing the father, "will rule the world; born for the sake of all that lives, he shall give up his royal estate, escape from the domain of sin, the five desires, with resolution and with diligence, practise austerities, and then, awakening, grasp the truth. The heavy gates of gloomy unbelief, fast kept by covetousness and lust, all living things confined within, he shall open, and give deliverance to all. Let the king, then, doubt not, nor in himself encourage thought of pain."

The horoscope finished, the king distributes gifts to all within his kingdom, and when the child was ten days old, he takes him to a temple of the gods and offers sacrifice; then going back, the child is carefully brought up within the palace. The poem then relates how universal prosperity prevailed throughout the land. There was no biting hunger, the soldiers' weapons were at rest, all diseases disappeared; throughout the kingdom all the people were piously affectioned, they sought their daily profit righteously, and no covetous or money-loving spirit ruled them. All practised the four rules of purity, and every hateful thought was banished. So then, because of such propitious signs, the child was called Siddhartha, perfection of all things.

And now his mother dies, and goes to the heaven where the thirty-three gods rule. Precious gifts are offered by members of the tributary states, presents of various kinds,—oxen and sheep, deer, horses, chariots, precious vessels, elegant ornaments fit to please the prince's heart: but his mind was not disturbed by glittering baubles such as these. "And now he was brought to learn the useful arts, when, lo! but once instructed, he excelled his teachers. His father, seeing his exceeding talent and his deep purpose to forsake the world, selected for the youth a wife, Yasodhara, majestic like the queen of heaven, constant ever, cheerful night and day, holding the palace pure and quiet, full of dignity and grace. So with such a wife and countless women as attendants on her, the prince lived in his palace. Then, as time went on, a son, Rahula, was born to them, on which the king, Suddhodana, was encouraged to believe that now his son would love his child and not forsake his home.

At length, the prince desires to leave his palace for a time to see the gardens. "Without are pleasant garden glades, pure refreshing lakes, and flowing fountains; every kind of flower and trees with fruit, arranged in rows, deep shade beneath." The prince desired, as a chained elephant longs for the desert wild, to visit these. The king accordingly takes the precaution to have the way prepared, to remove offensive matter, all persons old or sick, all who suffered grief or pain through poverty, these were all removed, so that his son might, in his present humour, see nothing to afflict his heart.

But it was in vain; a deva of the pure abodes assume the form of an aged man and stood beside the path, "struggling for life, weak and oppressed." The prince, beholding him, inquired, "what kind of man is this?" The charioteer, embarrassed, scarcely dared to answer truly, till the deva "added his spiritual power," and caused him to frame a true reply, "This is an 'old man,'—he was once a sucking child, brought up and nourished at his mother's breast, and as a youth full of sportive life, handsome, and filled with enjoyment; as years passed on, his frame decaying, he is brought to feel the waste of age." On this, the prince greatly agitated, asks, "Is yonder man the only one bent down with age, or shall I be such as he, and others also?" The charioteer again replies, "Throughout the world, this is the common lot; the youthful form must wear the garb of age."

Then the prince ordered his chariot to return, and "with speedy wheels take me to my palace." Reflecting there on the affliction of age, his mind seems to be ill at ease, and found no rest in anything within his home. After this, to alleviate his sorrow, the king arranges other excursions, but on each occasion another painful sight is brought before him by the deva:—first a sick man, "his body swollen and disfigured, sighing with deep-drawn groans, his hands and knees contracted, his tears flowing piteously." The prince again puts the question, "What sort of man is this?" and on receiving a reply similar to the former, he once more goes back to meditate.

On the third excursion, he beholds a dead man carried to the grave; "four persons carrying a corpse lifted on high appeared before the prince; the surrounding people saw it not, but only the charioteer and he; "What is this they carry?" said the prince. And now the gods constrained the charioteer to answer thus: "This is a dead man, all his power of body gone, life departed; his heart deprived of thought; his intellect dispersed; his spirit fled; his body withered and decayed, stretched out as a dumb log; family ties snapped; all his friends who loved him once, clad in white cerements, desiring to behold him not, are taking him to lie within the tomb," Then the prince, hearing the word Death, bent down his body on the chariot leaning-board, and stammered forth, with bated breath and struggling accents: "0 worldly men! how fatally deluded! beholding everywhere the body turned to dust, yet living more carelessly." Then he went back again to meditate.

After these painful sights, the prince is taken, by way of diversion, to see a ploughing match; but when he saw the ploughmen plodding along the furrows, and the writhing worms, his heart again is moved with piteous feeling, and anguish pierced his soul to see the labourers at their toil, struggling with painful work,—their bodies bent, their hair dishevelled, the dripping sweat upon their faces, their persons fouled with mud and dust; the ploughing oxen, too, bent by the yokes, their lolling tongues and gaping mouths. "The nature of the prince, loving, compassionate, his mind conceived most poignant sorrow, and "nobly moved to sympathy, he groaned with pain." He then retires to a solitary spot, and, seated beneath a flowering Jambu tree, he gives himself to deepest thought!

He is represented as then, for the first time, entering the mysterious condition of rapt ecstacy so frequently alluded to in Buddhist books, and called Dhyana, or Samadhi. It may, perhaps, be as well to quote the words of the poem itself on this point. "Lost in tranquil contempl-ation, he reflected that youth, vigour, strength of life, constantly renewed without long stay, in the end fulfilled the rule of ultimate destruction." This was the subject of his meditation: then, "without excessive joy or grief, without confusion, and with no hesitation in his thoughts, without dull dreaminess or excited longing, without aversion or discontent, but perfectly at peace, without impediment radiant with the beams of gathering illumination—thus he sat."

Whilst meditating thus a deva of the pure abode, transformed into a Sraman, or religious ascetic, came to the place. The prince, with due consideration, rose to meet him, and inquired respecting him who he was. In reply he said, "I am a Sraman. Depressed and sad at the thought of age, disease, and death, I have left my home to seek some way of rescue, but everywhere I find old age, disease, and death; all things hasten to decay; no permanency is there anywhere. Therefore, "he goes on, "I search for the happiness to be found in that which never perishes, that never knew beginning, that looks with equal mind on enemy and friend, that heeds not wealth nor beauty; the happiness to be found in solitude, in some lone dell, free from molestation, all thoughts about the world destroyed." And having spoken thus he disappeared.

This was the turning-point of the prince's history. From this time the idea of Nirvana deepened and widened in him. "His body as a peak of the golden mountain, his shoulder like the elephant's, his voice like the spring thunder, his deep blue eyes like that of the king of oxen, his mind full of religious thoughts, his face bright as the full moon, his step like that of the lion king, —thus he entered in the palace, and straightway sought his father's presence. Then he explained his dread of age, disease, and death, and sought respectfully permission to become a hermit."

We need not dwell on the account of his further struggle against a sense of duty or affection for his father. The culminating scene is when he awoke in the middle of the night and saw the sickly lamps, and the confusion of the music-and-dancing women as they slept upon the floor. "Now," he exclaimed, "I have awakened to the truth; resolved am I to leave such false society!" He forthwith summoned his equerry to bring his horse, and, notwithstanding all his protests, brought him to comply. "Forthwith, on that eventful night, he left the palace gates," the man streaming with light, the outcome of his high resolve; the horse like the white floating cloud. "Thus man and horse, both strong of heart, went onwards, lost to sight like streaming stars; but ere the eastern heavens flashed with the light of morn they had advanced three yojanas."

The prince forthwith dismisses his equerry and his horse. He sends back his jewelled turban, cuts off his hair, and assumes the brown robe of a hermit. After vainly seeking satisfaction in the company of some pain-practising ascetics, he resolves to seek wisdom for himself. Accordingly, he repairs to a quiet spot by the banks of a river called the Nairanjana, not far from the little town of Gaya, and there for six years practised the most severe penance, —each day, the legend says, "eating one hemp grain—his body shrunk and attenuated, his limbs exceeding weak, his heart of wisdom increasing more and more." At length he arrived at the conviction that these were not the means, to extinguish desire and produce ecstatic contemplation (Dhyana). He resolved, therefore, to refresh his members, and cause his mind to rest by partaking of food in moderation. He rose and bathed in the Nairanjana, but so weak was he that scarcely, with the help of a bending branch, he could mount the river bank.

At this time, a shepherd's daughter, called Nanda, was apprised by a deva of the opportunity she had of being the first to offer food to the Bodhisattva. She came forthwith, "upon her wrists the bracelets of chalcedony contrasted with her robes of blue, as colours of the rounded river bubble." She reverently offered him some rice-milk, sweet and perfumed. On eating it, he felt his strength come back afresh; and then, leaving the spot of painful penance, he wandered on alone towards the tree beneath which he hoped to reach perfect enlightenment. This tree, commonly known as the Bodhi tree, or tree of knowledge, was near at hand; and as he went, the legend says, the earth was shaken, and the rumbling of the earthquake heard. Various signs presented themselves, and, accompanied by devas and gazed on by Nagas, he came and took his seat, "with upright body, feet placed under him, not carelessly arranged, but with his limbs all firmly fixed and compact." Thus he sat, "nor shall he rise again," the Naga cried, "until his undertaking is completed."

This is the culminating point of the legend, and it is surrounded therefore with strange concomitants. We are told that Mara, the lord of the world of sense—that is, of sensuous indulgence—"enemy of religion, foe of those who seek deliverance from sin, and therefore rightly called the wicked'"—he alone was grieved, and sent his daughters to attempt to allure the princely hermit from his purpose. In vain they try their arts. Then Mara comes himself, and thus addresses the prince, "Rise up! begone!" and points his poisoned arrow at him. Equally in vain, for the Bodhisattva's heart remains unmoved: he felt no doubt, no fear. Then the scene changes, and Mara calls his army host, "of horrid shapes and monstrous forms," to attack his enemy. Some holding spears, some grasping trees, others wielding ponderous maces, with shapes and bodies terrible; thus the wicked goblin troop gathered round the tree, intent on tearing limb by limb the Bodhisattva's body. From the four sides the flames burst forth, and fiery steam ascended up to heaven; tempestuous winds arose on every side; the mountain forests shook and quaked; wind, fire, steam, and dust combined, produced a pitchy darkness, rendering all invisible.

But still the Bodhisattva, "silent and quiet in the midst remained, his face, unchanged, as calm as heretofore, like the great lion king placed amongst all the beasts howling and growling round him; so he sat, a sight unseen before, so strange and wonderful." At length Mara, wearied of his efforts, filled with fear, again took up his way to heaven [Mara's palace, as the lord of the world of pleasure, was in the heaven of "desire"], while all his hosts, "overwhelmed with grief and disappointment, fallen from their high estate, bereft of their warrior pride, their warlike weapons and accoutrements thrown away—like as when some cruel chieftain slain, the hateful robberband is all dispersed —so Mara's army, disconcerted, fled away."

Then comes the climax. "Bodhisattva now remained in peaceful quiet; the morning sunbeams brighten with the dawn; the dust-like mist, dispersing, disappears; the moon and stars pale their faint light; the barriers of the night are all removed'; whilst from above a fall of heavenly flowers pay their sweet tribute to the Bodhisattva." Then, passing through successive stages of rapt ecstacy, he traces back all suffering to the one cause of ignorance (avidya), that is, absence of light, and then himself attains the great awakened state of "perfect light."

Thus did he complete the end of "self"; as fire goes out for want of grass, thus he had done what he would have men do; he first had found the way of perfect knowledge, then, lustrous with all-wisdom the great rishi sat, perfect in gifts, whilst one convulsive throe shook the wide earth. This is the condition of the Buddha, or the awakened, and by this name henceforth he is to be called. At first, so says the legend, Buddha was disinclined to preach or teach among men, for who would have the power to comprehend the truth; but he is represented as being urged by Brahmadeva not to entertain such thoughts. "Oh, let your loving heart be moved with pity towards the world burdened with vexing cares," such is his appeal. Then Buddha's heart relents, and greatly was his pity nourished, and purposed was his mind to preach.

Having received food from some merchantmen, he set out towards Benares, intending to find the five men who had for six years shared his fast, but had left him when he took the rice-milk from Nanda. Step by step, like the king of beasts the lion, did he advance towards the Kasi city, bent on this design, "to preach Nirvana and convert the world." On his way, he meets a young Brahmin called Upali, who, struck with the appearance of the great Bhikshu stood with reverent mien beside the road. Having gazed upon him with astonishment, he asks him "of what noble tribe he was, and who his master." Buddha replies, "I have no master, no honourable tribe; but, self-taught in this profoundest doctrine, I have arrived at perfect wisdom." This wisdom he calls Sambodhi, or Sambuddhi, a word which cannot be accurately defined, but which evidently implies an innate consciousness of truth.

Then he goes on to say: "I have no name, I seek no profit; but, to declare the truth, to save all living things from pain, to fulfil my ancient vow, to rescue all not yet delivered. I go to sound the law-drum (i.e., to teach) in Benares." The young Brahmin astonished at the manner and the words of the Bhikshu, left him to pursue his journey: but yet he could not forget what he had heard. "At every turning of the road he stopped to think, embarrassed every step he took." The Buddha—called now Tathagata,—"the properly come"—proceeding slowly onwards, came to the Kasi city; there he seeks out the hermits, who at first resolve to avoid and ignore him, but, as he approached, they rose and conducted him to a place of rest. **And now Buddha is represented as turning the law-wheel of all that is, laying the foundation of this authority as a teacher or preacher. He declares to the five men the character of his doctrine, embodied in four leading truths.**

First of all, he says, his is a middle way; he discountenances asceticism. "The emaciated devotee," he says, "produces in himself, by needless suffering, sickly and confused thoughts; for he who tries to feed a lamp with water will not succeed in scattering darkness, and so the man who tries with wornout body to trim the lamp of wisdom, will not succeed, nor yet destroy his ignorance and folly." And then he goes on:— Who seeks with rotten wood to evoke the fire [i.e., by drilling one piece of wood into another] will waste his labour and get nothing for it; but drilling hard wood into hard wood the man of skill forthwith gets fire. So, in seeking wisdom, it is not by these austerities a man may reach the law of life.

But, on the other hand, he continues, the way is not by pleasure or unrestraint, for to indulge in pleasure is opposed to right—this is the fool's barrier against enlightenment. As some man, grievously afflicted, eats food not fit to eat and aggravates his sickness, so how can he get rid of lust who pampers lust? Scatter the fire and the desert grass dried by the sun, who shall put out the flames fanned by the wind? Such is the fire of hankering lust [concupiscence]. I then, he adds, reject both these extremes; my heart keeps in the middle way; all sorrow at an end and finished, now I rest in peace."

Buddha then goes on to explain the eightfold path by which the same end is to be sought. Of this we shall speak hereafter. But this eightfold path is the way, and the way is the last of the four truths. The three other truths are these—Sorrow exists, and then he explains what sorrow is. And he sums up his definition in these words:—The source of sorrow is in self; get rid of self, and sorrow ends. The second truth is, that sorrows accumulate, that is, that from this germ of self, countless sorrows grow and increase, amongst which old age and death are chief. The third truth is, these sorrows may be remedied. There is no hard and invincible fate or necessity in the case; but as sorrow began so it may end. And then the last truth before-named comes in, the way,—the eightfold line of duty, by which the fetters one by one are loosed, and the condition of an Arhat—a saint—is obtained.

This was Buddha's first sermon on the highest truth; and having spoken thus respecting truth, rhe men and 80,000 of the devas were thoroughly embued with saving knowledge. They put away defilement from themselves; they got the eyes of the pure law [i.e., sight to behold the true teaching]; then all the earth-spirits together raised a shout triumphant, 'Well done! Tathagata on this auspicious day has set revolving that which never yet revolved, and far and wide for gods and men has opened wide the gate *amratam*.'" I prefer leaving this last word untranslated, for it would be misleading to render it by our word 'immortality', and yet it means deathlessness, or, according to Buddha-ghosha, the great southern authority, it signifies that condition which, "not being born, does not decay nor die".

This is the literal account given us by Asvaghosha of the first sermon preached by Buddha. We cannot here notice any other point respecting it than this, that the devas, or beings who correspond somewhat with our idea of angels, are made, in the Buddhist dogma, hearers and learners of the doctrine as well as men. And countless numbers of these are represented as having been converted by the power of Buddha's teaching. In fact, the whole creation is brought within the same power, and from the lowest to the highest, for all living, the teaching of the great sage is made serviceable.

We have, after this, an account of various incidents in the active life of Buddha as a teacher. To these it is unnecessary here to allude. **He gathers round hin disciples; travels from place to place; frames rules for his society or order; and brings the poor as well as the rich within the community. He allows women also, after some delay, to enter the order and thus, during fifty years of life he matures his system, and leaves behind for the guidance of his followers a body of well-digested rules.**

And now he comes to die: he is an old man of eighty, and he knows the end is near. The account of his last journey from Rajagriha to Kusinagara, as it is embodied in the Mahaparinirvana Sutra, is precise, and probably authentic. It is found also in the concluding book of Asvaghosha's biography. There are one or two points in the narrative which deserve notice, and to these we will briefly allude. First, it is to be observed how the legend makes the lord of the world of pleasure, i.e., Mara, constantly track the steps of the teacher. He had tried, in the first place, to prevent him from attaining a condition of enlightenment; afterwards he is described as coming to him on Mount Girsha to exhort him to leave the world; and now, on his journey towards the scene of his death, Mara again appears.

The narrative, as it is found in Asvaghosha, runs thus—Buddha had received the gift of a grove of trees from a

Courtesan and was now about to leave Vaisali—he was sitting down beside a pool or tank of water (the Markatahrada)—when, shedding forth a flood of glory from his person, Mara, the wicked one, was roused, and came to the place where Buddha was, and then, approaching with his hands closed, spake thus: "Formerly, beside the Nairanjana river, when you had accomplished your enlightenment, you said, 'When I have done all I have to do, then will I leave the world [pass to Nirvana].' Now you have done all you had to do, you should, as then you said, depart." Then answered Buddha, "The time, of my complete deliverance is near, but let three months elapse and I shall die." Then Mara joyously returned to heaven. Then Buddha declared, "Now have I given up my term of years. I live henceforth by power of spiritual ecstacy; my body like a broken chariot stands; completely freed from life [the world], I go enfranchised as a chicken from its egg."

Thus determined, the teacher is represented as travelling on slowly, accompanied by Ananda, his personal attendant, "who loved so much," and his other disciples, towards Kusinagara. As he went, he preached his final sermons to the people of the various towns he passed. At length, arrived at Kusinagara, he took his seat between two sala trees, and directed Ananda to prepare his bed. "Ananda going, and weeping as he went," obeyed the order.

Then the Tathagata lay down, his head towards the northland on his right side, his hand beneath his head, with his feet crossed as any lion king. All grief is passed; from this one sleep his last-born body shall not rise again. His followers gather round him, the wind is hushed, the forest streams are silent, no sound is heard of bird or beast, the trees sweat out large flowing drop's, the flowers and leaves fall mournfully: and thus he passed away; and then, as Buddha died, "the great earth quaked throughout; the sun and moon withdrew their shining, the sturdy forests shook like aspen leaves whilst flowers and leaves untimely fell around like scattered rain."

6

Buddhism Spreads

It has been stated that a Life of Buddha, similar to that of Asvaghosha's great poem, was brought to China so early as the year 70 A.D. From this date, for 600 or 700 years following, a succession of Buddhist monks or priests continued to arrive in that country. They brought with them their books, which, by the orders of various sovereigns, were translated and placed in the monasteries; and so, as these books accumulated, they were entered in the different catalogues prepared from time to time, and at length, in the year 684 A. D., grouped together as a collection of a body of sacred writings. It would be impossible even to allude to the work of each of the translators during this period, but some remarks may be made by way of illustration. In the first place, with respect to the motive that induced these priests to wander away from their native country across the mountains and deserts to China, doubtless the knowledge of so promising a field for work and the patronage given them would cause many to find their way eastwards.

But there was also a strange impulse at work in the case of some of them to convert the world, and it was this which constrained them to travel from spot to spot. Thus we read of a translator in the second century 147 A.D. who worked for forty years at Loyang in translating books, "moved by a desire to convert men." Then immediately following him came a prince—so called, at least—of Parthia, who translated 176 distinct books. We should gladly know from what language these books were rendered, especially as we find one of them is the work called Dhammapada, showing that this book was known even at this early time in the north.

The expression generally used is, that these books were translated from the 'Fan' language; but that is no guide, for the word does not necessarily mean the language of the Brahmins or of Brahmadeva, but it is used as a general term for all languages of India and the neighbouring countries. We are told that, at the time when the Tibetan books were translated, there existed Buddhist works in the language of Li [Khotan or Nepal], Zahora [Panjab], Kashmir, etc.; and there is no doubt such books were brought to China, for the translations frequently contain bastard proper names, and are evidently made from non-Sanskrit originals. But how soon books written in other than Indian dialects, commonly understood, for example, among the Parthians (the Arsacidae), were brought to China is not determined. This much we know, that the last named translator, who is called a prince, and who is said to have given up the kingdom to his uncle in order that he himself might become a Buddhist mendicant, was an Arsacid, and that he came to China A.D. 149 with books. Considering the important place Parthia held in the east at this time, and its close relation with the west, this point is an interesting one. It is plain that many of the books translated were done from originals, not Sanskrit, but probably a corrupt dialect of Sanskrit commonly used in districts outlying the Indian frontier.

It is noticeable how rapidly the Buddhist movement and a knowledge of the books spread through China. **In 335 A.D. the Chinese were allowed to take monastic vows themselves, and as many as forty-two convents (or pagodas) had been built in Loyang alone.** It appears that much of this popularity was the result of a pretended power to work miracles. We read of a priest called Buddhasinha who claimed this power about the date just named, and, in consequence of his imposture, he persuaded the prince of the Chau kingdom to permit his subjects to become monks. These miraculous powers were sometimes an assumed ability to mount into the air without assistance but generally these miracles were connected with the Sariras, or relics of Buddha, or some great Bodhisattva; these were either some hair which would stretch indefinitely, or a bone relic that no power of man could break. But in no case were miraculous powers of a benevolent kind claimed; the signs, in fact, of their superior claims were wonder-working powers rather than miracles.

In agreement with this, we find priests occasionally put to death for practising magical arts; the account given is that "they used wild music to win followers, taught them to dissolve all ties of kindred, and aimed only at murder and disturbance." No doubt, in India power to work wonders was widely claimed by the Buddhists, and the miraculous virtues of the Sariras of Buddha when deposited in stupas is constantly referred to by the Chinese Buddhist pilgrims. Fa Hian, for example, tells us that when Buddha visited North India he left an impression of his foot in a kingdom called Udyana, and that in his time the impression was still there; but, he adds, it appears large or small according to the intensity of the religious feeling of the person who beholds it.

Again he tells us of Buddha's alms bowl, which poor people with a few flowers are able to fill, while the rich, though they offer thousands of bushels, can never fill. And every chapter in Huen Tsang's history of India contains accounts of wonders beyond all human ken wrought by the relics of Buddha. Sometimes the stupa emits a constant flood of light; sometimes it has the power of effecting an answer to the prayers of worshippers; at other times, a cover remains in mid air suspended by nothing; at other times, the cover moves with the worshipper.

We cannot wonder, therefore, that these magical powers were referred to similar relics and buildings in China, and hence to a great extent the rapid growth in popularity of the new creed amongst the people. At the beginning of the Tang dynasty (620-904 A.D.), a persecution was raised against Buddhism on the ground that the priests and nuns, by avoiding marriage, impoverished the revenue—what they hold about the condition of men depending on the will of Buddha is false; life and death are all determined by a self-governing fate; the monks are idle and unprofitable members of the community. So said Fu-yi, one of the ministers of Kaou-Tsu, the first emperor of this dynasty.

After some controversy, the Confucianists gained their point, and severe restrictions were placed on the foreign faith. These, however, were shortly afterwards removed; and during the reign of the second emperor fresh honours were bestowed on the priests, and in the person of Huen Tsang, the pilgrim, the cause was made an occasion for high court favour. Yet we read in the annals of frequently recurring persecutions. Early in the eighth century, A.D. 714, more than 12,000 priests were obliged to resume a secular life, and the writing of books, casting images, and building temples were strictly prohibited. But the cloud passed over, and in the year A.D. 763 Tae-tsung patronised the monks, because he believed that by propitiating the unseen powers he could preserve his empire from danger at less cost than by expending blood and treasure on the battlefield. This at least was a businesslike way of looking at the questions.

Again, the Emperor Huen tsung sent mandarins to escort a bone of Buddha to the capital, on which one of his ministers presented a strongly-worded remonstrance to his master: Why should a decayed bone, the filthy remain of a man long dead, be introduced into the imperial residence?

As for Buddha, he braved his vengeance and defied his power. This protest is still regarded with admiration by the Confucianists; the author of it, however, was banished to the Kwang-chow province, where some accounts state he was converted to Buddhism by a priest called Tai-Tien.

In the year 845 A.D., a third and very severe persecution broke out against the Buddhists. By an edict of the Emperor Wu-tsung, 4,600 monasteries were destroyed, and 40,000 smaller religious houses; the property of the houses was confiscated and used in the erection of secular buildings, and the copper bells and images were melted down and made into copper coins. More than 260,000 monks and nuns were made to return to secular life. Yet once again, as so frequently happens in history, this policy was reversed by Wu-tsung's successor, and unlimited tolerance proclaimed. Thus it was; the opposition of the Confucianists at one time was sufficient to check for awhile the advance of this creed—at another time, it recovered its lost numbers and seemed to ride over all misfortunes.

At length we read of a census being taken, towards the end of the thirteenth century, of the number of Buddhist temples and monks in the country—of the former it was reported there were 42,318, and of the latter 213,148—this was during the reign of Kublai Khan. If we remember that the ordained monks represent only a fractional portion of the professed adherents of the religion, and that beyond these again are the unattached professors or delievers in the externals of religion, we may conclude that at this time a majority of the people of the empire were Buddhistic if not Buddhists.

So the religion fared, until the time of Kanghi, the fourth emperor of the Manchu dynasty (1662 A. D.), who issued the so called Sacred Edict, in which the Buddhists are blamed for fabricating groundless tales about future happiness and misery. They are charged with doing this only for gain, and encouraging for the same object large gatherings of the country population at the temples, ostensibly to burn incense, but really to promote mischief. These sentiments are approved of at the present time. One of the sixteen lectures comprised in the edict is read at the periods of the new and full moon, in the temple of the patron god of each Chinese city. The town clerk, the local officers of Government, and a few rustic people, compose the audience. The Buddhist priests are denounced as drones of society, creatures like moths and mischievous insects, that thrive on the industry of others, whilst they do no work themselves. The people are warned not to go to their temples, nor take part in their village festivals.

Thus ostensibly the religion is proscribed, but yet it flourishes. The temples are still frequented; the monasteries, especially about Peking, are crowded with thousands and tens of thousands of monks, and books are issued from every quarter of the land, advocating or exhorting to the use of the Scriptures. It is our duty to look below the surface of this matter, and inquire what it is in Buddhism that keeps its hold on the minds of the people of China and Japan; and whether we may not deal with the question in a manner more suited to our own advantageous position, and the needs of the people, than we seem to have done hitherto.

7

The Worship of Kwan-Yin - Avalokitesvara

This god is the most common object of veneration among the Buddhists in China. Kwan-yin is a contraction of Kwan-shai-yin, a phrase signifying "a being who hears or perceives the cries of men." We will speak of this being, as is usual among the Chinese, as a female Pu-sa, or goddess. She is commonly known as the "Goddess of Mercy," from her attribute of "hearing." It is evident at once that such a being is foreign to the principles of Buddhism. There is no object of supreme worship among the Buddhists of the southern school. We must look on this culture, then, as a foreign introduction. The Indian name for Kwan-yin is Avalokitesvara, the "looking-down god," and the idea of such a being was probably derived from the old worship paid to the gods of the hills.

It seems probable that this Avalokitesvara was at first identical with Sumana, the god supposed to reside on Adam's peak in Sri Lanka. Reasons for this supposition will be given hereafter; it is enough now to say that this mount was visited according to the legend by Buddha, who left here an impression of his foot; according to the words of the "Mahavamsa," "rising aloft in the air, the divine teacher displayed the impression of his foot on the mountain of Sumanekuto," i.e., Adam's Peak. But, in the north, the legend is narrated under another form, that Buddha visited Lanka, and while there preached on Mount Potaraka or Potalaka a sutra, called Avalokitesvara, "with twelve faces." Now, the name given to this being by M. Burnouf is Samanta Mukha (Lotus of the Good Law), or, "the god who looks every way"; and one name of Sumana, the genius of the mountain, is Samanta, and the peak is called Samanta-kuta, so that we cannot doubt that Avalokitesvara (or the god who looks down, i.e., from the height of the mountain top) "with twelve faces," is the same as Samanta. This is rendered more likely if we consider the origin of the word Potaraka, or Potalaka. It is exactly the same word which is applied to Patala, at the mouth of the Indus, whence Nearchus with his fleet set out on their return homewards.

Whatever the true origin of this word, it means undoubtedly a harbour or a place for boats. Arrian tells us that the Indians call all the deltas at the mouths of their rivers "Patalas"; but this was probably hearsay only, as there is no such Indian word. General Cunningham supposes the origin of the word to be the Sanskrit Patala, a trumpet-flower, because of its shape, "in allusion to the trumpet shape of the province included between the eastern and western branches of the mouth ot the Indus, as the two branches as they approach the sea curve outwards like the mouth of a trumpet"; but this seems far-fetched. It would appear more probable that Potala was an old word for "harbour," or "place for boats"; at least, we find the word *pota*, a boat, an old Sanskrit word, and the termination *la* (or loka) a frequent one to signify "that which holds or keeps"; the word Potala, " the name of a seaport on the Indus," with which the Potalaka mountain is connected, would therefore signify the harbour or boat-place.

But there was also a Patala in Sri Lanka, and it is the harbour usually frequented by foreign ships; it is the present Putlam, formerly called Bhatala, and by Batuta, Battala. Concerning this port, Dr. Lee, in his Hebrew

Dictionary, has the following remarks—"If the Ophir from which this wood [the aloe] was brought was Sri Lanka, as Bochart seems to have shown, let us see whether we can find any such wood there. Ibn Batuta tells us that the whole shore of Battala abounded with cinnamon-wood and the Kalangi aloe, and that the merchants of Malabar and of the Maabar districts transport it without any other price than a few articles of clothing, etc." This name of Putlam or Battala, then, is connected with the mountain Potalaka. It was, doubtless, given to the mountain by those who visited the island and frequented this port—the mountain itself being visible to sailors nine days before reaching the land (Ibn Batuta).

But this same name of Potaraka, under the form of P'u-to, is given to an island in the Chusan archipelago in China. These islands of Chusan lie just off the entrance, to the great port of Hang-chau, from which in olden times, and to the present day the great trading junks called Chin-chew junks set sail for their distant voyages. The name of Potalaka or P'u-to, therefore, was given to this island, and the goddess Kwan-yin, or Avalokitesvara, was worshipped there; just as the Arab traders or others gave the name Potalaka to the mountain in Sri Lanka as the first land made on their adventurous voyages, and in both cases called Potala, from its proximity to the harbour, which they desired to find. So the god who looks down, Sumana, or Avalokitesvara, was worshipped in both places.

But there is a fourth Potaraka consecrated to the worship of this deity, in Tibet, where Lhasa is built. This, doubtless, is so consecrated in recollection of the origin of the cultus that of a hill-god who looks down; for this mountain of Potaraka in Tibet is one of the highest in that land of mountain ranges, and the god Kwan-yin, or Avalokitesvara, is the tutelary deity of the whole district. From what circumstance, then, did the worship of this being originate? It is highly probable that the merchants residing at Kandy, in the time of Fa Hian, and called by him Sa-pho, were Sabaens from the coast of Arabia. The trade being in their hands, they had taken up their residence in the island, and would, doubtless, introduce many traditions from their own country into the place of their residence. Now, we are told by Tiele that "in the religion of the Sabaens of South Arabia, made known to us by the decipherment of the Himyaritic inscriptions, by the side of the national gods of a genuinely Arabic character, such as the principal god Al-makah, 'the god who hearkens,' we meet with a number of purely Babylonian-Assyrian deities." This principal god, Al-makah, is found named in nearly all the Himyaritic records deciphered hy M. Halevy and others.

It might be supposed, therefore, that these Sabaen merchants would bring some knowledge of such a famous god into Sri Lanka. We are not surprised, therefore, to find that the Chinese merchants, who went back from Sri Lanka and introduced the knowledge of Mount Potaraka, with its tutelary deity of Sumana, or Avalokitesvara (Samanta), carried back also the knowledge of this name, "he who hears," or, " the god who hearkens"; and this is the meaning of Kwan-yin, "the god who hears the cries of men."' If this be so, here is a full explanation of the foreign character of this worship. As we know the idea of an objective worship is unknown to the early Buddhists. Whatever adoration was offered to the spots consecrated by Buddha's presence was offered as a subjective act, working as an *opus operatum*, and so also with regard to prayer; but now we see "an object" of worship introduced, and veritable worship and prayer offered to it.

This cultus, then, is the result of a necessity felt by the worshippers, who could never rest satisfied with the adoration of a logical abstraction or an invisible presence. We will confirm this historical connection by one or two further remarks. We are told by Dr. Edkins that "the worship of Kwan-yin was introduced into Indian Buddhism not long before the Christian era. In China, Kwan-yin was worshipped probably as early as the Han dynasty, i.e., down to 190 A.D." It was just at this time that the Arab sailors, by the discovery of the monsoons, traded regularly with South India and Sri Lanka. We might naturally expect to find this worship of Kwan-yin appearing in India at the same time.

But the worship of Kwan-yin is always associated with that of another deity called Amitabha, and their residence is in Sukhavat!, or the "land of the blest." But it is tolerably certain that the idea of Sukhavati is derived from the old name of Socotra, Sukhadhara, the happy land. There is a remark made by the old geographer Agatharcides, in his work De Mari Erythreo, that the happy islands lie off the mouth of the Red Sea.

Agatharcides tells us that on this island merchants from all parts, especially near the Indus, congregated; and the author of the Periplus says that the Sabaeans were accustomed from this island to set out on their voyage to Sri Lanka, and it was here they collected their goods. We argue, therefore, that the knowledge of this Sukhadhara, or Sukhavati, the island was brought to Sri Lanka by the same channel as the worship of the "hearing God," Almakah, by the Arab sailors who at an early date traded with the island, and many of whom settled in the chief town of Kandy, and were known to Fa-Hian (A.D. 400).

There is a remarkable confirmation of the supposition, that Socotora was from a very early period regarded as the island of the blessed, in some Egyptian records lately deciphered. In a paper read by Mr. W. Golenischeff at the Oriental Congress in Berlin, On an Old Egyptian Story, it is stated that in a papyrus he had just discovered in the Hermitage Imperial at St. Petersburg, he found an account of a voyage to the land of Pount, which it appears represents the two coasts of the Red Sea opposite each other at the straits of Bab-el-mandeb—the ship was 150 cubits long, 40 cubits broad, and manned by 150 of the best sailors of

Egypt. A storm having arisen, the ship was lost while they were on the sea, as it seems, beyond the straits, and the narrator was the only one of the crew saved. He was carried, as he clung to a spar, to an island, where he passed three days in entire solitude. At length he went to search for something to eat, and he found figs and grapes, every sort of magnificent Aaqt, the fruits Kaou and Neqou, melons of all kinds, fishes, and birds—nothing was wanting.

He dug a pit, lit a fire, and offered a sacrifice to the gods. Suddenly he heard a noise like the roaring of the sea, the trees shook, and the earth quaked again and he found that the commotion was caused by a serpent that was approaching him; it was 30 cubits long, and its beard more than 2 cubits, its members (scales) were encrusted with gold and of the colour of the true lapis lazuli. It coiled itself up in front of him. The narrator was filled with fear, and fell down before the creature. He goes on to tell how the serpent carried him in his mouth to a place of safety, and listened to his tale of shipwreck. "Fear not! fear not!" the creature said, "it is God who has preserved your life, and brought you to this enchanted isle. Nothing is wanting here; it is filled with everything that is good. You shall pass four months here, and then a ship will come with sailors and you shall return to your own town and die there."

Accordingly, after the time stated, he descended to the shore, and there he found a ship manned with sailors who brought him back to the land of Pharaoh. This papyrus, Mr. Golenischeff tells us, is extremely ancient, reaching back nearly 4,000 years. He connects with this ancient story of the enchanted island the tale of the adventures of Ulysses, and the Arab story of Sindbad. We need not follow him here, but pass on to his statement respecting the island off the coast of Pount. He says, "We have an inscription of the valley of Hammamat in which there is an account of a voyage of a certain Hannou, which he had undertaken in obedience to the orders of the Pharaoh Scanxkra, to the land of Pount, and which in style resembles the narrative found in the papyrus. In this account there is also mention made of a serpent, set to guard the incense accumulated on an island.

Where then is this island? The translator of the story says: "The description of the island of paradise, as we filled it in the papyrus, appears to explain itself naturally enough. The description of the island of Socotora leaves no doubt that the Egyptians who visited the land of Pount, very little distance from Socotora, were able, if not to see it, to hear accounts, more or less confused, which would give them an idea of that island, difficult of access, but rich in vegetation above all those on the north-east of Africa." If this conjecture be true, it would seem that the tale of "an island of paradise" must date from this old Egyptian belief, and the locality be identified with the isle of Socotora. In any case, this agrees remarkably with the Buddhist story of Sukhavati, or Sukhadhara, which is only another form of the word Socotora. It will, perhaps, be useful to give here the account of this supposed paradise, where Amitabha and Kwan-yin dwell.

Buddhist Paradise

The worship of Amitabha under the corrupted form Ome-to, is a prevalent form of superstition in China, The word "Amitabha" means "boundless glory, or light." He is regarded as the father of Kwan-yin. In this connection the worship was probably derived from Persia. He is the same as Mithras. He is also called Amitayus, i.e., "the Eternal." In this aspect he would correspond with the Persian "Zervan Akarana," or " boundless time." It was during the time of Artaxerxes Mnemon (380 B.C.) that the worship of Mithras, combined with foreign usages, spread over Western Asia to Europe, and in connection with Anahita (the goddess of pure water) was more widely diffused than that of any other deity of antiquity (Tiele). Hence among the altars found in such numbers on the Roman wall that stretches across our own island, not a few have been found dedicated to Mithras.

But we are told again by M. Reinaud that "the worship of the sun, and of the goddess Nancea or Anaitis at an early date penetrated the whole of the Indus valley." This double worship prohably gave rise to the Buddhist fiction of Amitabha and Kwan-yin. The latter, at any rate, has several of the attributes of the Persian Anahita, Anaitis, or Nancea. In the first place, she is worshipped as a female deity: she is also distinctly called "the pure" (tsing) as Anahita was; again, she is called "the high" (kao wang) corresponding to Ardvi, the epithet of Anahita (Ardvi sura Anahita); she is drawn sitting beside "a waterfall" (Bunyiu Nanjio's Catalogue of the Chinese and Japanese books in the Bodleian), thus indicating her association with "water"; and lastly, as Dr. Edkins tells us, the epithet of the Kwan-yin worshipped in Puto is Kwo-hai, "she who came across the sea."

Without dilating on this point, it will be enough to state that the double worship of Amitabha and Kwan-yin holds a conspicuous place in the Buddhism of the North. It is associated with the fiction of a paradise, or, "happy, or, pure land." We cannot doubt the idea of such a land is derived from a foreign source; and we may reasonably connect it with the introduction of the knowledge of Persian forms of worship joined with the fiction of a happy or fortunate land known to the Sabaeans who traded with India and Sri Lanka.

With respect to this paradise, the hoped-for rest of many thousands of Buddhists, the sutras tell us that it is so called because those born in it have no griefs or sorrows, they experience only unmixed joys. " This happy region is exquisitely adorned with gold and silver and precious gems. There are pure waters with golden sands, surrounded by pleasant walks, and covered with large lotus flowers. Thus this happy abode is perfected and adorned. Again, heavenly music is ever heard in this abode; flowers rain down three times each day; and the happy beings born there are able, by going to other worlds, to wave their garments and scatter flowers in honour of countless other Buddhas dwelling therein. Again, there are in this paradise birds of every kind, peacocks, macaws, kalavinchas, etc., who during the six watches, i.e., every four hours raise their notes in concert to sing the praises of religion, hearing which there rises in the minds of the auditors remembrance of Buddha, the law and the community. Again, the name of hell is there an unknown word; there is no birth in "an evil way," no fear of such births; and the birds that sing are but apparitional forms, made on purpose to sound the praises of religion. Again, the trees and strings of bells —curtains with bells in that paradise, when moved by the wind, produce sweet and enrapturing sounds; and, when these sounds are heard, thoughts of religion rise within the minds of all the auditors.

For what reason then is that Buddha called Amitayus Because the length of life (*ayus*) of that Buddha, and of those born there, is illimitable (*amita*); therefore he is so called. And why is he called Amitabha? Because the splendour (*abha*) of that Buddha is illimitable. And living there is a multitude of purified and venerable persons, difficult to count, innumerable, incalculable. And, therefore, all beings ought to make fervent prayer for that country. They require not to have good works as their qualification; but only let them keep in mind the name of Amitayus, and with thoughts undisturbed for one, two, three, four, five, six, or seven nights, treasure and repeat the name; then, when death draws nigh, this Buddha, with a company of saintly followers, will stand before them, and there will be perfect tranquillity. Therefore, let every "son and daughter pray to be born in that Buddha-country." And so the account goes on, and the paradise of Amitabha extolled. **It is difficult to describe the strong hold this**

belief has taken on the minds of the Buddhists in China. The repetition of the name of Amita is considered so meritorious, that believers in this strange myth go on incessantly repeating it counting their beads, till the ear wearies of the sound 'Amita Buddha!' 'Amita Buddha!' There is an anecdote, however, told by I-tsing, of a priest of this school, which will show the effect of such a belief in rather a favourable light. It is told of a contemplative priest called Shang-tih. "This man," he says, "longed for the joys of the western paradise, and, with the view of being born there, he devoted himself to a life of purity and religion, reciting the name of Buddha. He vowed to write out the whole of the Prajna-sutra, comprising 10,000 chapters. Wishing to pay reverence to the sacred vestiges of religion, and so to secure for himself greater merit with a view to be born in that heaven, he travelled through the nine provinces of China, desiring wherever he went to labour in the conversion of men, and to write copies of the sacred books.

"Coming to the coast, he embarked in a ship bound to Kalinga. Thence he proceeded to Malaya, and there embarked in a merchant ship to go to Mid-India. Being taken in a storm, the ship began to go down, and the sailors and merchants were all struggling together to get aboard a little boat that was near. The captain of the ship, being a Buddhist, was anxious to save the priest, and called out to him with a loud voice to come aboard the boat, but Shang-tih replied: 'I will not come, save the other people.' And so he remained silently absorbed, as if he were satisfied to die. Having refused all help, he joined his hands in adoration, and, looking towards the west, he repeated the sacred name of Amita, and as the ship went down these were his last words. He had a follower who remained by his master and perished with him, calling on the name of Amita."[1]

1. "Journal of the R. A. S.," October, 1881.

Ritual Services

It has long been supposed that India must have been permanently affected by the presence of a Greek kingdom in the neighbourhood of its north-west frontier. Alexander the Great, we are told, was accompanied by some 3,000 artists and actors, who belonged to Hellas—and the introduction of the new comedy into India is traced directly from Alexandria to Barygaza (Baroch) and thence to Ujjayini and North India. The plays of Aeschylus and Sophocles were read at the Parthian court, and the relationship between Parthian and Western Asia was a very close one. The Parthian prince, Pacorus, was, as Josephus tells us, in possession of Syria and Jerusalem. The close connection of Parthia with India and the northern invaders (the Yue-chi) at this time has already been referred to. Then again, the marriage of Chandragupta with a daughter of Seleucus, and the apparent knowledge possessed by the grandson of Chandragupta, the great Asoka, with the Greek King Antiochus, and his embassy to four other Greek kings, all this shows that there must have been some connection between India and the western world, from the time of the estalishment of Greek influence in the valley of the Oxus.

We read again, after the fall of the dynasty to which Asoka belonged, the Moriya, of a persecution of the Buddhists in India by Pushyamitra, whose son, Agnimitra, met the Greeks in battle on the banks of the Indus. The Greeks soon prevailed, however, and under Menander, about 150 B.C., their conquests were extended to the Ganges. It was with this Menander, probably, that the discussion occurred known in Pali as the 'Milindapanho,' or dialogues between King Milinda and the Buddhist sage, Nagasena. This book, probably written first of all in Sanskrit and translated into Pali, exists in China under the title of Questions of Nanda. It is occupied with discussion on certain abstruse points of philosophy, such as the existence of a personal self, the character of Nirvana, etc., sufficient, however, to show that these questions interested the minds of the Greek conquerors, and led to inquiries and examination.

In the western Buddhist caves in India, especially those at Ajanta, there are paintings the most of which curious and interesting are those which relate to Kwan-yin pictured there. This litany is a sort of prayer for deliverance addressed to Kwan-yin by those in distress. We will give a translation from the Chinese of the circumstances under which such supplications are offered:—

All hail, great compassionate Kwan-yin!
Though I were thrown on the Mountain of Knives
They should not hurt me!
Though cast into the lake of fire,
It should not burn me!
Though hurled down into hell,
It should not hold me!
Though surrounded by famished ghosts,
They should not touch me!
Though exposed to the power of devils,
They should not reach me!
Though changed into a beast,
Yet should I rise to heaven!
All hail, compassionate Kwan-yin!

Now, we are told that among the paintings in Ajanta are representations of these very calamities, and Kwan-yin, being invoked, is drawn as coming to rescue her suppliants from their misery. In this service, which is called the confessional of Kwan-yin possessed of a thousand arms and a thousand eyes, i.e., the all-powerful and ever-watchful. In the preface to the service, the Emperor Ch'eng Tsu, otherwise called Yung Loh, the third emperor of the Ming dynasty, states that he has heard that Avalokitesvara

[Kwan tseu-tsai] Bodhisattva, urged by his infinite compassion, has engaged himself under a great oath to become manifested in everyone of the innumerable worlds, for the purpose of saving the creatures who inhabit them." This is a widespread belief respecting the character of Kwan-yin. Hence, he is supposed to have gone down to the lowest hell for this same purpose; and, as this will illustrate the entire subject, it may be as well to notice the account as it is given us in one of the Buddhist sutras first of all.

The work is called the Karanda-vyuha, or arrangement of the basket of Avalokitesvara's excellences. It opens in the way adopted from very early times, as it was delivered by Ananda, the personal attendant of Buddha, and who introduces his sermons by the phrase, "Thus it was heard by me." He then proceeds to describe the occasion of the sermon he is going to record, and then proceeds: "When the vast assembly was met together, suddenly beams of light issued forth in the hell Avichi" This hell of Avichi is the lowest or deepest of the places of suffering, styled by the Chinese Buddhists "earth-prisons" ; in the language of China it is termed wu-kan, without interval, i.e., a place in which torments are endured without interval of relief. The account then proceeds to state that the beams of light reached the hall of assembly where Buddha was about to preach to his disciples, and "decorated the whole place." The pillars appeared to be inlaid with gems, the staircases to be covered with gold.

On this, one of the leading disciples stood up, and having laid one shoulder bare, and bent his right knee to the ground, he put his hands to his forehead, and turned reverentially to Buddha, and addressed him thus: "I am filled with excessive wonder, O holy one, whence come these rays? Of what lord [Tathagata] are they the visible majesty?" On which Buddha replied: "This is not the majesty of a Tathagata [i.e., of Buddha]. O noble youth, the glorious Bodhisattva, Avalokitesvara, has entered into the great hell

Avlchi, and, having delivered the beings there, is entering the city of the demons, pretas, hunger-stricken ghosts; hence it is that these my rays have been emitted." Then the same disciple addressed Buddha in these words: "O holy one! What beings are found in Avlchi? Does he preach the law there where no joy is found? Whose iron realm, surrounded by walls and ramparts, is, as it were, one uninterrupted flame, like a casket of flashing jewels? In what hell where there is a great wailing cauldron, wherein myriads of beings are thrown; just as beams or pulses rising and sinking in a pot full of boiling water, so do these beings endure corporeal pain in Avichi, how then, O holy one, does the Bodhisattva, Avalokitesvara, enter there?"

Buddha replies :—"O noble youth! just as an emperor enters a garden full of all precious things, attended with all his royal pomp, so Avalokitesvara enters the hell Avichi; but his body undergoes no change. When he approaches the hell it becomes cool. Then the guards of Yama, the sovereign of hell, bewildered and alarmed, begin to think: 'What is this inauspicious sign which has appeared in Avichi?' When Avalokitesvara enters there, there appear lotus-flowers large as chariot-wheels, the cauldron bursts open, and within that bed of fire a lake of honey is manifested. Then Yama's guards seizing all manner of weapon—sword, clubs, javelins, etc., and all the defensive armour of hell,—repair to Yama, the lord of justice, and address him thus: 'Let our king know that our "field of action" is destroyed and is become a place of pleasure, and is filled with all joy.' Yama replies:—'What is the reason thereof?' On which the guard, answers: 'Let our lord know that an inauspicious sign has appeared in Avichi. All has become quiet and cool, and a man assuming all shapes at will has entered there, wearing matted locks, and a diadem, and decked with divine ornaments, with his mind excessively benevolent, and like an orb of gold. Such is the man who has entered, and immediately on his entrance lotuses have appeared as large as chariot-wheels, and the cauldron has burst open, and within that bed of fire a lake of honey is manifested.' Then Yama reflected: 'Of what god is this the majesty?' "

Yama then proceeds to reflect as to the character of all the gods, but finds no one to correspond with the majesty of Avalokitesvara. Casting his eyes back, the ruler of hell beholds the visitor, and forthwith advances to worship him. Having delivered the sufferers in hell, Avalokitesvara proceeds to alleviate the torments of the famishing pretas—those wretched beings with forms like burning red hot pillars, tall as skeletons, with mouths like needles' eyes, are delivered by his mercy. "The city becomes cold, the thunderbolts cease, and the doorkeeper, with uplifted javelin, his hand busy with poison, his eyes red with anger, suddenly begins to feel the influence of mercy. Then Avalokitesvara causes cooling rivers to flow, and to cool the tongues of those suffering creatures."

Finally, they are all born in the paradise Sukhavati.

Such is the character of the oath of this imaginary merciful being, even as we read in the sutra just alluded to, where Avalokitesvara says: "I am visiting the innumerable hells in the universe, resolved myself not to grasp the perfect knowledge of a Buddha until all beings have been not only delivered from punishment, but are settled in the world of Nirvana."

This being the character of the oath undertaken by Kwan-yin, the emperor then proceeds to say that "for the purpose of securing this condition of salvation or deliverance, Avalokitesvara has formulated certain sentences, or mysterious words, which, if properly repeated, will render all creatures exempt from sorrow, and render them capable of attaining supreme wisdom. And, therefore, he adds, "We bring this service and these words to the knowledge of our subjects immersed in the affairs of the world and not acquainted with this mode of salvation, and we earnestly exhort all men carefully to study the characters of this work and faithfully to follow them."

The service which the writer has witnessed begins with a direction as to the preparation of the altar of the merciful one. In arranging the temple, the image of Buddha is to he placed on an altar on the south side of the building. The figure of Kwan-yin must be put on an altar in the west of the building. This figure may be either one with ten arms, or six, or four, or two. [The "arms" represent the number of faces, which, in the first place, were intended to represent the all-looking (samanta-mukha) character of this being; but the phrase, being perverted to a literal sense, was symbolised by the actual number of arms and hands, which appear so gross and offensive in connection with this idolatry.] On the day appointed for the recitation of the service the "7th, 14th or 15th, 21st, and 28th of the month" in the morning early, the sacred precinct, within which the worshippers are to say the words, is to be defined. This is done by the use of a marked line, made with a knife and accompanied by the repetition of certain words. Then pure water is sprinkled towards each quarter, i.e., at each corner of the precinct, then clean incense-dust is sprinkled on the floor, and afterwards a silken cord, composed of threads of five colours, is passed round the limits of the sanctuary, and the usual words repeated.

This having been done, the adjuncts of worship are arranged—lamps, incense, flowers, banners, and offerings of food. The incense is to be made of the finest sandalwood dust of the purest kind.

Then mats for kneeling, or stools for the same purpose, are to be arranged. The "hours" are thrice in the morning and thrice in the evening,—the days those named before.

Before entering to worship, the brethren are to be careful as to personal cleanliness. If the garments worn are not new, they are to be the best in their possession. An hour before and after service there should be no "mixed conversation"; on meeting one another there should be only the customary respectful salutation. The mind should be chiefly occupied in considering the character of the "ten obligations" (i.e., the ten vows of the order, not to kill, not to steal, etc.), before and after service.

If there be no real devotion during service, but only a confused way of going through an external duty, and if after it there be no right recollection, what benefit can be expected from these religious exercises? The rules and directions for the service must also be carefully studied, so that in going through it there may be outward decorum as well as inward devotion.

Finally, let the worshippers (laymen) strive after a firm faith, and excite in themselves an earnest perseverance and so, having purified the three faculties of thought, word, and deed, and engaging in the service in a proper way, they shall obtain their desires. The "service" begins with a direction. These " directions" are printed in smaller characters than the rest.

" When the procession enters the great hall [the hall of contemplation—the temple] they bow the head and pronounce this universal prayer:- "'Namo! great compassionate Kwan-shi-yin Bodhisattva.'"

The expression "Namo" is generally translated "Praised be," as, e.g., in the sentence commonly found at the beginning of all Buddhist compositions, " Namo tassa Bhagavato Arahato samma sambhuddassa,"— "Praise be to the blessed one, the holy one, the author of all truth."

Reciting this slowly and devotionally, let them enter the altar precinct, and having invested it three times successively, let them take their places in a standing position, and reflect thus : "All the Buddhas are the same with myself; it is only because we are self-deceived that we think otherwise; to remove the obstacles in the way of such right knowledge, I now come to worship the precious objects, and so desire to benefit all living things."

From this, and the other explanations which follow, it is plain that, at the time when this service was composed, Buddhism had assumed the "mystic" form of belief known in the last stage of its development. In this period, all things were considered as one with the supreme; the cause of the illusion which leads us to think of subject and object (*nang* and *so*) being removed, there will be illumination; that cause is "ignorance" (*avidya*, not-seeing-ness).

Now follows a hymn of incense: "Diffusive incense cloud! the brightness of holy virtue! [or, how bright is the character (*tih*) of the holy one!] Boundless is the heart of Bodhi! Wherever lights one ray of that wisdom there is worship, there is praise. We look up and adore the king in the midst of the law!"

The idea is here, that the canopy of the incense-cloud corresponds with the universal presence of the "heart of wisdom"—this is a euphemistic phrase for the universal essence. Bodhi, or wisdom, is supposed to be the one essence everywhere existing and diffused; as we recognise this, and learn such wisdom, we are made sharers in this "heart." "The king in the midst of the law," is another mystic phrase for the presence of Buddha, or the Dharma-kaya representing Buddha, in the character of "the law." It approaches in one sense to a "religious" presence.

Then repeat three times the following invocation:—

Namo! incense-cloud canopy Bodhisattva.

Here we see how the title Bodhisattva came to be "applied to denote a personification of a quality. The idea of Kwam-yin was, in the first instance, the quality of "mercy." This quality was personified, and on account of its chief excellency, the being representing it came to be considered as chief among the Bodhisattvas. So in this invocation, the canopy of incense, representing the immanent presence of the "king of the law," i.e., the presence of Buddha, in worship came to be personified as a Bodhisattva also.

The invocation of incense finished, let the officiating priest say—

"Reverent and attentive!"

Then chant the following. Bowing after each ascription.

With all my heart I adore the everlasting Buddhas of the ten regions!

With all my heart I adore the everlasting law of the ten regions!

With all my heart I adore the everlasting "order" [congregation] of the ten regions."

Then continue:

[Let] "This entire assembly, on their knees, reverently holding flowers and incense [or perfumed flowers] offer them as a religious offering."

Then let the assembly kneel, and, holding in their hands incense and flowers, let them. chant the following:

Oh! may the cloud of this incense [or the sweetness of these flowers] spread abroad and fill the worlds of the ten regions. Through every earth of all the Buddhas may it be perfected as a boundless incense-glory; fulfilling the way of a Bodhisattva, may it attain to the incense of a Tathagata!

It is plain, that in this there is nothing but mysticism. The cloud of incense being personified as a Bodhisattva, is expected to reach to the mystic condition of a Buddha.

Then let the congregation (the professors of religion, *hing-che*) light their incense and scatter their flowers, and then with their entire heart repeat the following mentally:

I scatter this incense and the sweetness of these flowers far and wide through the ten regions.

To represent the brightness of the mysterious presence or doctrine of Buddha,

[Symbol of] The music of the heavens and the precious incense of the devas,

Their heavenly food and precious robes.

Not to be understood is the dust [the nature] of the mysterious law.

Every grain of dust [i.e., every part of the incense] proceeding from the whole, so every part of the grain proceeds from the whole law. Circling round without impediment, it constitutes a glorious body;

Spreading abroad through the universe, it reaches to [the presence of] the three precious ones,

And to the three precious ones throughout the mysterious worlds of the ten quarters.

So this offering which I here present

Is offered thus throughout the universe,

In every place without hindrance or impediment;

And so the odour of the pious deeds done through endless time. At last shall spread through every world

And cause all creatures to return

And gain the birthless wisdom of our Buddha.

The above is a sample of the transcendental aspirations of Buddhist worshippers, belonging to this latest form of mysticism. The hope is evidently of a final restitution. As the atoms of incense unite and form a cloud, so by our pious deeds, the odour of which is spread through all the worlds, are we brought back to a complete union with Buddha.

The service then proceeds:

Let all be reverent!

The head priest having said this bows once.

The congregation then reflects that the three precious objects of worship are separated from us only by our own impurity. If we cleanse our thoughts and words and actions, then they will be united with us and we with them.

Let them, therefore, chant,

With all our hearts we hail thee and worship, O Sakya Muni, lord of the world!

Then consider that the object worshipped and the worshipper are but one; let the obstacles of impurity be removed and he will come and give us rest.

The service proceeds in this way, with similar invocations to other objects of worship and similar reflections.

After the invocations, there is a prayer to Amitabha, and the other objects, finally to Kwan-yin. The prayer is of this character:

May the all-seeing and all-powerful Kwan-yin, in virtue of her vow, come hither to us as we recite the sentences and remove from us the three obstacles of impure thought, word, and deed.

We shall now merely give the succession of parts, as the portion translated is enough to show the character of the whole.

After the prayer of incense, except on the first day, the service proceeds with an introductory prayer to Kwan-yin. After this, there are ascriptions or praise to all the Buddhas and Bodhisattvas.

Next follows the lesson beginning thus—

The Sutra saith, etc. : —

After this, the litany of earnest request in this way-

All hail, compassionate Kwan.yin!
May I soon acquire perfect knowledge!
All hail, compassionate Kwan-yin!
May I soon attain divine wisdom!

Then follows the act of faith-

Though I were cast on a mountain of knives,
It should not hurt me.
Though thrown into a lake of fire,
It should not burn me, etc.

Then, after ten invocations to Kwan-yin, repeated quickly, and ten to Amitabha, the officiating priest continues with a second reading from the books, recording the vow of Kwan-yin to deliver all living things.

Now follows the repetition of the "sacred words," mostly in Sanskrit, not undetstood by the priests or people, but supposed to have a magical effect and bring deliverance by their inherent virtue.

After the repetition, there are various prayers of confession and strong aspiration after deliverance.

Finally, a further invocation, a procession round the altar, a prayer for "all that lives," and an ascription of praise; after this the assembly leaves the sanctuary.

It must be evident from a consideration of this outline of the service, that it is framed on a foreign model. It is opposed to the original creed of Buddhism, in which there can be no objective worship or real prayer to a superior power; and the character of the ritual, the succession of parts, and the language of the various portions, has nothing in keeping, so far as is known, with any Buddhist service elsewhere. In the southern school, so far as we can gather, the chief and most solemn service is the bimonthly repetition of the Pratimoksha and the assemblies held on festival days, when the Sutras are read, and sometimes the Jatakas, or birth-stories, are narrated for the amusement of the people. The following is the Rev. Spence Hardy's account:

"It is to be supposed that an atheistical system will pay little regard to acts of worship. The people, on entering the vihara the chapel, prostrate themselves before the image of Buddha, or bend the body, with the palms of the hands touching each other and the thumbs touching the forehead. They then repeat the threefold formulary of protection, called the Tun-sarana, stating that they take refuge in Buddha, in the dharma, and in the Sangha, or they take upon themselves a certain number of the ten obligations, the words being first chanted in Pali by a priest, or in his absence by a novice. Some flowers and a little rice are placed on the altar, and a few coppers are thrown into a large vessel placed to receive them; but no form of supplication is used, and the worshipper goes through the process with feelings kindred to those with which he would irrigate his field or cast his seed-corn into the ground, knowing that in due time, as a natural consequence, he will reap the reward of his toil. When special offerings are made, or a ceremony attended that is out of the common course, it is usually with the expectation of receiving some specific boon which may be relative either to this world or the next." This seems to be the usual form of daily worship in the south.

In Japan at least, in that part which the present writer visited in 1854-5 the Buddhist temples were daily frequented by the people. The usual course was to bow on entering, and then lay some flowers on the altar, and repeat some prayers kneeling. The women used to touch respectfully, and sometimes to kiss, the head of a red-lacquered figure of Ananda, in recognition of their gratitude to him for gaining Buddha's permission to admit women into the community. After this, a few prayers were repeated, and the act of worship was over. In other cases, an assembly of priests was called and the sutras read by one of their number, with some interruptions arising from interjaculatory utterances denoting either approval, or, as it sometimes seemed, the contrary. But only at the Hai-choang Temple, near Honan, was the service just referred to ever witnessed. And its peculiar ritual made a lasting impression on the present writer's mind. The service appears to be framed on the model of a Christian liturgy.

The Buddhist service was brought to China during the Tang dynasty, i.e., after the sixth century, and appears not to have been translated, as we have it, until the Ming dynasty, that is the fifteenth century.

AMITABHA

This being, as before stated, represents "the eternal," or the infinitey-glorious. The usual method of venerating him is by the repetition of his name. In China and Japan there is a school called the "Tsing tu," or "pure land" school of Buddhists, who place their reliance on the virtue of this name for securing them birth in the western paradise. The name "Amita" is repeated incessantly, and the beads counted in connection with the repetition, until the sound becomes wearisome. Regarding this kind of worship, or invocation, the books say: "Every person desirous of invoking this Buddha should first of all excite in himself a believing heart. By means of this invocation we obtain endless happiness. If a man has no faith, his exercises will be all fruitless. Therefore, the sutra says, 'Faith is the first requirement for the man who enters on the practice of religion.'" Again, we read, "If there be a virtuous man, or a virtuous woman, who has heard the name of Amitabha mentioned, and who, with firm purpose, retains the name and recites it or repeats it for one day, or two days, or for seven days, with undivided attention without any confused thoughts, this man, when about to die, shall behold Amitabha with all his saints appearing before him, and he shall pass away to be born in that most blissful paradise called Sukhavati."

There is a large amount of native literature, especially in the south of China, relating to this form of belief. Among other popular expositions of it, one particularly attracted my notice. It is the representation of Amitabha under the character of one who "draws as by a rope" (*tsee yin*) to the repetition of the name of Buddha, and so secures for the virtuous man a birth in the western region. There is a picture of Amitabha standing on a lotus flower the symbol of birth in his paradise, and with a rope in his right hand. On his breast is the figure of another lotus, and in his left hand his *patra*, or alms-dish. The rope is connected with a ship under full sail, evidently crossing the sea to the blissful paradise. It is full of male and female disciples. The ship is called "the boat of knowledge and love"; on the flag is an inscription: "The world of supreme bliss," Sukhavati. There is a pendant flag on the bow of the boat, on which is inscribed "He who draws to the western region." At the post of command is a figure, with an exact representation of a mitre on his head, giving directions and overseeing the crew and passengers: he is probably Kwan-yin.

On the sail is the following legend written: "The one word Mi-to [Amita] is the precious sword for cutting down the crowd of heretical opinions. The word Mi-to is the method for crushing down the terrors of hell. The word Mi-to is the bright lamp which gives light in darkness. This is the ship of love that crosses over the sea of sorrow. This word Mi-to is the direct road for escaping the circle of transmigration. This word Mi-to is the pleasant way to shake off the bonds of further birth and death. This word Mi-to is the secret power that perfects the character of the saint [*rishi* or *isi*, in Chinese, *sin*]. This word Mi-to is the divine elixir that leads to a thorough change of conduct or to conversion [*hwan kwuh*]. These six words are a perfect substitute for the 84,000 gates of the law modes of salvation,—referring to the 84,000 sections, or words, of the original Scriptures of Buddhism. The six words are "Na-mo-O-mi-to-fuh," i.e., Praise to Amita Buddha.

There are other six words, also sometimes referred to in connection with this form of belief: "Om-ma-ni-pat-nie-hum," i.e., Om, mani padme, hum; but the reference in the passage before us is to the former sentence: they are the knife that in a moment severs the 1,700 trailing creepers [tangled vine, or rattan sprouts]. This one word Mi-to, without any other, is sufficient in the snapping of a finger to transport to the western paradise. There is another scroll, or legend, on the body of the paper, which is to this effect:— "Among the various expedients laid down in the sacred books as methods of salvation, there is none equal to this method of invoking the name of Buddha. This one method or means is called seeking to be born in the western paradise. Again, it is called practising 'the pure land' method of religion.

The superlatively happy land of the west is the pure land referred to, so called because it is the land of the pure Buddha. In all the Sutras of the twelve divisions of the sacred canon Tripitaka, San-ts'ong, men are exhorted to return, and are led to this happy land. The 84,000 gates of the law all lead to this. This invocation of Buddha is the most excellent and incomparable method of deliverance. An old priest says, 'Other methods of learning are like the progress of a small insect up a high mount, covering one pace in half an hour; but practising this pure land method is like a ship running before a fair wind and tide, 1,000 li in a moment.' Once entering this paradise, we are eternally safe; those in the highest state forthwith ascend the ladder of Buddha, i.e., are in a direct way to perfection; those in a lower state enjoy the highest bliss of Deva heaven.

The reward, indeed, is excellent; the method very easy. There is no inquiry here about rich or poor, about wise or foolish, about old or young, male or female, about lay or religious, about secular or ascetic,—all can practise this mode of religion. All are exhorted, therefore, whether virtuous men or faithful women, everywhere to practise it. Only get faith and repeat this one word. Seek to be born in this paradise. If the whole mind cannot be given to this subject, owing to worldly engagements, then, by repeating the name of Buddha each day, 3,000 or 5,000 times, there will be abiding merit. But if not able to do this, then reading through this scroll, and making one prayer that you may be born there, or that your father or mother may be born there, or that your father or mother, if suffering from sickness, may recover and obtain increased happiness, or that they, or any of your relations, may obtain conversion. In either case, your prayer shall be granted, and your own merit be greatly increased.

It is needless to describe at any greater length the character of this belief in Amitabha. It is the prevalent form of Buddhism in many parts of China, and especially in the island of Pu-to; and the ease with which its rules are attended to, and the general admission of male and female, rich and poor, into the privileges it pretends to offer, secure for it a large share of popular favour. In another sense, this paradise is regarded as a figurative description of our moral nature pure and at rest. "Amitabha means the mind clear and enlightened. The rows of trees supposed to surround the material heaven represent the mind cultivating the virtues. The music means the harmony in the mind. The flowers, and particularly the lotus, mean the mind opening to consciousness and intelligence. The beautiful birds mean the mind becoming changed and renovated." "The object," Dr. Edkins observes, "of this figurative interpretation of the western paradise of Amitabha was doubtless to redeem the Tsing-tu [pure land] school from the discredit into which it had fallen, by abandoning the Nirvana in favour of a sensuous heaven. The original inventors of it must have had such a notion of it as has been given that of an imaginary heaven, but they did not try to prevent its being accepted as real by the ignorant and uninquiring." Hence the effort of the Yun-tsi school to restore the fable to its original mystic form.

We have thus regarded Buddhism in China as a form of religion implying faith and worship.

8

The Sangha

Little can be added to what has already been said with respect to the order, or Sangha, the congregation, of the Buddhist community. The rules for admission are the same in the northern school as in the south. A child of eight years of age, or as soon as he is old enough to drive away crows, may be admitted into the order as a novice (*shami, samanera*). He must, however, have the consent of his parents, and be free from physical disqualifications. The word Shami is defined in the Chinese "Daily Manual," as "ceasing from worldly occupations, and engaging in loving duties to all creatures." Both the shami and the shamini, i.e., male and female novices, have to take the following vows:-(1) not to kill; (2) not to steal; (3) not to marry; (4) not to lie; (5) not to drink wine; (6) not to use perfumes, or flower-wreaths, etc.; (7) not to attend dances or theatres; (8) not to sit on high and luxurious seats; (9) only to eat at fixed hours; (10) not to possess cattle, gold and silver, or precious stones.

The "Daily Manual," in commenting on these rules, says: "Drinking wine causes a person to lose control of himself; his guardian spirits are grieved at such conduct, and when dead he falls into the hell apportioned for drunkards. Scents and flowers on the person produce libidinous thoughts. Music and dancing are opposed to modesty, and produce dissipation. These are the amusements of the world, not of religious persons. High and luxurious seats produce idle habits, and are not allowable. To eat at improper times refers to the rule only to take one full meal at noon. To be always wanting food is the great impediment in the way of deliverance from the bonds of life.

"To possess wealth and jewels is the root of covetousness; to get money and to desire to be always eating, i.e., covetousness and gluttony are the two first of the five evil desires. The rule is to eat in order to nourish life—this is allowable and for worldly men to possess wealth is allowable, but not for the religious.'"

At the age of twenty the novice if he desires may be admitted into full orders; he then takes upon him the 250 rules of the Pratimoksha. He must then also receive the tonsure and wear the robes. He then selects the monastery in which he proposes to reside, and is admitted to the sangha, or congregation.

There are different rules of conventual discipline, according to the school to which the priest attaches himself. In the contemplative school, which has taken root in southern China, the chief duty is profound and continued meditation; the practice of external means is not so much employed. The founder of this school, Bodhidharma, was a native of South India, and came to China A.D. 526. He is spoken of as the twenty-eighth patriarch of the Buddhist church; this succession of patriarchs, however, is unknown in the Theravadi school of Sri Lanka. "He represents a school that despises books, and reduces Buddhist teaching to the simplest possible rules. He decried book-reading, and his system made the monasteries much more mystical and meditative than before." This mystic school has kept its hold in southern China to the present day.

There are two volumes of a work commonly met with in the Canton province, called Shan-lin-shun-pih-shwo, or sayings of the **Shan, or meditative school** of priests, in which the opinions of these mystic Buddhists are largely quoted. Their one aim seems to be to acquire the "nature " of Buddha by giving up all active employment. This agrees with what we read of Bodhidharma, who, on arriving in China it is sometimes said he arrived there on the leaf of the tea-plant, was invited to Nanking, where the emperor of southern China held his court. The emperor said to him: "From my accession to the throne I have been continually building temples, transcribing sacred books, and admitting new monks to take the vows; how much merit may I be supposed to have accumulated?" The reply was, "None." The emperor: "And why none?" The patriarch: "All this is but the insignificant effect of an imperfect cause not complete in itself: it is the shadow that follows the substance, and is without real existence." The emperor: "Then what is true merit?" The patriarch: "It consists in purity and enlightenment, depth and completeness, and in being wrapped in thought while surrounded by vacancy and stillness. Merit such as this cannot be found by worldly means." The emperor then asked: "Which is the most important of the holy doctrines?" To which the monk replied: "Where all is emptiness, nothing can be called 'holy.' " The emperor rejoined: " Who then is it that replies to me?" The patriarch: "I do not know." '

This extract exhibits the character of the mystic school of Buddhism. It discourages book-learning; the attainment of perfection is the work of the heart—hence, we are not surprised to find the class of priests belonging to this school described as being imbecile in appearance and idle in their lives. It is the natural consequence of their "do-nothing" axiom. Bodhidharma himself, we are told, passed many years gazing at a wall, and was called the "wall-gazing Brahmin". He died finally of old age, and was buried in the Hiung-er mountains between Honan and Shansi.

The **Tian-tai school** of priests, on the other hand, allow the necessity of knowledge as well as meditation. This school was founded by Chi-k'ai, not long after the arrival of Bodhidharma in South China. He had left his home in Honan, and wandered to a romantic spot in the Cheh-kiang province, where he founded a monastery. It is called the Kau-ming convent. It was, however, at a place called Si-tsoh, not far from the present Tan-nian monastery, that he composed the system of doctrine called **Chi-kwan**, that has ever since distinguished his school. He had at first followed the doctrine of the contemplative school, but he was dissatisfied with it; he did not approve of the rejection of study or the teaching of the sacred books. He taught, therefore, the union of knowledge (*chi*) and meditation (*kwan*) as being the true means of enlightenment.

I may be allowed here to quote that I have written elsewhere, concerning the teaching of this school: "The system of Chi-k'ai was founded on principles advocated in the 'Chung-lun', a treatise written by Nagarjuna Bodhisattva. This treatise advocates a middle way in the exposition of Buddhist doctrine; it rejects all anti-theses, and endeavours to find the middle truth in the reconciliation of opposites. 'So,' Chi-k'ai said, 'the true secret of Buddha's doctrine is found neither in book-learning nor external practices, nor yet in sole attention to ecstatic contemplation, neither in the exercise of pure reason, nor in reveries of fancy; but, he said, 'there is a middle course which includes all and rejects none'; this system he called Chi-kwan [fixity in learning and meditation], in agreement with the saying found in the Dhammapada: 'Without knowledge there is no meditation, and without meditation there is no knowledge; he who has knowledge and meditation is near Nirvana.' "

With regard to the school as it now exists, we have the testimony of a visitor, that the priests of the Kwo-tsing-sze, one of the establishments of the sect, in Cheh-kiang, are both numerous and respectable. The Superior is a middle-aged man, surrounded by a number of persons well-acquainted with the principles of Buddhism. They maintained that all systems were alike, and all led to one result. As to image-worship, they said that the most advanced Buddhists worshipped without the use of any images; the middle-class used images in their worship as helps to devotion; and the rest used neither images nor worship. As for themselves, they could worship without any images at all, and they thought it best to do so. They were asked, What was the need, then, for images? They said they were necessary for the vulgar.

The ground of this system is found in the stanza-which Chi-k'ai places at the beginning of one of his books:

Scrupulously avoiding wicked actions,
Reverently performing virtuous ones,
Purifying the intention from selfish desire,
Is the doctrine of all the Buddhas.

This verse is found in "Dhammapada," and represents a fundamental principle: "Do nothing wrong; do all that is right." The guide to determine the right and wrong is the moral teaching of Buddha, which is to be gathered from the books. The way to advance is to meditate therein. There is a good deal said about this system of the Tian-tai priests in the book before quoted, and to that work the reader is referred.

The third school of Buddhists to which we shall briefly allude is the **Kiau-men, or school of learning** or doctrine only. These Buddhists are opposed to contemplation as a means, and advocate attention to the literal teaching of Buddha found in "the books." They belong to the "exoteric" branch of the religion. Dr. Edkins, in speaking of this school, quotes from a native writer, who thus compares Buddha and Bodhidharma: "Tathagata taught great truths, and the causes of things. He became the instructor of men and devas. He saved multitudes, and spoke the contents of more than 500 works. Hence arose the Kiau-men, or exoteric branch of the system, and it was believed to hold the tradition of the words of Buddha. Bodhidharma brought from the 'western heaven' the seal of truth [true seal], and opened the fountain of contemplation in the east. He pointed directly to Buddha's heart and nature, swept away the parasitic growth of book-instruction, and thus established the exoteric branch of the system containing the tradition of the heart of Buddha. Yet the two branches, while presenting of necessity a different aspect, form but one whole."

Without enlarging on this point, we may allude to the little book called the "Daily Manual of the Sraman," as giving an account of the duties of the disciple adopting the teaching of this school as his guide. There are duties prescribed for every event of the day. On awaking in the morning, he must sit up in a grave posture and repeat a verse, to recall his mind to the duties of religion:

On first awaking from my sleep,
I ought to wish that every breathing thing
May wake to saving wisdom.

On hearing the convent-bell calling to prayers, he ought to say:

Oh, may the music of this bell, wherever heard,
Produce in all a sense of rest,
And quiet every care, etc."'

On getting out of bed, say:

On putting down my feet and standing up,
Oh, let me wish that every living thing
May gain release of mind and self
And stand upright in perfect rest!

On putting on the vestments, say:

Assuming this my upper robe,
I pray that every living thing
Obtaining the true principles of religion
May safely reach the other shore.

And so on for all the duties, even the most trivial, of the day. There is direction given how to bow to a sacred object, how to read the sutras, how to walk on the road when begging, and so throughout.

It is plain that this school must have considerablc influence in keeping alive a healthy tone in a system otherwise full of the elements of decay; for mysticism, by itself, cannot endure; but when supplemented by action, or united with practical aim and duties, it may take its place in, and perhaps give a character to, the complex system which we call Buddhism.

The Tantra School, or The Practice of Charms and Magical Signs

The repetition of words not understood by the people has always taken its place, in the estimation of the superstitious, among religious practices, and in Buddhism it has obtained singular authority. This may be owing to the prevalence of such beliefs or customs among the northern nations that adopted Buddhism as their religion; or it may result from the natural development of Buddhist modes of thought. It is plain that, if there is no recognition of a personal and supreme being, and yet no distinct denial of a superior power or an occult principle that may be brought into harmony with our own being, the use of prayer can only be for the purpose of bringing into play a virtue residing in the act itself: the step from this to the belief in a virtue residing in the words is a very small one. We find, then, as the theory of a universal essence or force, or, as the Chinese love to call it, "heart," was accepted, so the use of words for adjusting the relationship between the subjective and this universal "heart" came into use.

In the service of Kwan-yin, the sacred part of the function, or, as we should say, "the mystery," consists in the repetition of the words. These words must be effectual, if properly repeated. This superstition has taken deep hold on northern Buddhists. Everyone knows how the magic formula of "Om mani padme hum!" is repeated in Tibet; and it is no less common in China. There is an instance of this in the inscription found on the limestone archway at Keu-yung-kwan, in North China. This archway stands about five miles north of the entrance of the Nankow pass. It is covered with mythological and symbolical sculptures, evidently of Indian origin. It is probably the bottom part of an old pagoda that was built "across the street," as it is still known by that name.

This pagoda, we are told, though erected for the benefit of the locality, proved an object of such terror to the superstitious Mongols coming south from their native wilds, that they could not be induced to pass under it; and so it was necessary, in the early part of the Ming dynasty, to remove the upper part of the pagoda, the policy of the government being to conciliate and attract these wild nomads. Several Europeans, who had passed that way, had noticed the village and the archway. Father Gerbillon, who was there on his way to Mongolia, in 1688, says: "The village might pass for a little town. The gate by which it is entered is like a triumphal arch"; and the Russian Timkowski, in 1820, says; "Here the road begins to be very difficult, especially for carriages, and does not change for a distance of five verst, as far as the fort of Kiu Young (Kouan), the principal defence of this passage. The interior of the middle gate is ornamented with figures of heroes sculptured on the walls."

A. Wylie, however, was the first to draw attention to the inscription found on the archway, and in a paper read before the Royal Asiatic Society, in 1870, he produced the whole of it with a translation. Without introducing all of it here, we may select one or two sentences such as these: *"Om! namo bhagavate! om bhur om bhur om sodhaya, sodhaya, visodhaya visodhayasama,"* etc. The words are repeated by the people with no knowledge of their meaning.

The translation of the first portion of the inscription is as follows: "Om! adoration to the holy Buddha, who art exalted above the three worlds—adoration to thee! which is equivalent to Om Bhur om! Bhur om! Bhur om! Purify, purify, completely purify! O thou incomparable one, who embracest all space, and whose splendour has appropriated the sphere of knowledge! thou who art welcome of all the Tathagatas, whose speech is blessing, and who art immortal, consecrate me by sprinkling me with holy water and the great mudra [the seal or sign made with the fingers] with the words of mystic prayer," etc. The inscription is mixed up with disconnected charm words, and if any meaning can be assigned to it, the object of the words is to produce a mystical purity and deliverance for all who repeat it right.

In all the little manuals which occur in such numbers throughout China, similar mystic sentences are given as necessary for assisting the worshipper. Such phrases as *"Om, lam! Svar! Seou li seou li [sri, sri] Mo-ho seou-li,"* occur throughout their pages, used as invocations or magical charms for bringing the heart into union with the principle of being. It would be needless to produce other examples, as they are all of one character, and consist of broken, corrupt sentences, extracted from Indian books, and drawn up at a late period in the history of the religion. These sentences are called To-lo-ni (dharani), and are used not only in the usual recitation of prayers, but on special occasions, such as the service for asking for rain.

There is a special treatise for this purpose published by royal mandate in China, and called the "great cloud-wheel rain-asking sutra." The preface to it was written so recently as 1780 A.D., by an emperor of the present dynasty, Kien-lung. The theory of compelling rain to fall is connected with the very old belief in the existence of dragons, or nagas, who either withhold or grant rain according to their benevolent or malevolent disposition. Buddha revealed certain sentences which would have the power, when properly repeated, to overcome all evil influences and produce a good disposition among the nagas, and so cause rain to fall. These sentences he delivered to the great dragon-king and they are recorded in the sutra. They are like the rest: *"Tan-chi-ta To-lo-ni, To-lo-ni, Yan-to-lo-ni San-po-li-ti-see-che, pi-che-ye,"* etc. These being repeated in the order given are supposed to have the power required, and they are so repeated by the Chinese.

But perhaps the most complete body of magic sentences to be found in any Chinese work are those which occur in a popular sutra called the Ling-yen-king; and as a consideration of this work will illustrate the late philosophical character of Buddhism, perhaps this is the proper place to refer to it.

It has long been suspected, that the development of Buddhism led to the later forms of Hindu superstition known as the worship of Vishnu, Siva, etc. There is much to support this opinion. We might refer to the account given by Huen Tsang, in the tenth book of the Si-yu-ki, referring to the construction of the Brahmins convent by King Sadvaha, a patron of Nagarjuna, a most distinguished Buddhist scholar. This convent, which was probably somewhere near Nagpur, was consecrated to Parvati, under her name of "The Black Bee"; we are told that Brahmins and Buddhists lived together in its caves, until the latter were expelled by force by the former. What happened here occurred also at a celebrated convent called Nalanda, in south Bihar, south-east of Patna. This monastery at one time held as many as 10,000 monks, forming the most splendid Buddhist establishment in India. It was celebrated as a place for study, both for Brahminical books and those of Buddhism. In the end the two systems coalesced.

Among other works originating from this establishment is the one called briefly by the name given above, Leng-yen-king,—but when written in full "Sheu-leng-yen-king," or "Surangama Sutra," It was brought to China and translated by Paramiti in A.D. 705. Now, on page 30 of the ghth book of this sutra, it is stated, that "this volume as brought from India and belongs to the Kwan-ting :hool." The school so named is, in Sanskrit, called the Iurddhabhishiktas, or the "head-baptised." The xplanation of this title given in the passage referred to is ıis, that those who hold the principles of this book, on ıem the wisdom of Tathagata descends and washes the ıead of the heart," just as the Kshatriya king is baptised t his consecration. This explanation is a plausible one, nd may probably account for the custom of sprinking vater on the head commonly practised in Tibet, but only dministered in China to high personages, who are thereby dmitted into the Buddhist church and solemnly invested s protectors of religion.

But there is another, and more probable, derivation of he term, as applied to a Buddhist school. We are told by Colebrooke that among the mixed classes in India there is ne called Murdhabhishikta, which consists of those born rom a Brahmin and a woman of the Kshatriya class.

Now, the application of this term to a Buddhist school seems to intimate the mixed character of the tenets held by those belonging to it, that they were Buddhist and Brahmin intermixed; and such is the character of the book we are considering. Its principles are these, that there is but one universal soul, which by a sort of inversion is conceived of as multiplied, but only in error; that this is the one "ever-quiet yet ever-shining" reality; that we and all that lives are one with it. By removing the dust from the mirror all is clear; so by removing false and inverted thoughts about ourselves from the heart, we are restored to our one and true condition.

The subject is illustrated in many ways, but to mention only one: Buddha desires to show that our ideas of multiplicity are a delusion, he therefore takes a soft and embroidered handkerchief, and in the sight of the congregation tied in it a knot, then, showing it to Ananda, he said, "What call you this, Ananda?" He answered: "It is called a knot." On this, Buddha repeated the act, and tied a second knot above the first, and asked again, " What call you this?" He replied again: "This is a second knot," and then he repeated the same thing and the same question until six knots had been tied. Buddha then addressed Ananda and said: "When I first tied the handkerchief you said it was made into a knot; yet the handkerchief itself is one piece of silk: how then can you speak of a second, third, and fourth knot as distinct from the first and the handkerchief?" On this Ananda replied: "Lord! this valuable embroidered handkerchief, originally woven from silken threads into its present form, although in itself essentially one substance, may, when tied up into knots, be spoken of as knotted, even if there were a hundred knots; on what ground then does Buddha demur to the name?"

Buddha addressed Ananda: "You allow, with respect to this embroidered silk, that in its original character it is but one, but when I tied each successive knot you said it was each time a distinct knot; you should, therefore, clearly understand the nature of this inquiry, that substantially and essentially this silk handkerchief is one and the same, but that accidentally, by circumstances, it is called by the name of each successive knot. Now then, tell me what you think: Each knot I tied down to the sixth you told me was a different knot. I propose now to undo this sixth knot: do I thereby affect the handkerchief as one, or the remaining five knots?" Ananda replied: "No! Lord, the last knot is different from the first, and yet the handkerchief remains the same."

"So is it," Buddha said, "with your six organs of sense and the great unity. If you keep the knots tied, there must of necessity rise the thought, ' This knot is this and not that,' so the question of this and that is raised. If you want to get rid of this thought, all you have to do is to tie no knots, or untie them all, you will then have the same handkerchief without knots—so is it with the senses. From he first, your mind and nature being in disorder and confusion, there has arisen a false excitement of a knowledge derived from senses, e.g., from sight, and this knowledge wildly exercised has produced endless deceptions; at last, worn out with excessive action, the sight has caused the belief in objects of sense, as the eye fatigued sees in space fanciful objects, figures, and sky-flowers. But really in the depth of the true sight-power there lies no cause or ground for this deception; thus from excess of action have sprung up as qualities and characteristics of this false appearance the ideas of worldly phenomena, mountains and rivers, the great earth, death, and Nirvana; these all alike are but perishing qualities (*siang*) of a conditioned existence."

Ananda said: " The excessive action and confusion of which you speak I take to correspond to the tying of the knots; tell me then how to get rid of it." Then Tathagata, with his hand taking the knotted handkerchief, smoothed out the left part of it, and said: "Is it now untied, Ananda?" To which he answered, "No." Then the lord, shaking out the other part with his hand, smoothed it to the right, and said: "Is it now untied, Ananda?" To which he answered, "No!" The lord then added, "I have smoothed the silken napkin out, on the right and left, and yet you say it is not untied; tell me then, how is it to be unloosed?" To which Ananda answered: "You must take the middle part, the heart of the knot, then separate each part, and it will come untied." Buddha replied: "Good! good! Ananda, if you wish to untie the knots and make all smooth begin at the heart."

By this enigmatical method Buddha is supposed to exhibit the non-reality of qualities or distinctions, and to show that the mode of recovery is by undoing or doing away with the inversions or delusions of sense. In order to accomplish this, we must begin at the heart; and to get the heart right and the delusions corrected, he imparts to his followers a long series of sacred words, or charms l the repetition of which the end will be reached. The dharanis, are 427 in number, and consist of Sanskr words, including the objects of common Hindu worsh such as Parvati, Narayana, Kuvera, and so on conjoine with the names of the Buddhas and the sacred books. S that here we find the idea fully developed, of the power words, whenceso-ever derived, to govern the heart an produce magical effects. These dharanis are explained i a fanciful way in a work published at Canton in the twenty seventh year of the reign of Taou-Kwang (A.D. 1848). Eac syllable is restored to its true sound, and the whole pu together so as to appear to make some sense. It is plai the priest who undertook the task did not understand hi work, for he gives us the most random explanations o ordinary Sanskrit words. It is enough for us, however, t gather that the use of these charmed words was introduce into Buddhism at a time when the system was losing it distinct character from connection with Brahminism.

It will be plain, from what has been said, that th practical teaching of Buddha has been to a great exten effaced in China by the later growth of Pantheism an mystic fancies. The "heart" is regarded as the substantiv basis of all things, and to get this heart or heart of Bodhi is the aim of the disciple.

This he attempts by the practice of meditation or reverie or else by the repetition of words. And while he is forbidden by the first principles of his faith to do any harm, he is no encouraged to practise any good. We do not wonder therefore, that the Buddhists are sometimes compared to drones or noxious insects. The character of the Chinese as a practical and industrious race, forbids them to attach importance to idle and fruitless habits of dreaming away life; but yet, on the other hand, their natural superstition prevents them from wholly discountenancing those who pretend to have magical powers over the elements and the future world, hence the strange medley of practical common sense and helpless resignation to supernatural influences found among them.

The very boatman, who works hard for his few cash, will burn his paper and make the sign with his fingers before he makes his morning venture. And the scholar, who pretends to despise Buddhism and the teaching of Buddha, has got at his fingers' end the sentences contained in the books supposed to possess magical virtue. The present writer had great difficulty in persuading his teacher to go over with him and explain the short sutra known as the "Heart-Sutra"; but on one occasion, when the book had accidentally been mislaid, he found that the *sin-sang* knew the whole of it by heart, and there was no occasion to seek for the book. And so also, when the Yamen of Yeh Ming-shin, the governor of the two provinces, was entered, in 1857, by the troops under Sir M. Seymour, there was found in the innermost chamber a massive gilt image of Kwan-yin, with the two attendant figures, one on either side; and to all appearances, this image was the object of daily worship to those within the palace. So in practice they contradict themselves.

9

Final Assessment

We shall now consider the influence which Buddhism probably exerted on the prevailing opinions of the Chinese people after its introduction among them.

Confucianism—which is, in fact, not the teaching of Confucius, but the transmitted doctrine of an early age—had already shaped itself into a rigid code when Buddha's disciples came to Loyang from India. How would the two systems adjust themselves? The only parts of early Confucianism that require notice are the implied acknowledgment of a belief in a personal God (Shang-ti) and the duty of sacrifice.

Shang-ti is viewed, in the first instance, as the highest of all spirits to whom the ancient Chinese offered their sacrifices; secondly, as the creator and preserver of all, who has conferred upon men a moral sense; next, as one who governs the world, and can put down mighty kings and exalt those of low degree; next, as one who only wishes to do men good, but punishes the evildoers; next, as one with whom good emperors are after their death; next, as one who by dreams and visions of the night opens the understanding of men; next, as a holy being whom the impure cannot approach; and finally, as one who is also gracious and merciful to penitents.

With reference to this belief, the Buddhists deny the existence of a personal God. They attribute creation, as we term it, to the action of fixed laws of destruction and renovation. They say, that it is by the "mutual excitation of wind and water" that everything is changed and renovated, and that the process is an eternal one. They deny, also, that reward comes from God, or punishment; they affirm that actions in themselves bring their results, and that all we do tends to this result. They do not deny the existence of spirits; like the Chinese, they will speak of the six honoured ones, the spirits of hills, and rivers, and trees, and the host of lower spirits occupying the depths beneath; but they will not worship any the highest of all spirits.

The old ritual of the Chinese or dained sacrifices. The emperor was commanded to sacrifice to heaven; and at the present day (19th century) the imperial worship of Shang-ti on the round hillock to the south of the city of Peking is surrounded with all the solemnity of which such an occasion is capable. "The altar is a beautiful marble structure, ascended by twenty-seven steps, and ornamented by circular balustrades on each of its three terraces. Here the emperor kneels, surrounded first by the circles of the terraces and their enclosing wall, and then by the circle of the horizon.He thus seems to himself and to his court to be the centre of the universe, and, turning to the north, assuming the attitude of a subject, he acknowledges by prayer and by his position that he is inferior to Heaven alone. As might be expected, careful distinctions are made in the sacrifices. The animals ordinarily used for food by the ancient Chinese, and the fruits of the earth known to them, are almost all included. But the great distinguishing sign of superiority is the offering of a whole burnt offering to heaven a first-born male.

The Buddhists denounce sacrifices. In his interview with the hermits called Bhargavides, on his road to Vaisali, the young prince who was to become Buddha, watched their modes of worship and inquired as to their sacrifices. "What is the nature of the religion which consists in offering up sacrifices?" he said. "It is a custom which has been handed down from very remote time," they replied, "that those who worship the Gods must sacrifice." "I will ask you, then," said the prince, "if a man, in worshipping the gods, sacrifices a sheep and so does well, why should he not kill his child and so do better? Surely there can be no merit in killing a sheep?"

And, consequently, in the Buddhist system all bloody sacrifices are abolished. They offer flowers and incense, and sometimes cakes and other food of that sort, but no flesh or the life of any creature.

So in China, the monasteries are, many of them at least, receptacles for living creatures, who find asylums there. The Haichwang temple of Honan, which has so frequently been described by European visitors, has its special department for "preserving life." And in a popular work, largely circulated among the lower orders, describing the future punishments of the wicked, special wrath is threatened against those "who take life" while the bliss of a happy metempsychosis is freely offered to all those who are instrumental in saving the life even of the meanest creature. Although sacrifices are freely offered to Confucius, of which we read in 'The History of the Temples of the Sage',[1] yet it is impossible to deny that tenderness for life must have been increased among the people by the presence of the vast number of Buddhist fraternities in their midst; and, very probably, in the system of sacrifices, which are now very much identified with the burning of paper and the cracking of squibs, at least in the daily and popular worship of the crowds.

1. According to this work, 6 bullocks, 27,000 pigs, 5,800 sheep, 2800 deer, and 2,700 hares are sacrificed in the temples of Confucius annually. (Douglas)

How different is this from of worship of the Buddhists! If it be true they worship only a principle, yet it is a principle embodied in a life. The mercy of Kwan-yin was illustrated in the mercy of the living Buddha. Her willingness to save is only the expression of Buddha's aim in being born; not only being born once, but through a succession of ages; and the thought rises even higher, when the recollection of his sufferings for the sake of "all that breathes" is joined with the sentiment of mercy.

We may suppose, therefore, that the introduction of Buddhism among the Chinese tended some way to elevate their thoughts and give some tinge of spirituality to their worship. At any rate, it must have brought them to a knowledge of a worship distinct from that of the mere powers of nature, or deified intellect, and as it did this, or tends to do this, it has answered a great purpose.

The Chinese regard what is called the "superior man" as holding rank next below Confucius. The "sage" was incapable of evil. The Buddhist represents this character in his description of a Bodhisattva. This being has all human qualities, but is possessed of Bodhi, or perfect wisdom. And he exercises this wisdom for the good of others, "having benefited himself, he desires to benefit all,"—this is the phrase usually employed to indicate such a character. The effect of this teaching is exhibited in the fact, that the Chinese, whether Buddhists or not, term their idols or figures by the general term of Pu-sa. It is used for all purposes of this kind, and doubtless the character of the Bodhisattva has been transferred in some degree to these idols.

There is a work in the Buddhist collection in China, written by Fa-lin, to confute the sceptical opinions of Fu-yi. Fu-yi was a stern enemy of Buddhism. He lived in the time of the Emperor Kaou-Tsu (A.D. 618-627), the first of the Tang dynasty. He proposed to the emperor that the monks and nuns should be obliged to resume secular life and bring up children, and so benefit the state. "The reason they adopt the ascetic life," he says, "is to avoid contributing to the revenue"; and then he proceeds to accuse the priests of idleness and superstition. To this, it was replied that Buddha was a sage, and it was wrong to speak ill of him; but Fu-yi replied that loyalty and filial piety are the greatest virtues, and that the monks, disregarding both these, were guilty of gross neglect. His opponent, the Buddhist, replied simply by stating that the punishment of hell awaited his vilifier.

The Confucianists do not believe in future punishment—they affect to ignore it; but Buddhist teaching is very distinct on the point. The earliest school of Buddhists say, that below the earth there are eight great hells. Besides these "great earth-prisons" (the word for "hell," in Chinese, is earth-prison), there are others called frontier or side-prisons, through which the sufferers emerge. The time of suffering in each of these places is determined—after the expiry of the years, the released being may be born either on earth again as a beast or a man, or else in heaven.

There is no need to describe the heavens of the Buddhists. Those called Kama-lokas, which include that of the Olympus-dwelling gods, all admit of the enjoyment of sensuous pleasure. The superior heavens are free from this, and the happiness consists in thought or pure being. The highest heavens admit of no thought, nor do they exclude it; the condition here is purely transcendental. Such was the belief imported into China when the Buddhist books were brought there. They had known hitherto nothing about such places "in the next world"; Confucius never spake about angels or other spiritual beings; consequently, the Chinese regarded the present life, the happiness of society, as the end of all.

The ground was now changed, and the effect of the new religion on the people was to introduce a dread of the hereafter on account of these threatened punishments.

There is a book, widely distributed among the people; which relates to this subject, —it is called the "Kin-kong-king-in-kwo-tsiang-chu," or "Explanations relating to the causes and fruits [deeds and consequences] of the Diamond Sutra. In this book are pictures of the courts of the infernal regions and the character of the punishments assigned to the culprits brought before the tribunals.

Throughout the book the eye is pained at the horrible scenes attempted to be drawn—the tortures of the wicked, and the delight of the demons engaged in the disgusting details of dismemberment, disembowelling, and hacking the bodies of their victims. At the conclusion of the work are represented the ten courts presided over by ten judges, of whom the Indian Jemma (Yama), with his two dogs, is the fifth. And, in conclusion, the wheel of metempsychosis is figured, in which we observe no birth as "a deva".

The Tolerant Spirit

One marked effect on the masses in China resulting from the intermixture of Buddhism with Confucianism and Taoism has been to produce a common indifference to the distinctive character of each. "These three religions," Dr. Edkins says, "are truly national, because the mass of the people believe in them all. They are far from feeling it inconsistent to do so."

It seems to the present writer that very much of this is due to the direct tolerance inculcated by Buddhism, or, at least, preached by the Buddhists. They do not attach weight so much to the doctrine as to life or conduct. If we hang on doctrine, they say, we are depending on a " quality" (*siang*); but the object of religion is to get rid of such dependence, and to free oneself from self-assertion. This spirit of quietism, or indifference, is illustrated by the whole tenor of their history. Passive submission has marked the conduct of the Buddhist wherever he is found, and opposed to this passive condition is all contention for mastery—hence the mutual accommodation found among the Chinese.

An important feature in the Buddhist doctrine is the supposed impossibility of the supreme God being capable of causing or allowing suffering. In the Buddhist controversy held at Pantura, in Sri Lanka, this was the point most frequently urged by the native priests **against the Christian doctrine that the Jehovah of the Old Testament was capable of anger and repentance, and that he caused suffering in punishment of sin.** In China the universal worship, or honour, paid to Kwan-yin is a proof that this idea of mercy is a paramount one in thier estimate of divinity.

With respect to its social aspect, the Buddhist doctrine has tended to strengthen ties between parent and child, by representing filial duty as one of the chief virtues. There is a weird sort of story told in the life of Buddha, known as the Abhinishkramana Sutra, of a merchant youth who was condemned to wear a red hot iron ring round his forehead for having struck or, kicked his mother; and the duty of obedience and attention to parents is indeed one of the most attractive features in the character of this religion. The youthful Sama is painted (sculptured) at Sanchi waiting on his blind parents, bringing them fruits and water daily, and because of his piety he was restored to life. So in the history of Asoka's son, Kunala. He had resisted the importunities of his step-mother, and incurred her hatred. He was sent to a distant appenage of the kingdom, and there by her craft his eyes were put out. He submitted to the indignity without complaint, and came playing his lute to the home of his childhood, anxious to know why he had incurred his father's displeasure, but with no resentment. This feature of the Buddhist belief must have recommended the system to the notice of the Chinese, with whom this duty of filial piefy is paramount.

And so it would seem that Buddhism not only supplemented the national faith in supplying a metaphysical side to it, but it added in some points to the strength of the morality of the people, and in other points raised and elevated their conceptions.

Aesthetic Contribution

There is a point of view from which we may regard the result of Buddhism as highly advantageous, that is, in promoting a correct aesthetic taste, especially in religious architecture. Buddhism illustrates the rule, that the highest divinity was not to be figured by any human form or shape that led to the idea of the rounded topes and the ascending towers or tees above the tope, which called for all the power of man to erect, as the idea had required all his power to conceive. The Pagoda in China is the expression of the highest expansion of the thought; and nothing, we may say, has more guided and fostered a correct taste in landscape effect and right proportions, combined with beauty of detail, than the almost universal adoption of this Indian model of a Bhagavat, or Pagoda-house.

The symbolism of the tope or stupa, from the crowning spire of which the Pagoda originates is, like that of other sacred edifices, intended to figure out an idea of the world, or universe, ruled over or occupied by one superme spirit or being.

So the stupa is a high, solid structure, designed to be based on a square foundation or platform, from which rises into the air a semi-circular dome, which is crowned by a square railing, or sometimes a solid cube with eyes on every side. The square platform represents earth, the semi-circular dome figures out air, the railed structure on the top denotes the heaven where watch the four gods indicated by eyes. This was the first effort to describe in stone the idea of the world, or the three worlds, over which the spiritual presence of Buddha was supposed to rule. In this stupa were his relics, denoting his presence, the only authorised substitute for himself; but, as the system grew, the idea of the universe expanded also, and it was not only earth, and air, and heaven that had to be represented, but the towering worlds above the heaven, and after that the platforms or plateau—it is the only word we can use—of heavens extending upwards and towards the eight points of space,—hence the symbolism expanded also, and above the cubical structure was erected a high staff with rings or umbrellas, to denote a world soaring above world to the uppermost empyrean.

Now, it is this crowning pole, with its rings or umbrellas, that originated the idea of the Pagoda. Each platform in this structure denotes a world, and, as they tower upwards in beautifully decreasing size, they offer to the eye an effort of the mind of man to represent in stone the idea of the infinite. On each side of these platforms there are bells and tinkling copper leaves, to denote the eternal "music of the spheres" ; and the beautifully carved balustrades and projecting eaves are ever described as proper emblems of the habitations of the happy beings who enjoy the presence of the Buddhas dwelling in these supernal regions. This is the origin of the Pagodas; and there is nothing which gives China its distinctive architectural character so much as these Buddhist structures, not used for worship, but to figure out the illimitable nature of the space in which dwells the "spiritual essence of all the Buddhas."

From the universal practice of offering flowers at the shrines of Buddha has grown a taste in the cultivation of beautiful flowers and the arrangement of the garden temples which distinguishes the Chinese and the people of Japan. When the present writer was residing at Hakodate, in Japan, he had the opportunity of frequently visiting the temple gardens there and the graveyards in the town. The arrangement of the flowers was a subject of wonder to him—the varied effects of colour and grouping, and the careful way in which every available corner of ground was utilised for the purpose of cultivation. These flowers were used daily for the decoration of the different altars of the temples; and in the graveyards there were small joints of bamboo sunk in the ground at the head of most of the graves, which were daily filled with water, and a few choice flowers placed therein, by the priests on the deceased one's relatives.

In China, this love of flowers, and taste produced thereby in the arrangement of colour and shape, is exhibited in their art and ornamentation on every hand. There is an artificiality sometimes noticeable not found in Japan, but this is just the result we should expect from the unequal division of the public taste between **the cramped and artificial ritual of Confucianism and the free and unfettered Buddhism;** yet it will not be disputed that the taste is the result of an aesthetic sentiment, excited, in the first instance, by religious conceptions, and sustained and cultured by the growth of such ideas, until it has become natural.

It would be out of our way to describe the effect of Buddhism on the native literature of China; but we may allude to the introduction of the folklore of the west among these people. **The Jatakas and other tale-books now form a part of their literature—these must have had their influence.** There is a celebrated tale, translated by Stas. Julien, under the title of "La Blanche et Bleu," of two fairy spirits, or nagas, who carry on a sort of innocent intrigue with a young apothecary of Hankow. This tale is founded on a Buddhist story called "Nagananda," which was probably written at the time of Raja Siladitya A.D. 650, in India. The ideas run into one another naturally, but the Chinese plot is borrowed from the Indian tale—and this is true in other points: the tales we find in Aesop are current in China, but in both cases derived from a Buddhist source. Many of these tales appear trivial, but compared with the stories found, for instance, in the "Gesta Romanorum," they are well conceived and sustained, and they must have produced a result, in many cases beneficial, on those who read them.

We sum up, therefore, our estimate of the effect of Buddhism, morally and socially, on the character of the Chinese people in these words:—While it has not answered any great end in raising the religious tone of the masses of the people, it has certainly tended to promote a love of morality, and a healthy society, by guarding it agaist vice or profligacy; and it has helped to raise the mind to a love of the beautiful in nature, and assisted in the advancement of art and literature.

II. They Walked to India

The Adventurous Seekers of the First World Religion

1. Fa Hian
2. Huen Tsang

Fa Hian, the Pioneer Pilgrim whom Buddha Saved from the Hurricane

1

Started with Four Companions

Fa Hian, when formerly resident at Tchang'an, now called Se-ngan, was grieved at noticing the fragmentary character of the Rules of the Buddhist Discipline (Vinaya Pitaka) as they were then known in China. Whereupon, in the second year of Hung Chi, the cyclical characters being Ki Hae, he agreed with Hwui king, Tao Ching, Hwui Ying, and Hwui Wu, to go together to India to seek for complete copies of these Rules.

Setting out, therefore, from Tchang'an, they first of all crossed the Lung Mountains and arrived at the country of the Prince Kon Kwei, where they sojourned during the season of the rains. After this they pushed forward, and arrived at the country of the Prince Niu Tan; then crossing the Yang Lau Hills they reached the great frontier station of Chang Yen in the province of Kansu. This place was in such an unsettled condition that the roads were unsafe for passengers. The Prince Tun Nieh of the country prevailed on them to remain there for some time, and himself afforded them hospitality. It was here they fell in with Chi Yen, Hwui Kan, Sang Chau, Po Wan, and Sang king, and pleased to find they all had one common aim in view, they remained together during the season of rains.

After this they again set out and arrived at Tun Wang in the province of Tangui. There are fortifications here extending about eighty li (i.e., about sixteen miles) east and west, and half that distance north and south. They all stopped here a month and some odd days, after which Fa Hian and his four companions made arrangements to set out in advance of the others, and so they were again separated. The military governor of Tun Wang, Li Ho by name, provided them with all necessaries for crossing the Gobi Desert. In this desert there are a great many evil demons, there are also sirocco winds, which kill all who encounter them. There are no birds or beasts to be seen; but so far as the eye can reach, the route is marked out by the bleached bones of men who have perished in the attempt to cross the desert. After travelling thus for seventeen days, a distance of about fifteen hundred Ii, they arrived at the kingdom of Shen-Shen.

In Shen-Shen

This land is rugged and barren. The people dress like the Chinese, except they wear garments made of felt and woollen stuff. The king of this country is well affected to the Law of Buddha. In his dominions are about four thousand priests, all of whom belong to the religious system known as the Little Vehicle (Hinayana). The common people and the Sramans of this and the neighbouring kingdoms all follow the religious customs of India, only some more exactly than others. All the kingdoms westward from this, as a rule, have the same characteristics, except that their languages differ—each using its own dialect of the Tartar language. All the followers of Buddha (Pravrajikas), however, practice themselves in reading Indian books, and conversing in that language. Remaining here one month and some days, they again set out in a north-westerly direction, and after journeying for fifteen days, arrived at the kingdom of the Oui (Ouigours). This kingdom has about four thousand priests, all professing the doctrines of the

Little Vehicle. When Fah Tsih and Tsai Tch'ang, two Buddhist priests of the land of Thsin, arrived in this country, they were unable to conform to some of the customs of the religious community.

Fa Hian, therefore, having obtained a pass, proceeded to the palace (hall) of the reigning Prince Kung Sun, where he remained two months and some days; after which, he returned to Po Wan and the rest who had by this time arrived at the country; but as there was a general dissatisfaction with the want of politeness which the people of the country showed towards their guests, three of the pilgrims, Chi Yan, Hwui Ran, and Hwui We, resolved immediately to retrace their steps towards Kao Tchang, for the purpose of obtaining there the provisions necessary for their journey. Fa Hian and the others, in consequence of their possessing a pass, were furnished with all they needed by Kung Sun. After having provided themselves with these things, they immediately set forward in a southwesterly direction. On their route they found neither dwelling-houses nor people. The miseries they endured in crossing the rivers, and in surmounting the natural difficulties of the road along which they had to journey, exceed all conception. After being on the road a month and five days, they at last arrived at Khoten (Yu-tien).

In Khoten

This country is exceedingly prosperous; the people are very wealthy, and all of them, without exception, reverence the Law of Buddha, and take delight in attending to their religious duties. The body of priests may, perhaps, amount to ten thousand men, and principally belong to the system of the Great Vehicle. They all partake of their meals in common. The people of the country build their houses in clusters. Before the doors of their houses they erect small towers. The smallest are about twenty-two feet high. They also construct apartments for foreign priests, where they entertain them as guests, and provide them with all they require.

The ruler of the country located Fa Hian and his companions in a Sangharam (Seng-Kia-Lan in Chinese) which was called Gomati (Kiu-Mati). The priests of this temple belong to the system known as the Great Vehicle (Mahayana). At the sound of the gong, three thousand priests assemble together to take their meal. Whilst entering the dining hall they observe the greatest decorum and propriety of conduct; one after another they take their seats. Silence is observed amongst them all; they make no noise with their rice-bowls, and when they require more food there is no chattering one with the other, but they simply make a sign with their fingers and so are supplied.

Hwui king, Tao Ching, and Hwui Ta, set out in advance towards Ki'a-Cha (Kartchou), while Fa Hian and the rest, wishing to witness the ceremony of the procession of images, halted here for a period of three months and some days. In this country there are fourteen large Sangharamas, without reckoning the smaller ones. On the first day of the fourth month, they begin within the city to sweep and water the roads, and to decorate the streets.

Above the chief gate of the city they stretch out a large cloth screen, and ornament the covered space in every possible way, then the king and the court ladies, with their attendants, take their places there. The priests of the Gomati temple, belonging to the Great Vehicle, being chiefly honoured by the king, first take their images in procession. They construct a four-wheeled image-car about three or four li from the city, its height is about thirty-five feet, and in appearance like a moving royal pavilion. It is adorned with the seven precious substances, and silken streamers and flags and curtains. The chief image is then placed upright in the centre of the carriage, with two Bodhisattvas in attendance, and surrounded by all the Devas. All are made of gold and silver, while glittering gems are hung suspended in the air.

When the image is about one hundred paces from the city gate, the king removes his royal head-dress, and putting on new garments, with bare feet he proceeds from the city to meet the procession, holding flowers and incense in his hand, and followed by his suite. On meeting the car he bows down with his face to the ground in adoration, while he scatters the flowers and burns the incense. At the time when the image enters the city, the court ladies and their attendants throw down from the pavilion above the gate flowers in endless variety. Thus everything is sumptuously arranged.

Each Sangharama has its own car, and its own day, for the procession. Beginning on the first day of the fourth month, they continue till the fourteenth day, after which they conclude, and the king and the ladies return to the palace. Seven or eight li to the west of this city is a Sangharama, called the Royal New Temple. During the last eighty years three kings have contributed towards its completion. It is about two hundred and ninety feet high. There are many inscribed plates of gold and silver within it. Jewels of every description combine to give a perfect finish to the pinnacle above the roof.

There is a hall of Buddha behind the main tower, which is perfectly adorned and very magnificent. The beams, pillars, doors, and windows are covered with gold plates. Besides this, there are priests, chambers elegantly finished and adorned, so that no words can adequately describe them. All the kings of the six kingdoms to the east of the great mountain range called Tsung Ling send as religious offerings to this temple whatever most costly gems they have, and in such abundance that but few of them can be used.

The religious processions of the fourth month being over, one of the pilgrims, called Sang Chau, set out in company with a fellow disciple belonging to the country of the Ouigours, towards Ki-pin (Cophene); Fa Hian and the rest pressed on towards the country of Tseu-ho, and after a journey of twenty-five days they arrived there. The king of this country, by the determined energy of his character, has collected round him about one thousand priests, chiefly belonging to the system known as the Great Vehicle. The pilgrims rested in this country fifteen days, and then going southward for four days, they entered the Tsung Ling mountains, and reached the country of Yu-hwui, where they rested. After this, proceeding directly onwards for twenty-five days, they arrived at the country of Rie-cha (Kartchou, the Kie-pan-to of Huen Tsang), where they rejoined Hwui king and the others.

In Kie-Cha

The king of this country holds the quinquennial assembly known as the Pan-che-yu-sse. At the time of the assembly he invites the Sramans of the four quarters (of every country) to attend. A vast concourse of them having come together, they then proceed to decorate the priests' session-place with silken flags and canopies. In the midst they erect a draped throne adorned with gold and silver lotus flowers, and behind it they arrange the seats for the priests. The king and his attendant ministers then proceed to make their religious offerings.

Principally in the spring time that the king convokes the assembly, either during the first, second, or third month. After it is over, the king again exhorts his ministers to prepare and present further religions offerings. This occupies from one to five days more. After this is all done, the king further makes an offering of the horse which he rides, with its trappings, while the chief minister of the country, and the principal nobles and officers of the land, offer theirs also; moreover, they make presents of white woollen stuff and every kind of precious things which the Sramans require. All these things are given as votive offerings by various ministers of the king.

But, after being thus publicly presented by vow, they are redeemed from the priests for a certain value. These mountainous regions are so cold that they will produce no cereal but wheat. As soon as the ecclesiastics have gathered in their harvest or, received their dues, the weather becomes cloudy and overcast. The king, therefore, usually supplicates the priests to allow all the wheat to ripen before they begin to gather in or receive theirs. In this country is a stone spitting (Pikdan) vessel of Buddha; it is the same colour as his alms-bowl. There is also one of Buddha's teeth, over which the inhabitants have raised a tower. There are about 1,000 or more priests here, all of them belonging to the system called the Little Vehicle.

Everywhere to the eastward of these mountains the ordinary people wear coarse garments like those of China, with the exception of some woollen stuffs and felt, which are different. The variations and additions of the religious observances of the Sramans of these different countries I am unable fully to record. This country is reputed to be in the midst of the Tsung Ling mountains. From these mountains onwards, the plants and fruits are, as a rule, different from those of China, except the bamboo, the pomegranate, and the sugar-cane.

2

Arrives in India

From this country, proceeding westward towards North India, after a journey of one month, we succeeded in passing the Tsung Ling mountains. These mountains are covered with snow both in winter and summer. They shelter venomous dragons also, which, if once provoked, spit out their poison against the traveller. Scarcely one person out of ten thousand survives after encountering the various difficulties which oppose their advance—the wind, and the rain, and the snow, and the driving sand and gravel. The men of these districts are also known as men of the Snowy Mountains.

On passing this mountain chain we arrive in North India. On the confines of this region is a little kingdom called To-li, in which, likewise, there is a congregation of priests, belonging to the Little Vehicle. In this kingdom there was, formerly, an Arhat, who, by his spiritual power, transported a sculptor up to the Tushita Heavens, to observe the size, colour, and general appearance of Maitreya Bodhisattva, so that, on his return, he might carve a wooden image of him. Having first and last made three ascents for the purpose of correct observation, he finally completed the image. It was 94ft high, and the length of the foot of the image is 9ft. 4in. On festival days it always emits an effulgent light. The princes of all the neighbouring countries vie with each other in making religious offerings to it. It still exists in this country.

Keeping along the incline of the Tsung Ling mountains, in a south-westerly direction, they travelled onwards for fifteen days. The road is difficult and fatiguing. Steep crags and precipices constantly intercept the way. These mountains are like walls of rock, standing up 10,000 ft. in height. On looking over the edge the sight becomes confused, and then, on advancing, the foot loses its hold and you are lost. At the base there is a stream called the Sin-to (Indus). Men of old days have cut away the cliff so as to make a passage, and have carved out against the rock steps for descent, amounting altogether to 700 in number.

Having passed these, there is, suspended across the river, a bridge of ropes, by which travellers pass over it. From one side of the river to the other is eighty paces. According to the records of Kau Yih, neither the Chinese Generals Chang Kian nor Kan Ying of the Eastern Han dynasty, reached so far as this.

All the priests asked Fa Hian what he knew as to the time when the law of Buddha began to spread eastward from their country. Hian replied, "On enquiry, men of those lands agreed in saying, that, according to an ancient tradition, Sramans from India began to carry the sacred books of Buddha beyond the river, from the time when the image of Maitreya Bodhisattva was set up." Now this image was set up 300 years or so after the Nirvana of Buddha, which corresponds with the time of Pingwang, of the Chau family. Hence it may be said that the diffusion of the great doctrine may be attributed to the influence of this image. For apart from the power of the great teacher Maitreya, following in the footsteps of Sakya who would have been sufficient to cause the knowledge of the three precious ones—Buddha, Dharma, Sangha—to be spread so far, that even men on the outskirts of the world acquired that knowledge? We may conclude, therefore, with certainty, that the origin of this diffusion of the law of Buddha was no human work, but sprang from the same cause as the dream of Ming Ti.[1]

In Udyana

Crossing the river we arrive at the country of Ou-chang (Udyana). This is the most northern part of India. The language of middle India is everywhere used. Middle India is that which is called the Middle Country (Madhya Desa). The clothes and food of the ordinary people are, likewise, just the same as in the Middle Country. The law of Buddha is universally honoured. The name given to places where the priests take up their fixed abodes is Sangharama. There are altogether about 500 of these in this country, all of which are attached to the system called the Little Vehicle. If any foreign Bhikshu arrives amongst them, they are all ready to entertain him for three days, after which they bid him seek for himself a resting place.

Tradition says, "When Buddha visited North India, he at once came to this country. When he left he bequeathed to them an impression of his foot." The appearance of the impression is large or small, according to the intensity of the religious feeling of the person who beholds it. It exists to the present day. The stone on which Buddha dried his clothes, and the place where he converted the malevolent

1. Ming Ti, the second emperor of the Eastern Han dynasty, began to reign A.D. 58. In the fourth year of his reign he had a dream of this sort —he thought he saw a Divine Being with a body like gold, and of a vast height (70ft.), his head surrounded by a glory like the Sun, fly down towards him and enter his palace. This dream was interpreted as referring to Buddha (Fo), and, consequently, an embassy was despatched to the country of the Tai-yue-chi (the Great Getae), and to India, to seek diligently after the law of Buddha. After eleven years the members of this embassy returned, bringing with them Buddhist books and figures, and also several foreign Sramans. From this time Buddhism began to prevail in China.

dragon (Apalala), still remain. The stone is about 12ft. high and 24ft. square, and smooth on one side.

From this place the three pilgrims, Hwu King, To Ching, and Hwui Ta, went on in advance towards the kingdom of Na-kie (Nagrak or Nagarahara), where the shadow of Buddha is to be seen. Fa Hian and the others remained in this country during the season of the rains. After this they descended towards the south, and arrived at the kingdom of Su-ho-to (Swat).

In this country also the law of Buddha is in a flourishing condition. This is the place where, in ancient times, the divine ruler Sakra (Indra), with a view to tempt Bodhisattva, caused the appearance of a hawk, pursuing a small bird like a dove on which, Bodhisattva tearing his own flesh, gave it in substitution for that of the bird. When Buddha had arrived at complete wisdom, he passed by this place with his disciples, on which he spake to them thus: "It was here that, in one of my former births, I tore my flesh in substitution for that of a bird." The people of the country having thus gained knowledge of this event, erected a stupa upon the spot, and enriched it with gold and silver ornaments.

Gandhara

From this point, still descending in an eastward direction, after five days' journey, we arrive at the country of Kin-to-wai (Gandhara). This is the kingdom formerly governed by Fa Yih, the son of Askoa.

At the time when Buddha was Bodhisattva, he also, in this country, performed an act of sublime charity by sacrificing his eyes. Men have erected on this spot likewise a stupa, enriched with gold and silver.

From this spot, going eastward seven days, there is a country called Tchu-sha-si-lo (Takshasila). This word, being interpreted, signifies, "the severed head."[1] Buddha, when

1. This is an error of Fa-Hian, as the name seems to be derived from the root Taksa, to build (or, figuratively, to cut to pieces), and Sila, a rock

he was Bodhisattva, in this place gave his head in charity; men, therefore, have given this name to the country. Still going to the eastward two days' journey, you come to the place where he gave his body to feed a starving tiger[2]. In these two places they have raised great towers, adorned with all the precious substances. The kings, ministers, and people of all the surrounding countries vie with each other in making religious offerings at these places, in scattering flowers, and burning incense continually. Including the two mentioned in the previous section, men of that district call these four the four great Stupas.

Purushapura

From Gandhara, going south four days' journey, we arrive at the country of Fo-lau-sha (Purushapura or Peshawar). In olden times Buddha, in company with all his disciples, travelled through this country, on which occasion he addressed Ananda thus, "After my Nirvana there will be a king of this country called Ka-ni-ka (Kanishka), who on this spot will raise a Pagoda."

In after times King Kanishka was born, and, on one occasion, as he was going on a tour of inspection, the divine ruler Sakra, wishing to originate the first thoughts of such a purpose, caused to appear before him a little shepherd boy making a Pagoda on the road. The King then stopped and asked him what he was doing, to which he replied, "I am making a tower in honour of Buddha." The King said, "You are a very good boy," and immediately set about building a great tower over that of the little shepherd boy.

(instead of Sira, a head). Our author's mistake, however, is easily accounted for, by considering the legend which follows in the text, and which is also related by Huen Tsang.

2. The tower erected on this spot has been identified as the Great Tope at Manikyala, explored by General Court, close to the Huta-Murta Vihara, or the Body-oblation Vihara, referring to Buddha's sacrifice of his body to feed some starving tiger cubs.

The height of it was 470ft. and more, and it was decorated with every sort of precious substance, so that all who passed by and saw the exquisite beauty and graceful proportions of the tower and the temple attached to it, exclaimed in delight, "These are incomparable in beauty." Tradition says that this was the highest tower in Jambudwipa. When the King had finished his tower, the little one, built by the shepherd boy, immediately came out of it, and removed itself to the south of the great tower, its height was about 3ft. 6in.

Buddha's alms-bowl is also preserved in this country. In former times a king of the Yu-chi, having raised a great army or soldiers, came with them all to invade this country, desiring to carry off the alms bowl. When he had subdued the country, the king of the Yu-chi, being a firm believer in the law of Buddha, wished to take the bowl and to go. He, therefore, prepared to make religious offerings, and, having performed his vows to the three Sacred objects of worship, he caparisoned a great elephant, and placed the alms bowl upon its back. No sooner had he done so, than the elephant fell to the ground, and was unable to advance a step. He then caused a four-wheeled car to be constructed to convey the alms-bowl, and eight elephants to be harnessed to it; but once more they were unable to advance.

The king was then convinced that the destiny of the alms bowl in that kingdom was not yet completed, and, being deeply ashamed of himself, he forthwith raised a tower upon the spot, and also a Sangharama; moreover, he delayed his own departure, and remained to guard the relic, and performed every kind of religious service in its honor. There are about 700 priests at present in this temple. When mid-day approaches, the members of the community bring forth the alms-bowl, and, in company with the laity, who are in attendance, pay it every kind of religious honour. So, again, after the mid-day meal, as evening approaches, at the time of burning incense, i.e., evening service, they do likewise. The bowl contains about two Tau (a dry measure, equal to 1.2 gallons). It is of a mixed color, but mostly black. The seams where the four parts join together are bright. It is about two inches thick, and it is kept well polished and bright. Poor people, with the few flowers which they cast into it, are able to fill it; whilst there are very rich men who, being wishful to pay their devotions with very many flowers, are unable to fill it up, though they offer a hundred, or a thousand, or ten thousand bushels.

The two pilgrims, Po Wan and Tsang King, having merely paid their reverence to the alms bowl of Buddha, forthwith returned homewards. The three pilgrims Hwui King, Hwui Ta, and To Ching, as we have before stated, had gone on in advance to the country of Na-kie, to pay their devotions to the shadow of Buddha, as well as his tooth and skull-bone. Hwui King, however, having fallen sick, To Ching remained with him at Na-kie, to take care of him, so that Hwui Ta alone returned to Peshawar, and, after a conference with the two former pilgrims, Po Wan and Tsang King, who had not yet set out, they all three resolved to return to China. Meanwhile, Hwui King having set out for the temple of Buddha's alms-bowl, after his arrival, died there. On this Fa Hian went on by himself, towards the place of Buddha's skull bone.

3

The Bone of Buddha

Going westwards sixteen yojanas, we arrive at the borders of the country of Na-kie (Nagrak). In the city of Hi-Io (Hidda), is the vihara, containing the relic of the skull-bone of Buddha. This vihara is entirely covered with plates of gold, and decorated with the seven precious substances. The king of the country reverences, in a high degree, this sacred relic. For fear lest any man should carry off the true bone and substitute another in its place, therefore he appoints eight persons belonging to the principal families of the country to seal up every night the door of the shrine, each one with his own seal, so as to guard and protect it.

At early dawn these eight men all go to the temple, and each one observes if his seal is as he left it. They then open the door, and having washed their hands with perfumed water, they take out the bone of Buddha, and place it upon a lofty throne which is erected outside the shrine. On this throne is a circular table composed of the seven precious substances, with a crystal bell-shaped cupola on the top. Both the table and the cover are highly decorated and enriched with gems.

The bone is of a yellowish-white colour, about four inches square, and somewhat elevated in the middle. Each day after it is thus removed, certain men appointed for the purpose ascend a lofty belfry and beat a great drum, blow the conch, and clash the cymbals. When the king hears it he immediately repairs to the vihara and offers flowers and incense; having done this, he repeatedly bends his head to the ground in adoration and departs. He enters by the eastern gate and departs by the western one. Thus does the king discharge his religious duties every morning, and after worship he proceeds to attend to governmental affairs.

The chief men and nobles also attend to these acts of worship first, and then to their household duties, this, in fact, is the first and unfailing duty of every day. After the acts of worship are over, they then return the relic to its shrine. In this vihara is a Dagoba ornamented with the seven precious substances, partly solid and partly hollow, and about five feet in height. In order to enable worshippers to present their offerings at this Dagoba there are men appointed to sell flowers and incense at the gate of the vihara every morning, so that all those who desire to make religious offerings may purchase everything necessary for the purpose.

All the neighbouring princes depute commissioners to present religious offerings in this chapel. The site of the chapel is a square of forty paces a side. Though the heavens should quake, and the earth open, this place would remain unmoved.

Going north from this place one yojana, we arrive at the chief city of the country of Na-kie (Nagrak). This is the place where Bodhisattva, in one of his former births, gave money in exchange for some five-stalked flowers with which he might pay religious reverence to Dipankara Buddha. In this town also is a tower of Buddha's tooth-relic, which is worshipped in the same way as the skull-bone.

One yojana to the N.E. of this city we reach the entrance of a defile where is preserved Buddha's religious staff. A vihara is erected in which religious offerings are made to it. The staff is made of sandalwood, of the kind called Gosirchandana, and is about one chang and six or seven tenths long (between 19 and 20 feet). It is contained in a wooden tube case, from which no human power can remove it. Entering the defile and travelling westward for four days there is a vihara erected for the purpose of paying religious reverence to Buddha's robe (Sanghati). When there is a drought in that country the chief personages of the kingdom assemble together, and taking out the robe of Buddha, they worship it and pay to it religious devotions. The heavens then yield abundance of rain. To the south of Nagrak, half a yojana, is a cave on the S.W. face of a large mountain. In this cave Buddha left his shadow.

At about ten paces off you may see it, like the true resemblance of Buddha, of a golden color, with all its characteristic signs perfectly bright and shining. On turning away or going nearer, the resemblance to the reality becomes less and less distinct. The kings of all the surrounding countries have deputed skilful artists to take a copy of the figure, but they have been unable to accomplish it. A tradition common amongst the men of that country says that all the thousand Buddhas of the present Kalpa will leave their shadows in this place.

About a hundred paces west of this is a place where Buddha during his lifetime shaved his head and pared his nails. Here Buddha, assisted by his disciples, raised a tower from seventy to eighty feet high, as a model for all future buildings of the sort, and this still exists. By the side of this tower is a temple in which, about 700 priests reside. In this place also is a tower erected in honor of all the Arhats and Pratyeka Buddhas of whom as many as a thousand in number have dwelt in this place.

In the second month of winter, Fa Hian and his two companions To Tchang and Hwui Ying, going to the South, crossed the Little Snowy Mountains (probably the highest part of the Khyber range). The snow continually accumulates on these mountains, both in winter and summer. The exceeding cold which came on suddenly in crossing the northern slope of the mountain, which lies in the shade, caused the men generally to remain perfectly silent—to shut their mouths—through fear. The pilgrim Hwui Ying was unable, after repeated efforts, to proceed any further. His mouth was covered with a white foam; at last he addressed Fa Hian and said, "It is impossible for me to recover; while there is time you do press forward, lest we all perish," and upon this he presently died. Fa Hian cherished him to supply warmth and piteously invoked him by his familiar name, but it was all ineffectual to restore life. Submitting therefore to his destiny, he once more gathered up his strength and pressed forward.

Having at length surmounted the ridge of the mountains and passed to the southward of them, they arrived at the country of Lo-I (Roh or Rohi, another name for Afghanistan). In this neighbourhood there are 3000 priests belonging both to the Little and Great Vehicle. The two pilgrims remained here during the season of rest in the rainy months; after this they proceeded to the south ten days' journey, and arrived at the country of Po-Nu (Bannu). Here also there are about 3000 priests, all belonging to the system called the Little Vehicle. From this, going eastwards three days' journey, they again crossed the river Indus. Both sides of the river are now level and plain country.

4

Mathura, Madhya Desa

On the other side of the river is a country called Pi-cha (Panchanada or Punjab). The Law of Buddha is prosperous and flourishing here, and is known both in connection with the Little and Great Vehicle. On seeing disciples from China coming among them they were much affected and spoke thus, "How wonderful to think that men from the ends of the earth, should know the character of this religion (lit., that there is a system of religion requiring one to leave one's family), and should come thus far to seek the laws of Buddha." We received from them all that we required and were treated according to the provisions of the law.

From this, proceeding in a south-easterly direction somewhat less than eighty yojanas, we pass in succession various temples, containing very many priests, in all amounting to 10,000 and more. Having passed by all these places, we arrived at a certain kingdom called Ma-teou-lo (Mathura). Here, again, we followed the course of the river Po-Na (Jumna). [The force of "again" seems to be that they had followed previously the course of the Indus.] On the banks of this river there are twenty Sangharamas, containing perhaps 3000 priests. The Law of Buddha is in a reviving condition.

All the kingdoms beyond the sandy deserts are spoken of as belonging to western India. The kings of all these countries firmly believe in the Law of Buddha. When they pay their religious offerings to the priesthood, they uncover their heads. Both they and the members of their households and the ministers of state frequently conduct the priests to their several palaces, for the purpose of providing them with food. Having placed their entertainment before them, they spread a carpet on the ground opposite the lofty dais on which the priests sit, and there take their places in front of them, for in the presence of the priesthood it is not allowed to laymen to sit on a loftier seat. These rules for the conduct of princes when offering their religious devotions, have been handed down by tradition from the time when Buddha was in the world to the present day.

To the south of this, the country is called Madhya Desa, the middle country. The climate of this region is exceedingly equable, there is neither frost nor snow. The inhabitants are prosperous and happy. There are no Boards of Population and Revenue. Those only who farm the Royal demesnes, pay a portion of the produce as rent. Nor are they bound to remain in possession longer than they like. The king in the administration of justice, inflicts no corporal punishment, but each culprit is fined in money according to the gravity of his offence; and even in cases where the culprit has been guilty of repeated attempts to excite rebellion, they restrict themselves to cutting off his right hand.

The chief officers of the king have all allotted revenues. **The people of this country kill no living creature nor do they drink intoxicating liquors. And, with the exception of the Chandalas, they eat neither garlic nor onions.** The word "Chandala" signifies a wicked man, who lives apart from others. If such a man enters a town or a market place, he strikes a piece of wood, in order to keep himself separate; people, hearing this sound, know what it means and avoid touching him or brushing against him. In this country they do not keep swine or fowls, they do not deal in living animals, nor are there shambles or wine shops round their markets. They use shells for money in their traffic. The Chandalas alone go hunting and deal in flesh.

From the time of Buddha's Nirvana, the kings and nobles of all these countries began to erect viharas for the priesthood, and to endow them with lands, gardens, houses, and also men and oxen to cultivate them. The records of these endowments, being engraved on sheets of copper, have been handed down from one king to another, so that no one has dared to deprive them of possession, and they continue to this day to enjoy their proper revenues. All the resident priests have chambers, beds, coverlets, food, drink and clothes provided for them without stint or reserve. Thus it is in all the places. The priests, on the other hand, continually employ themselves in works of benevolence, in reciting their Scriptures, or in profound meditation.

When a strange priest arrives amongst them, the senior brethren go out to meet him, and conduct him on his way, carrying for him his clothes and alms-dish. They then present him with water to wash his feet and cleanse them from mire, and they prepare an extraordinary repast. After a little pause, when the stranger has rested, they ask him his age, according to which they allot him a chamber with proper materials, in every respect as the Law directs. In every place where the priests take up their fixed abode, they erect towers in honour of Sariputra, Mogalan, Ananda, and also towers in honour of the Abhidharma, Vinaya, and Sutra Pitakas.

After the first month of residence the principal religious families in the neighbourhood exhort them to commence their religious services. On this, the priests partake of an extraordinary collation, and being assembled in a great congregation they repeat the Law; this being over, they present religious offerings to the tower of Sariputra, every kind of incense and flowers, and throughout the whole night they burn lamps provided by those men for the purpose.

Sariputra was originally a Brahmin. On one occasion having met Buddha, he sought to become a disciple. So also did the great Kasyapa and the great Mogalan. The Bhikshunis principally affect the worship of the tower of Ananda, because it was Ananda who requested Buddha to permit females to become disciples. The Samaneras (novices) principally affect the worship of Rahula, the son of Buddha. The preachers of the Abhidharma pay their religious offerings to that work, and so also with the masters of the Vinaya.

Every year there is one such religious service, each individual having his own day. Men who belong to the Great Vehicle worship the Prajna Paramita, Manjusri, and Avalokiteswara. The priests' harvest being finished—or it may be—the season when the priests receive presents being over, then the nobles, and householders, and Brahmins, all provide themselves with different sorts of material for making garments such as priests require and present them to the clergy. The priests likewise make presents one to another.

These rules of courtesy for the direction of the holy congregation, have been handed down without interruption from the time of Buddha's nirvana till now. From the river Sin-to (Indus) to South India, where it borders on the southern sea, a distance of forty or fifty thousand li, the land is all plain and level. There are no great mountains or valleys, but still there are rivers.

5

At Sankasya where Buddha Descended from Heaven

Going S.E. from Mathura eighteen yojanas, there is a kingdom called Sang-ka-shi (Sankasya). When Buddha went up to the Triyastrinshas heaven, to say Bana (Law) for the sake of his mother, after three months he descended at this place. On this occasion he exerted his spiritual power so that his disciples did not know where he had gone. Seven days before the completion of the three months, he again scattered his spiritual influence, so that Aniruddha a cousin, of Buddha, by his divine sight was able to behold the World-Honored one afar off. Immediately he addressed the venerable Maha Mogalan, "You now can go and pay reverence to the World-Honoured one." Mogalan forthwith proceeded and prostrated himself in adoration of the marks on the foot of Buddha. This act of adoration being over, Buddha addressed him and said, "After seven days more I shall descend to Jambudvipa." Then Mogalan returned.

At the appointed time the Maharajas of the eight kingdoms and all the ministers and people, not having seen Buddha for so long, greatly desired to meet him. They flocked therefore in great crowds to this country to await the return of the World-Honoured one. Then the Bhikshuni Utpala began to think thus with herself, "Today the king, ministers, and people are all going to meet Buddha and render homage to him, but I—a woman—how can I contrive to get the first sight of him." Buddha immediately, by his divine power, changed her into a holy Chakravarti Raja, and in that capacity she was the very first to reverence Buddha on his return.

Buddha was now about to descend from the Triyastrinshas heavens. At this time there appeared a threefold precious ladder. Buddha standing above the middle ladder which was made of the seven precious substances began to descend. Then the king of the Brahmakayikas—followers of Brahma, one of their heavens—caused a silver ladder to appear, and took his place on the right hand, holding a white chowry in his hand. Whilst the divine Sakra caused a bright golden ladder to appear, and took his place on the left hand holding a precious parasol in his hand. Innumerable Devas were in attendance while Buddha descended. After he had accomplished his return the three ladders all disappeared in the earth except seven steps, which still continued visible.

In after times king Asoka, wishing to find out the utmost depth to which these ladders went, employed men to dig and examine the matter. They went down till they came to a spring of yellow water, but yet had not arrived at the bottom. The king deriving from this an increase of faith and reverence, forthwith built over the ladders a vihara, and in the middle of it placed a standing figure of Buddha sixteen feet high. Behind the vihara he erected a stone pillar thirty cubits high, and on the top placed the figure of a lion. Within the pillar on the four sides are placed figures of Buddha; both within and without it is shining and bright as glass (lapis lazuli).

It happened once that some heretical persons had a contention with the Sramans respecting this, as a place of residence. Then the Sramans agreed to any condition for settling the question that might be considered reasonable on which they all bound themselves to this compact, "If this place properly belongs to the Sramans, then there will be some supernatural proof given of it." Immediately on this, the lion on the top of the pillar uttered a great roar. Witnessing this testimony, the unbelievers were abashed and withdrew from the dispute and submitted.

The body of Buddha, in consequence of his having partaken of divine food during the three months he was in the Triyastrinshas heavens, emitted a divine fragrance, unlike that of men. Immediately after his descent, he bathed himself. Men of after ages erected in this place a bath house, which yet remains. There is also a tower erected on the spot where the Bhikshuni Utpala was the first to adore Buddha on his return. There is also a tower on the spot where Buddha when in the world cut his hair and his nails, and also on the following spots, where the three former Buddhas, as well as Sakya Muni, sat down, and also where they walked for exercise, and also where there are certain marks and impressions left on the stones by the feet of the different Buddhas; these towers still remain.

There is also one erected where Brahma, Sakra and the Devas attended Buddha when he came down from heaven. In these different places there are perhaps 1000 male and female disciples who in their several establishments have their meals in common. They belong promiscuously to the systems of the Great and Little Vehicle, and agree to occupy the same place. A white-eared dragon or Naga or, the dragon Yih-pih-i, i.e., one white ear, is the patron of this body of priests. It is he who causes fertilizing and seasonable showers of rain to fall within their country, and preserves it from plagues and calamities, and so causes the priesthood to dwell in security. The priests, in gratitude for these favours, have erected a Dragon-chapel, and within it placed a resting place for his accommodation, and, moreover, they make special contributions, in the shape of religious offering, to provide the dragon with food.

The body of priests every day select from their midst three men to go and take their meal in this chapel. Towards the end of each season of rest, the dragon incontinently assumes the form of a little serpent, both of whose ears are edged with white. The body of priests, recognizing him, place in the midst for his use a copper vessel full of milk cream. The serpent then proceeds to come down from the highest part of the alcove, constructed for his accommodation, to the lowest part, all the while moving as though he would pay his respects to all those around him. He then suddenly disappears. He makes his appearance once every year.

This country is abundantly productive; the people in consequence are very prosperous, and rich beyond comparison. Men of all countries coming here, may without any trouble obtain all they require.

Fifty yojanas to the north of this temple is another temple called "Fire Limit," which is the name of an evil spirit. Buddha in one of his incarnations converted this evil spirit, whereupon men in after ages raised a vihara on the spot. At the time of the dedication of the vihara, an Arhat spilt some of the water, with which he was cleansing his hands, on the earth, and the place where it fell is still visible; though they have often swept and cleansed the place, yet the mark still remains and cannot be destroyed.

There is, besides, in this place, a tower of Buddha which a benevolent Spirit ever keeps clean water, and which at first was built without a human architect. There was once a heretical king who said, "Since you are able to do this, I will bring a great army and quarter it here, which shall accumulate much filth and refuse. Will you be able to clear all this away, I wonder?" The Spirit immediately caused a great tempest to rise and blow over the place, as a proof that he could do it.

In this district there are a hundred or so small towers; a man might pass the day in trying to count them without succeeding. If anyone is very anxious to discover the right number, then it is customary to place a man by the side of each tower and afterwards to number the men. But even in this case, it can never be known how many or how few men will be required. There is also a Sangharama here, containing about six or seven hundred priests. In this is a place where a Pratyeka Buddha ate the fruit of Nirvana; the spot of ground where this took place is just in size like a chariot wheel, all the ground around it is covered with grass, but this spot produces none. The earth also where he dried his clothes, is bare of vegetation; the traces of the impress of the clothes remain to this day.

6

The Glory of Sravasti

Where Buddha Lived for 25 Years

Fa Hian resided in the Dragon Vihara during the summer rest. After this was over, going south-east seven yojanas, he arrived at the city of Ki-jou-i (Kannauj). This city borders on the Ganges. There are two Sangharamas here, both belonging to the system of the Little Vehicle. Going from the city six or seven li in a westerly direction, on the forth bank of the river Ganges, is the place where Buddha delivered the Law for the good of his disciples. Tradition says that he preached concerning impermanency and sorrow, and also on the body being like a bubble and so on. On this spot they have raised a tower, which still remains. Crossing the Ganges, and going south three yojanas, we arrive at a forest called Ho-li. Here also Buddha preached the Law. They have erected towers on this spot and also where he sat down and walked for exercise.

Going South-East from this place ten yojanas, you arrive at the great country of Sha-chi (Kasi). Leaving the southern gate of the capital city, on the east side of the road is the place where Buddha once located himself. While here, he bit off a piece from the Dantakachta stick with which he cleansed his teeth, and fixing it in the earth it immediately grew up seven feet high, neither more or less. All the unbelievers and Brahmins, filled with jealousy, cut it down, and tore away and scattered the leaves far and wide, but yet it always sprang up again in the same place as before. Here also they raised towers on the place where the four Buddhas walked for exercise and sat down. The ruins of these still exist.

Going eight yojanas northwards from this place, we arrive at the country of Kiu-sa-lo (Kosala) and its chief town She-wei (Sravasti). There are very few inhabitants in this city, altogether perhaps about two hundred families. This is the city which king Prasenjit governed. Towers have been erected in after times on the site of the ruined vihara of Maha Prajapati, also on the foundations of the house of Sudatta the Nobleman, also on-the spot where Angulimala was burnt who was converted and entered Nirvana; all these towers are erected in the midst of the city. The unbelieving Brahmins, entertaining a jealous feeling, desired to destroy these various edifices, but on their attempting to do so the heavens thundered and the lightnings flashed, so that they were unable to carry their design into execution. Leaving the city by the south gate, and proceeding twelve hundred paces on the road, on the west side of it is the place where the nobleman Sudatta built a vihara (Jetavana Vihara). This chapel opens towards the East. The principal door is flanked by two side chambers, in front of which stand two stone pillars, on the top of the left hand one is the figure of a wheel, and on the right hand one, the image of an ox. The clean water of the tanks, the luxuriant groves, and numberless flowers of variegated hues, combine to produce the picture of what is called the Vihara of Chi-un (Jeta).

When Buddha ascended into the Triyastrinshas heavens to repeat the Law for the sake of his mother, after ninety days absence, king Prajapati desiring to see him again, carved out of the sandalwood called Gosirsha-chandana (ox-head) an image of the saint and placed it on the seat that he usually occupied. When Buddha returned and entered the vihara, the image immediately quitting its place, went forward to meet him. On this Buddha addressed these words to it, "Return, I pray you, to your seat. After my Nirvana you will be the model from which all my followers (lit. the members of the four schools or classes) shall carve their image of me." On this the figure immediately returned to its seat.

This image, as it was the very first made of all the figures of Buddha, is the one which all subsequent ages have followed as a model. Buddha subsequently removed and dwelt in a small vihara on the south side of the greater one, in a place quite separate from that occupied by the image, and about twenty paces from it. The Chi-un Vihara originally had seven stories. The monarchs of all the surrounding countries and their inhabitants vied with each other in presenting religious offerings at this spot. They decked the place with flags and silken canopies, they offered flowers and burnt incense, while the lamps shone out day after day with unfading splendor.

Unfortunately, a rat gnawing at the wick of one of the lamps caused it to set fire to one of the hanging canopies, and this resulted in a general conflagration, and the entire destruction of the seven stories of the Vihara. The kings and people of the surrounding countries were all deeply grieved, supposing that the sandalwood figure had also been consumed. Four or five days afterwards, on opening the door of the eastern little chapel, they were surprised to behold the original figure there. All the people were filled with joy, and they agreed to rebuild the chapel. Having completed two stories they removed the image from its new situation back to where it was before.

When Fa Hian and To Ching arrived at this chapel of Chi-un, they were much affected to think that this was the spot in which Buddha had passed twenty-five years of his life. Around them stood many strangers, all occupied in similar reflections. They had traversed a succession of strange countries. Perhaps they might be spared to return home, perhaps they would die. Gazing thus upon the place where Buddha once dwelt, but was no longer to be seen, their hearts were affected with very lively regret. Whereupon the priests, belonging to that community, came forward and addressed Fa Hian and his companion thus, "From what country have you come," to which they replied, "We come from the land of Han." Then those priests, in astonishment, exclaimed, "Wonderful! to think that men from the remotest corner of the earth should come so far as this, from a desire to search for the Law;" and then talking between themselves they said, "Our various Superiors and Brethren who have succeeded one another in this place, from the earliest time till now, have none of them seen men of Han come so far as this before."

Four li to the North West of the Vihara is a copse called "Recovered Sight" (Aptanetra Vana). Originally there were five hundred blind men dwelling on this spot who were in the habit of attending the chapel. On one occasion Buddha declared the Law on their account; after listening to his sermon, they immediately recovered their sight. The blind men, overcome with joy, drove their staves into the earth and fell down on their faces in adoration. The staves forthwith took root and grew up to be great trees. The people, from a feeling of reverence, did not presume to cut them down, and so they grew and formed a grove, to which this name of "Recovered Sight" was given. The priests of the chapel of Chi-un resort in great numbers this shady copse to meditate after their midday meal. Six or seven li to the North East of the Vihara of Chi-un is the site of the chapel which Visaka-matawi built, and invited Buddha and the priests to occupy. The ruins of this chapel still exist.

The great Garden enclosure of the Vihara of Chi-un has two gates, one opening towards the East, the other towards the North. This garden is the plot of ground which the nobleman Sudatta bought, after covering it with gold coins. The chapel is placed in the exact centre of it; it was here that Buddha resided for a very long time and expounded the Law for the salvation of men. Towers have been erected on the various spots where he walked for exercise or sat down. These towers have all distinctive titles given them, as for example, the place where Buddha was accused of murdering the Chandala woman. Leaving the garden of Chi-un by the eastern gate, and going north seventy paces, on the west side of the road is the place where Buddha formerly held a discussion with the followers of the ninety-six heretical schools. The king of the country, the chief ministers, the landowners and people all came in great numbers to hear him.

At this time a woman, who was an unbeliever, called Chinchimana, being filled with jealousy, gathered up her clothes in a heap round her person so as to appear big with child, and then accused Buddha, in the midst of the great assembly, of having acted towards her contrary to the Law. On this, Sakra, the heavenly king, taking the appearance of a white mouse, came and gnawed through the sash which bound the woman's clothes up in the heap; on this the whole fell down, and then the earth opened and she herself went down alive into Hell.

Here also is the place where Devadatta, having poisoned his nails for the purpose of destroying Buddha, went down alive into Hell. Men in after times signalised these various places so that they might be known. Where the discussion took place they raised a chapel, which was more than six cheung (seventy feet) high, and within it placed a sitting figure of Buddha. To the east of the road is a temple (Devalaya) belonging to the heretics, which is named "Shadow-covered." It is just opposite the vihara erected on the place of the discussion, and of the same height. It has received the name of "Shadow-covered" from the fact that when the sun is in the west, the shadow of the Vihara of Buddha the honourable of the age covers the temple of the heretics, but when the sun is in the east the shadow of the latter is bent to the north, and does not at all overshadow the chapel of Buddha.

The heretiesbeing in the habit of appointing persons to take care of their temple, to sweep and water it, to burn incense and light lamps for religious worship, it was found that, towards the approach of morning their lamps disappeared and were discovered in the middle of the Buddhist chapel. On this the Brahmins, being angry, said,

"These Sramans take our lamps for the purpose of their own religious worship, why do we not put a stop to it?" Whereupon, the Brahmins, placing themselves in watch at night, saw how the thing was done, for lo! their own gods came and taking the lamps proceeded with them to the chapel of Buddha, and having three times moved round the building in solemn procession, and thus paid their homage to Buddha, they suddenly disappeared. On this the Brahmins, recognising the greatness of Buddha's spiritual power, forsook their families and became his disciples.

Tradition says that about the time when these things happened, there were ninety Sangharamas surrounding this chapel of Chi-un, all of which, with one exception, were occupied by priests. In this country of mid-India there are ninety-six heretical sects, all of whom allow the reality of worldly phenonena. Each sect has its disciples who beg their food, but do not carry alms-dishes. They build hospices by the side of solitary roads (lit. "houses of merit," i.e., for obtaining merit) for the shelter of travellers, where they may rest, sleep, eat and drink, and are supplied with all necessaries. The followers of Buddha also, as they pass to and fro, are entertained by them, only different arrangements are made for their convenience. Devadatta also has a body of disciples still existing; they pay religious reverence to the three past Buddhas, but not to Sakya Muni.

Four li to the South-East of Sravasti is the place where the World-Honoured one stood by the side of the road; on this spot there is a tower built. Fifty li to the west of the city we arrive at a town called To-wai (Tadwa), this was the original birthplace of Kasyapa Buddha. Towers are erected on the spot where he had an interview with his father and also where he entered nirvana. A great tower has also been erected over the relics of the entire body of Kasyapa Tathagata.

7

Where Buddha Was Born

Leaving the city of Sravasti, and going twelve yojanas to the South-east, we arrive at a town called Na-pi-ka. This is the birthplace of Krakuchanda Buddha. There are towers erected on the spots where the interview between the father and son took place, and also where he entered nirvana. Going north from this place less than one yojana, we arrive at a town where Kanakamuni Buddha was born; there are towers also erected here over similar places as the last.

Kapilavastu in Rains

From this spot going eastward less than a yojana we arrive at the city of Ka-wei-lo-wei (Kapilavastu). In this city there is no government or people, it is just like a great desert. There is simply a congregation of priests and about ten families of lay people. In the place where stand the ruins of the palace of Suddhodana, there is a picture of the Prince-apparent and his mother (supposed to be) taken at the time of his miraculous conception. The Prince is represented as descending towards his mother, riding on a white elephant. Towers have been erected on the following spots; where the royal Prince left the city by the Eastern gate; where he saw the sick man, and where he caused his chariot to turn and take him back to his palace. There are also towers erected on the following spots: at the place where the Rishi Asita calculated the horoscope of the royal Prince; where Nanda and the others struck the elephant and seized it; where the arrow going south-east thirty li, entered the earth, from which bubbled up a fountain of water, which, in after generations, was used as a well for travellers to drink at; also on the spot where Buddha, after arriving at Supreme Wisdom, met his father; where the five hundred Sakyas, having embraced the faith, paid reverence to Upali; at the place where the earth shook six times in succession; at the place where Buddha expounded the Law on behalf of all the Devas, while the four Heavenly Kings guarded the four gates of the hall, so that his father could not enter; at the place where Maha Prajapati presented Buddha with a Sanghati (robe) while he was sitting under a Nyagrodha tree, with his face to the East, which tree still exists; at the place where Virudhaka Raja killed the offspring of the Sakyas, who had previously entered on the path Srotapanna. All these towers are still in existence.

A few li to the north-east of the city is the royal field, where the Prince, sitting underneath a tree, watched a ploughing match. Fifty li to the east of the city is the royal garden, called Lumbini; it was here the Queen entered the bath to wash herself, and having come out on the northern side, advanced twenty paces, and then holding a branch of the Sala tree in her hand, brought forth the Prince. When born he walked seven steps; two dragon Kings washed the Prince's body,—the place where this occurred was afterwards converted into a well, from which the priests draw their drinking water.

All the Buddhas have four places universally determined for them: 1. The place for arriving at Supreme Wisdom; 2. The place for turning the wheel of the Law; 3. The place for expounding the true principles of the Law, and refuting the heretics; 4. The place for descending to earth after going into the Triyastrivishas heaven to explain the Law to their mothers. With respect to other places, they are chosen according to the time when the several Buddhas come into the world. The country of Kapilavastu is now a great desert, you seldom meet any people on the roads, for they are much in dread of the white elephants and the lions which frequent the neighbourhood, and render it impossible to travel negligently. Going east five yojanas from the place where Buddha was born, there is a country called Lan (Ramagrama).

Ramagrama

The king of this country obtained one share of the relics of Buddha's body. On his return home he built a tower over these relics which is the same as the Tower of Ramagrama. By the side of it is a tank, in the middle of which resides a Dragon, who constantly guards and protects the tower, and performs religious service in it, morning and night. When King Asoka was born and came to the throne, he wished to destroy the eight towers which had been erected over the different portions of the relics and to build eighty-four thousand there throughout the land. Having destroyed seven of them, he next proceeded to treat this one in the same way. The Dragon therefore assumed a body, and conducted the king within his abode, and having exhibited to him all the vessels and appliances he used in his religious services, he addressed the king, and said: "If you can excel me in these particulars, then you may destroy the tower, go and do so at once, I will have no quarrel with you." King Asoka, knowing that these vessels were of no human workmanship, immediately returned to his home without carrying his purpose into execution.

In the midst of this sacred spot grass and weeds were allowed to grow. There was no one either to water it or sweep it; but ever and anon a herd of elephants, carrying water in their trunks, piously watered the ground, and also brought all sorts of flowers and perfumes to pay religious worship at the Tower. Buddhist pilgrims from all countries came here to pay their vows and worship at the shrine. On one occasion some of these, or, one of these, being very much frightened, concealed themselves amongst the trees. They then saw the elephants perform their Service according to the Law. The disciples of Buddha on this were greatly affected. They grieved to think that in this sacred spot there was neither temple nor priests to perform religious service, so that the very elephants had to water and sweep it.

On this they immediately gave up the great Precepts of the lay disciple, and took upon them the vows of a Samanera. They then began to pluck up the brushwood, and level the ground, and arrange the place so that it became neat and clean. They further stimulated the king of the country to help make residences for the priests. Moreover, they built a temple, in which priests still reside. From about the time when these things occurred there has been a regular succession of priests till now, only the Superior of the temple has always been a Samanera. Three yojanas east of this place is the spot where the royal Prince dismissed his charioteer Tchandaka and the royal horse, previous to their return. Here also is erected a tower.

Kusinagara

Proceeding eastward from this place four yojanas we arrive at the tower raised over the ashes selected after the burning of Buddha's body. Here also is a Sangharama. Again advancing twelve yujanas to the eastward we arrive at the town of Kusinagara. To the north of this town, on the place where the world-honoured Buddha, lying by the side of the Hiranyavati river, with his head to the north, and a Sal tree on either side of him, he entered nirvana. Also in the place where Subhadra was converted, the very last of all his disciples. Also where, for seven days, they paid reverence to the world-honoured Buddha, lying in his golden coffin. Also where Vajrapati threw down his golden mace, and where the eight kings divided the relics;

in each of the above places towers have been raised and Sangharamas built, which still exist.

In this city also there are but few inhabitants; such families as there are connected with the resident congregation of priests. Going south-east twelve yojanas from this place we arrive at the spot where all the Litchavis, desiring to follow Buddha to the scene of his nirvana, were forbidden to do so. On account of their great affection to Buddha, they were unwilling to go back, on which Buddha caused to appear between them and him a great and deeply-scarped river, which they could not cross. He then left with them his alms-bowl as a memorial, and exhorted them to return to their houses. On this they went back and erected a stone pillar, on which they engraved an inscription.

8

Vaisali, Pataliputra, Gaya

Going eastward from this spot five yojanas we arrive at the country of Vaisali. To the north of the city of this name or to the north of the capital city of Vaisali, there is the vihara of the great forest, Mahavana Vihara, which has a double tower or a tower of two stories. This chapel was once occupied by Buddha. Here also is the tower which was built over half the body of Ananda. Within this city dwelt Amradarika (Amrapali) who built a tower in honour of Buddha, the ruins of which still exist. Three li to the South of the city, on the west side of the road, is the garden which Amradarika presented to Buddha as a place for him to rest in.

When Buddha was about to enter nirvana, accompanied by his disciples, he left Vaisali by the western gate, and turning his body to the right as a token of respect (Pradakshina) he beheld the city and thus addressed his followers: "In this place I have performed the last religious act of my earthly career." Men afterwards raised a tower on this spot. Three li to the north-west of the city is a tower called "the tower of the deposited bows and clubs."

The origin of this name was as follows:—On one of the superior affluents of the river Ganges there was a certain country ruled by a king. One of the concubines of this monarch gave birth to an unformed foetus, whereupon the wife of the king, being filled with jealousy, said, "Your conception is one of very bad omen." So they immediately closed it up in a box of wood and cast it into the middle of the Ganges. Lower down the stream there was a certain Raja, who, as he was taking a tour of observation, caught sight of the wooden box as it floated on the surface of the stream. On bringing it to the shore and opening it, to see what was inside, he beheld a thousand little children very fair and just of a size. The king thereupon took them and brought them up. Afterwards, when they grew up, they turned out to be very brave and warlike, and were victorious over all whom they went to attack. In process of time they marched against the kingdom of the monarch, their father. The king was filled with great consternation in anticipation of their approach. On this his concubine asked the Raja why he was so terrified, to whom he replied, "The king of that country has a thousand sons, brave and warlike beyond compare, and these are coming to waste my territories, this is why I am alarmed." To this the concubine replied, "Fear not! but erect on the east of the city a high tower, and when the robbers come, place me on the top of it, and I will restrain them."

The king did as she requested, and when the invaders arrived the concubine, from the top of the tower, addressed them, saying, "Are you my children all? Then why are you engaged in such rebellious acts as these?" They replied, "Who are you, that say you are our mother?" The concubine replied, "If ye will not believe me, all of you look up towards me, and open your mouths." On this the concubine, with both her hands, compressed her breasts, and from each breast forthwith proceeded five hundred jets of milk, which fell into the mouths of her thousand sons. On this the robbers, perceiving that she was indeed their mother, immediately laid down their bows and clubs. The two royal fathers, by a consideration of these circumstances, were able to arrive at the condition of Pratyeka Buddha, and two Towers, erected in their honour, remain to the present day.

In after times, when the world-honoured Buddha arrived at Supreme Reason, he addressed all his disciples in these words, and said, "This is the place where I formerly laid aside my bow and my club." Men in after times coming to know this, founded a tower in this place, and hence the name given to it. The thousand young children are in truth the thousand Buddhas of this Bhadra Kalpa. Buddha, when standing beside this tower, addressed Ananda in these words, "After three months I must enter nirvana," on which occasion Mara Raja so fascinated the mind of Ananda that he did not request Buddha to remain in the world.

Going east from this point three or four li there is a tower. One hundred years after the nirvana of Buddha there were at Vaisali certain Bhikshus who violated the rules of the Vinaya by their conduct, in ten particulars, justifying themselves by saying that Buddha had said "thus it was"—at which time all the Arhats and the orthodox Bhikshus, making an assembly of seven hundred ecclesiastics and more, compared and collated the Vinaya Pitaka afresh. Afterwards men erected a tower on this spot, which still exists.

Where Ananda Died

Going four yojanas east of this, we arrive at the confluence of the five rivers. When Ananda was going from the country of Magadha towards Vaisali, desiring to enter nirvana, all the Devas acquainted king Ajatsatru of it. The king immediately placed himself at the head of his troops, set out after him and arrived at, or, towards the banks of the river. All the Litchhavis of Vaisali, hearing that Ananda was coming, likewise set out to meet him and arrived at the side of the river. Ananda then reflected that if he were to advance, king Ajatsatru would be much grieved, and i he should go back, then the Litchhavis would be indignant Being perplexed he forthwith entered the samadhi, callec the "brilliancy of flame," consuming his body, and enterec nirvana in the very midst of the river. His body was dividec into two parts, one part was found on either side of the river, so the two kings, each taking the relics of half his body, returned and erected towers over them.

The City of Asoka

Crossing the river, and proceeding towards the south one yojana, we arrive at Magadha, and the town of Pa-liu-fou (Pataliputra). This is the town in which king Asoka reigned. In the middle of the city is the royal palace, the different parts of which he commissioned the genii tc construct. The massive stones of which the walls are made the doorways and the sculptured towers, are no humar work. The ruins of this palace still exist. The younger brother of king Asoka having arrived at the dignity of ar Arhat, was in the habit of residing in the hill Khi-chi-kiu (Gridhrakuta), finding his chief delight in silen contemplation. The king, having a great regard anc reverence for his brother, requested him to come to his house to receive or present his religious offerings. His brother, pleased with his tranquility in the mountain declined the invitation.

The king then addressed his brother, saying, "If you will only accept my invitation, I will make for you a hil within the city." The king then, providing all sorts of mea and drink, invited the Genii to come, addressing them thus "I beg you all to accept my invitation for tomorrow, but as there are no seats fit for you, I must request you each tc bring his own." On the morrow all the great Genii came each one bringing with him a great stone, four or five paces square. Immediately after the feast, he deputed the Geni to pile up the great stones and make a mountain of them and at the base of the mountain with five great square stones to make a rock chamber, in length about thirty-five feet and in breadth twenty-two feet, and in height eleven feet or so.

In this city once lived a certain Brahmin, called Lo-tai-sz-pi-mi, of large mind and extensive knowledge, and attached to the Great Vehicle. There was nothing with which he was unacquainted, and he lived apart occupied in silent meditation. The king of the country honoured and respected him, as his religious superior guru. If he went to salute him he did not dare to sit down in his presence. If the king, from a feeling of affectionate esteem, took him by the hand, the Brahmin immediately washed himself from head to foot. For something like fifty years the whole country looked up to this man and placed its confidence on him alone. He mightily extended the influence of the Law of Buddha, so that the heretics were unable to obtain any advantage at all over the priesthood.

By the side of the tower of king Asoka is built a Sangharama belonging to the Greater Vehicle, very imposing and elegant. There is also a temple belonging to the Little Vehicle. Together they contain about six or seven hundred priests, all of them exceedingly well conducted. In the college attached to the temple one may see eminent Sramans from every quarter of the world, and whatever scholars there are who seek for instruction, they all flock to this temple. The Brahmin teacher is also called Manjusri. The great Sramans of the country, and all the Bhikshus attached to the Great Vehicle, universally esteem and reverence him; moreover, he resides in this Sangharama.

Of all the kingdoms of mid-India, the towns of this country are especially large. The people are rich and prosperous and virtuous. Every year on the eighth day of the second month there is a procession of images. On this occasion, they construct a four-wheeled car, and erect upon it a tower of five stages, composed of bamboos lashed together, the whole being supported by a centre post resembling a large spear with three points, in height twenty two feet and more. So it resembles a Pagoda. They then cover it over with fine white linen, on which they afterwards paint all sorts of gaily-coloured pictures. Having made figures of all the Devas, and decorated them with gold, silver, and coloured glass (lapis lazuli), they place them under canopies of embroidered silk. Then at the four corners of the car they construct niches (shrines) in which they place figures of Buddha, in a sitting posture, with a Bodhisattva standing in attendance.

There are perhaps twenty cars thus prepared, and decorated each one differently from the rest. During the day of the procession, both priests and laymen assemble in great numbers. There are all sorts of games and amusements for the latter whilst the former offer flowers and incense in religious worship. The Bramacharis come forth to salute Buddha, and one after the other the cars enter the city. After coming into the town they take up their several positions. Then all night long the people burn lamps, indulge in games, and make religious offerings. Such is the custom of all those who assemble on this occasion from the different countries roundabout.

The respected nobles and landowners of this country have founded hospitals within the city, to whicn the poor of all countries, the destitute, cripples, and the diseased may repair for shelter. They receive every kind of requisite help gratuitously. Physicians inspect their diseases, and according to their cases, order them food and drink, medicine or decoctions, everything in fact that may contribute to their ease. When cured they depart at their own convenience. King Asoka having destroyed seven of the original pagodas, constructed 84,000 others. The very first which he built is the great tower which stands about three li to the south of this city. In front of this pagoda is an impression of Buddha's foot, over which they have raised a chapel, the gate of which faces the north. To the south of the tower is a stone pillar, about a chang and a half in girth (eighteen feet), and three chang or so in height (thirty-five feet). On the surface of this pillar is an inscription to the following effect, "King Asoka presented the whole of Jambudwipa to the priests of the Four Quarters, and redeemed it again with money, and this he did four times." Three or four hundred paces to the north of the pagoda is the spot where Asoka was born or resided. On this spot he raised the city of Ni-lai[1] and in the midst of it erected a stone pillar also about thirty-five feet in height, on the top of which he placed the figure of a lion, and also engraved an historical record on the front of the pillar, giving an account of the successive events connected with the city of Ni-lai, with the corresponding year, day, and month.

New Rajagriha

From this city, proceeding in a south-easterly direction nine yojanas, we arrive at a small rocky hill standing by itself, on the top of which is a stone cell facing the south. On one occasion, when Buddha was sitting in the middle of this cell, the Divine Sakra took with him his attendant musicians, each one provided with a five-stringed lute, and caused them to sound a strain in the place where Buddha was seated. Then the divine Sakra proposed forty-two questions to Buddha, writing each one of them singly with his finger upon a stone. The traces of these questions yet exist. There is also a Sangharama built upon this spot.

Going south-west from this one yojana we arrive at the village of Na-lo (Nalanda). This was the place of Sariputra's birth. Sariputra returned here to enter nirvana. A tower therefore was erected on this spot, which is still in existence.

Going west from this one yojana we arrive at the New Rajagriha. This was the town which king Ajatsatru built. There are two Sangharamas in it. Leaving this town by the

1. The town of Nala (mentioned in the Singhalese Annals) is situated to the south-east of the gates of Pataliputra.

west gate, and proceeding 300 paces, we arrive at the tower which king Ajatsatru raised over the share of Buddha's relics which he obtained. Its height is very imposing. Leaving the south side of the city, and proceeding southwards four li, we enter a valley situated between five hills. These hills encircle it completely like the walls of a town. This is the site of the old town of king Bimbasara. From east to west it is about five or six li, from north to south seven or eight li. Here Sariputra and Mogalan first met Asvajit. Here also the Nirgrantha made a pit with fire in it, and poisoned the food, of which he invited Buddha to partake.

Here also is the spot where king Ajatsatru intoxicating a black elephant, desired to destroy Buddha. To the north-east of the city, in the middle of a crooked defile, the physician Jivaka (Ki Kau) erected a vihara in the garden of Ambapali, and invited Buddha and his 1250 disciples to receive her religious offerings. The ruins still exist. Within the city all is desolate, and without inhabitants.

Gridhrakuta, Where Buddha Meditated

Entering the valley, and skirting the mountains along their South-eastern slope for a distance of fifteen li, we arrive at the hill called Gridhrakuta (Ki-che-kiu). Three li from the top is a stone cavern facing the south. Buddha used in this place to sit in profound meditation. Thirty paces to the north-west is another stone cell, in which Ananda practised meditation. The Deva Mara Papiyan having assumed the form of a vulture, took his station before the cavern, and terrified Ananda. Buddha, by his spiritual power (of Irrdhi), penetrated the rock, and with his outspread hand touched the head of Ananda. On this he bore up against his fear, and found peace. The traces of the bird and of the hand-hole still plainly exist, and from this circumstance the hill is called "the hill of the vulture cave" (Gridhrakuta).

In front of the cave are spots where each of the four Buddhas sat down. Each of the Arhats likewise has a cave in this neighbourhood celebrated as the place where he practised meditation. Altogether there are several hundreds of these.

Here is the place where, during the lifetime of Buddha, when he was walking to and fro, from east to west, in front of his cell, Devadatta, standing on the mountain between the northern eminences, rolled down athwart his path a stone which wounded a toe of Buddha's foot. The stone is still there. The hall in which Buddha delivered the law has been overturned and destroyed; the foundations of the brick walls still exist however. The peaks of this mountain are picturesque and imposing; it is the loftiest one of the five mountains that surround the town. Fa Hian having bought flowers, incense, and oil and lamps, in the New Town, procured the assistance of two aged Bhikshus to accompany him to the top of the peak. Having arrived there, he offered his flowers and incense, and lit his lamps, so that their combined lustre illuminated the gloom of the cave.

Fa Hian was deeply moved, even till the tears coursed down his cheeks and he said, "Here it was in by' gone days that Buddha dwelt, and delivered the Surangama Sutra. Fa Hian, not privileged to be born at a time when Buddha lived, can but gaze on the traces of his presence, and the place which he occupied." Then taking his position in front of the cave, he recited the Surangama Sutra, and remained there the entire night.

Venuvana Vihara

Returning towards the New City, after passing through the old town, and going more than 300 paces to the north, on the west side of the road, we arrive at the Kalanda Venuvana Vihara (the chapel in the Bamboo Garden of

Kalanda). This chapel still exists, and a congregation of priests sweep and water it. Two or three li to the north of the chapel is the Shi-mo-she-na (Samasana) which signifies the field of tombs for laying the dead. Skirting the southern hill, and proceeding westward 300 paces, there is a stone cell called the Pipal (Pin-po-lo) cave, where Buddha was accustomed to sit in deep meditation after his mid-day meal.

Going still in a westerly direction five or six li, there is a stone cave situated in the northern shade of the mountain called Che-ti (Sattapanni cave). This is the place where 500 Arhats assembled after the Nirvana of Buddha to arrange the collection of sacred books. At the time when the books were recited, three vacant seats were specially prepared and adorned. The one on the left was for Sariputra, the one on the right for Maudgalyayana. The assembly was yet short of 500 by one Arhat; and already the great Kasyapa was ascending the throne, when Ananda stood out of the gate unable to find admission; on this spot they have raised a tower, which still exists. Still skirting the mountain we find very many other stone cells used by all the Arhats for the purpose of meditation. Leaving the old city and going north east three li we arrive at the stone cell of Devadatta, fifty paces from which there is a great square black stone.

Some time ago, there was a Bhikshu who spent his time in walking forward and backward on this stone meditating on the impermanency, the sorrow, and vanity of his present life. Arriving thus at an unsound state of mind, disgusted at the sorrows of life, he drew his knife, and would have killed himself but then he reflected that the world-honoured Buddha had forbidden self-murder in the precepts left for his followers, but then again he thought "although that is so, yet I am simply anxious to destroy the three miseries that rob me of my rightful enjoyment (i.e., *raga, dwesa, moha*—evil desire, hatred, ignorance). Then again he drew his knife and inflicted a wound upon himself to cut his throat. On the first gash he obtained the degree of Su-to-un (Sowan); when he had half done the work he arrived at the condition of A-na-hom (Anagami); and after completing the deed he obtained the position of Arhat, and entered nirvana.

At Gaya, Now Deserted

Going west from this four yojanas we arrive at the town of Gaya. All within this city likewise is desolate and desert. Going south twenty li, we arrive at the place where Bodhisattva, when alive, passed six years in self-inflicted austerities. This place is well wooded. From this spot, proceeding westward three li, we arrive at the spot where Buddha, entering water to bathe himself, the Deva held out the branch of a tree to him to assist him in coming out of the water. Again, going north two li, we arrive at the place where a village girl gave milk and rice to Buddha. From this, going north two li, is the spot where Buddha, seated on a stone under a great tree, and looking towards the cast, ate the rice and milk. Both the tree and the stone remain to the present day. The stone is about six feet square, and two in height.

In mid-India the heat and cold are so equalized that trees will live for thousands of years, and even so many as ten thousand. Going north-east from this half a yojana, we arrive at a stone cell, into which Bodhisattva entering sat down with his legs crossed, and his face toward the west. While thus seated, he reflected with himself: "If I am to arrive at the condition of perfect wisdom, then let there be some spiritual manifestation." Immediately on the stone wall there appeared the shadow of Buddha, in length somewhat about three feet. This shadow is still distinctly visible. Then the heavens and the earth were greatly shaken, so much so that all the Devas resident in space cried out and said, "This is not the place appointed for the Buddhas past or yet to come should arrive at Perfect Wisdom; at a distance less than half a yojana south-west from this, beneath the Pei-to (Patra Leaf) tree, is the spot where all the Buddhas past or yet to come should arrive at that condition."

The Devas having thus spoken immediately went before him, singing and leading the way with a view to induce him to follow. Then Bodhisattva, rising up, advanced after them. When distant thirty paces from the tree, the Devas presented to him the grass mat of Ki-tseung (Santi). Bodhisattva, having accepted it, again advanced fifteen paces. Then 500 blue birds came flying towards him, and having encircled Bodhisattva three times in their flight, departed. Bodhisattva, then going forward, arrived under the Pei-to tree, and spreading out the mat of Santi, sat down upon it, with his face towards the east.

Then it was that Mara Raja dispatched three pleasure girls from the northern quarter to come and tempt him, whilst Mara himself coming from the south, assailed him likewise. Then Bodhisattva striking the toe of his foot against the earth, the whole army of Mara was scattered, and the three women were changed into hags. On the place above-mentioned, where he inflicted on himself mortification for six years, and on each spot subsequently mentioned, men in after times erected towers and placed figures of Buddha, which still remain. Buddha having arrived at Supreme Wisdom for seven days, sat contemplating the Tree, experiencing the joys of emancipation.

On this spot they have raised a tower, as well as on the following, where he walked for seven days under the Pei-to tree, from east to west; where all the Devas, having caused the appearance of a hall composed of the seven precious substances, for seven days paid religious worship to Buddha; where the blind dragon Manlun (Moucha-linda), for seven days encircled Buddha in token of respect; also where Buddha seated on a square stone beneath a Nyagrodha tree, and with his face to the east, received the respectful salutation of Brahma; also where the four

Heavenly Kings respectfully offered him his alms-bowl; also where the 500 merchants presented him with wheat and honey; also where he converted the Kasyapas, elder and younger brothers, each of whom was at the head of 1,000 disciples.

In the place where Buddha arrived at perfect reason, there are three Sangharamas, in all of which priests are located. All the ecclesiastics are supplied with necessaries by the people, so that they have sufficient and lack nothing. They scrupulously observe the rules of the Vinaya with respect to decorum. They exactly conform to the regulations established by Buddha when he was in the world, which relate to sitting down, rising up, or entering the assembly; and they have ever done so from the first till now. The sites of the four great Pagodas have always been associated together from the time of the nirvana. The four great Pagodas are those erected on the place where he was born, where he obtained emancipation, where he began to preach, and where he entered nirvana.

9

The Tree Where Asoka Prayed

Formerly, when King Asoka was a lad, when he was playing on the road, he encountered Sakya Buddha going begging. The little boy, rejoiced to have the opportunity, immediately presented him with a handful of earth, as an offering. Buddha received it, and on his return sprinkled it on the ground on which he took his exercise. In return for this act of charity the lad became an iron-wheel king, and ruled over Jambudwipa. On assuming the iron wheel (i.e., when he became a universal monarch) he was on a certain occasion going through Jambudwipa in the administration of justice, at which time he saw one of the places of torment for the punishment of wicked men, situated between two mountains, and surrounded by an iron wall. He immediately asked his attendant ministers, "What is this place?" To this they replied and said, "This is the place where Jemma, the infernal king, inflicts punishment on wicked men for their crimes." The king then began to reflect and said, "The Demon King, in the exercise of his function, requires to have a place of punishment for wicked men. Why should not I, who rule these men on earth, have a place of punishment likewise for the guilty?"

On this he asked his ministers, "Who is there that I can appoint to make for me a Hell, and to exercise authority therein for the punishment of wicked men?" In reply they said, "None but a very wicked man can fulfil such an office." The king forthwith dispatched his ministers to go in every direction to seek for such a man. In the course of their search they saw, by the side of a running stream, a lusty great fellow of black colour, with red hair and light eyes, with feet like talons, and a mouth like that of a fish. When he whistled to the birds and beasts they came to him, and when they approached he mercilessly shot them through, so that none escaped.

Having caught this man, he was brought before the king. The king then gave him these secret orders, "You must enclose a square space with high walls, and with this enclosure plant every kind of flower and fruit, and make beautiful lakes and alcoves, and arrange everything with such taste as to cause men to be anxious to look within the enclosure. Then, having made a wide gate, the moment a man enters within the precincts, seize him at once, and subject him to every kind of infernal torture. And whatever you do, let no one who has once entered ever go out again. And I strictly enjoin you, that if even I should enter the enclosure, you torture me also and spare not. Now then, I appoint and constitute you Lord of this place of Torment!".

It happened that a certain Bhikshu, as he was going his rounds begging for food, entered the gate. The Infernal Keeper seeing him, seized his person and made preparations to put him to torture. The Bhikshu, being very much frightened, suppliantly begged for a moment's respite, that he might, at least, partake of his mid-day meal. It so happened that just at this moment another man entered the place, on which the keeper directly seized him, and, putting him in a stone mortar, began to pound his body to atoms, till a red froth formed on the surface of the mass. The Bhikshu having witnessed this spectacle, began to reflect on the impermanence, the sorrow, the vanity of bodily existence, that it is like a bubble and froth of the sea, and so he arrived at the condition of Arhat. This having transpired, the Infernal Keeper laid hold of him and thrust him into a cauldron of boiling water. The heart of the Bhikshu and his countenance were full of joy. The fire was extinguished and the water became cold, while in the middle of it there sprung up a Lotus, on the top of which the Bhikshu took his seat.

The keeper on witnessing this forthwith proceeded to the king and said, "A wonderful miracle has occurred in the place of Torture—would your Majesty come and see it." The king said, "I dare not come, in consideration of my former agreement with you." The keeper replied, "This matter is one of great moment; it is only right you should come; let us consider your former agreement changed." The king then directly followed him and entered the prison; on which the Bhikshu, for his sake, delivered a religious discourse, so that the king believed and was converted.

Then he ordered the place of Torture to be destroyed, and repented of all the evil he had formerly committed. From the time of his conversion he exceedingly honoured the three sacred symbols of his faith: Buddha, Dharma, and Sangha, and went continually to the spot underneath the Pei-to tree for the purpose of repentance, self-examination, and fasting. In consequence of this, the queen on one occasion asked, "Where is the king perpetually going?" on which the ministers replied, "He continually resides under the Pei-to tree." The queen thereupon, awaiting an opportunity when the king was not there, sent men to cut the tree down. The king, repairing as usual to the spot, and seeing what had happened, was so overpowered with grief that he fell down senseless on the ground. The ministers, bathing his face with water, after a long time restored him to consciousness. Then the king piled up the earth on the four sides of the stump of the tree, and commanded the roots to be moistened with a hundred pitchers of milk. Then, prostrating himself at full length on the ground, he made the following vow: "If the tree does not revive, I will never rise up again."

No sooner had he done this than the tree immediately began to force up small branches from the root, and so it continued to grow until it arrived at its present height, which is somewhat less than 120 feet.

Kukkuta-pada Giri

From this place, going south three li, we arrive at a mountain called the Cock's-foot (Kukuta-pada Giri). The great Kasyapa is at present within this mountain. On a certain occasion he divided the mountain at its base, so as to open a passage for himself. This entrance is now closed up. At a considerable distance from this spot, there is a deep chasm; it is in this fastness as in a receptacle that the entire body of Kasyapa is now preserved. Outside this chasm is the place where Kasyapa, when alive, washed his hands. The people of that region, who are afflicted with headaches, use the earth brought from the place for anointing themselves with, and this immediately cures them. In the midst of this mountain, as soon as the sun begins to decline, all the Arhats come and take their abode. Buddhist pilgrims of that and other countries come year by year to this mountain to pay religious worship to Kasyapa; if any should happen to be distressed with doubts, directly the sun goes down, the Arhats arrive, and begin to discourse with the pilgrims and explain their doubts and difficulties; and, having done so, forthwith they disappear. The thickets about this hill are dense and tangled. There are, moreover, many lions, tigers, and wolves prowling about, so that it is not possible to travel without great care.

Deer Park in Benares

Fa Hian returning towards Pataliputra kept along the course of the Ganges, and after going ten yojanas in a westerly direction arrived at a vihara called "Desert" (Kwang ye) in which Buddha resided. Priests still reside in it. Still keeping along the course of the Ganges, and going west twelve yojanas, we arrive at the country of Kasi and the city of Benares (Po-lo-nai). About ten li or so to the north-east of this city is the chapel of the Deer Park of the Rishis. This garden was once occupied by a Pratyeka Buddha. There are always wild deer reposing in it for shelter.

When the world-honoured Buddha was about to arrive at Supreme Wisdom, all the Devas who resided in space began to chant a hymn and say: "The son of Suddhodana Raja, who has left his home that he may acquire Supreme Wisdom, after seven days will arrive at the condition of Buddha." The Pratyeka Buddha hearing this, immediately entered nirvana. Therefore, the name of this place is the Deer Park of the Rishi. The world-honoured Buddha having arrived at complete knowledge, men in after-ages erected a vihara on this spot. Buddha being desirous to convert Adjnata Kaundinya (Keou lun) and his companion, known as the five men, they communed one with another and said: "This Sraman Gotama, having in his own person for six years practised the severest mortifications, reducing himself to the daily use of but one grain of millet and one of rice, and in spite of this, having failed to obtain Supreme Wisdom, how much less shall he now obtain that condition, by entering into men's society and removing the checks he placed upon his words and thoughts and actions; today when he comes here, let us carefully avoid all conversation with him.

On Buddha's arrival the five men rose and saluted him, and here they have erected a tower—also on the following spots, on a site sixty paces to the north of the former place, where Buddha, seated with his face to the east, began to turn the Wheel of the Law to preach for the purpose of converting Kaundinya and his companions, commonly known as "the five men;" also on a spot twenty paces to the north of this, where Buddha delivered his prediction concerning Maitreya, also on a spot fifty paces to the south of this, where the Dragon Eapatra asked Buddha at what time he should he delivered from his Dragon form; in all places towers have been erected which still exist. In the midst of the Park there are two Sagharamas which still have priests dwelling in them.

Proceding north-west thirteen yojanas from the Park of the Deer, there is a country called Kau-chang-mi (Kausambi). There is a vihara, here called Gochira Vana (the Garden of Gochira) in which Buddha formerly dwelt; it is now lying in ruins. There are congregations here, principally belonging to the system known as the Little Vehicle. Eight yojanas east of this place is a place where Buddha once took up his residence and converted an evil demon. They have also erected towers on various spots where he sat, or walked for exercise, when he was resident in this neighbourhood. There are Sangharamas still existing here and perhaps one hundred priests.

In the South, at Perhaps Ellora

Going two hundred yojanas south from this, there is a country called Ta-Thsin (Dakshina, Deccan). Here is a Sangha ram a of the former Buddha Kasyapa. It is constructed out of a great mountain of rock, hewn to the proper shape. This building has altogether five stories. The lowest is shaped into the form of an elephant, and has five hundred stone cells in it. The second is in the form of a lion and has four hundred chambers. The third is shaped like a horse and has three hundred chambers. The fourth is in the form of an ox and has two hundred chambers. The fifth story is in the shape of a dove and has one hundred chambers in it. At the very top of all is a spring of water which flowing in a stream before the rooms, encircles each tier, and so, running in a circuitous course, at last arrives at the very lowest storey of all, where, flowing past the chambers as before, it finally issues through the door of the building. Throughout the consecutive tiers, in various parts of the building, windows have been pierced through the solid rock for the admission of light, so that every chamber is quite illuminated and there is no darkness throughout the whole.

At the four corners of this edifice they have hewn out the rock into steps, as means for ascending. Men of the present time point out a small ladder which reaches up to the highest point of the rock by which men of old ascended it, one foot at a time. They derive the name which they give to this building, Po-lo-yu, from an Indian word signifying pigeon. There are always Arhats abiding here. This land is hilly and barren and without inhabitants. At a considerable distance from the hill there are villages, but all of them are inhabited by heretics. They know nothing of the law of Buddha, or Sramans, or Brahmins, or of any of the different schools of learning.

The men of that country continually see persons come flying to the temple. On a certain occasion there were some Buddhist pilgrims from different countries who came here with a desire to pay religious worship at this temple. Then the men of the villages, alluded to above, asked them saying, "Why do you not fly to it? We behold the religious men who occupy those chambers constantly on the wing." These men then answered by way of excuse, "Because our wings are not yet perfectly formed."

The country of Ta-Thsin (Deccan) is precipitous and the roads dangerous and difficult to find. Those who wish to go there ought to give a present to the king of the country, either money or goods. The king then deputes certain men to accompany them as guides, and so they pass the travellers from one place to another, each party pointing out their own roads and intricate bye-paths. Fa Hian, finding himself in the end unable to proceed to that country, reports in the above passages merely what he has heard.

10

Gets Books, Learns Sanskrit, Stays for Three Years

From Benares going eastward in a retrograde order, we arrive at the town of Pataliputra again. The purpose of Fa Hian was to seek for copies of the Vinaya Pitaka. But throughout the whole of Northern India the various masters trusted to tradition only for their knowledge of the Precepts, and had no written copies of them at all. Wherefore Fa Hian had come even so far as Mid-India without effecting his purpose. But here in the Sangharama of the Great Vehicle at Patna he obtained one copy of the Precepts, the collection used by the school of the Mahasanghikas which was that used by the first great assembly of priests convened during Buddha's lifetime. In the chapel of Chi-un (Jetavana) there is a tradition that this was originally their copy, or, that this school originally sprang from them. The eighteen sects in general have each their own Superior, but they are agreed in their dependence on the Great Refuge found in Buddha, Dharma and Sangha. In some minor details of faith they differ, as well as in a more or less exact attention to some matters of practice.

But the collection is generally regarded as most correct and complete. Moreover, he obtained one copy of Precepts in manuscript, comprising about 7,000 gathas. This copy was that used by the assembly belonging to the school of the Sarvastivadins, the same, in fact, as is generally used in China. The masters of this school also hand down the Precepts by word of mouth, and do not commit them to writing. Moreover, in this assembly he obtained an imperfect copy of the Abhidharma, including altogether about 6,000 gathas. Moreover, he obtained a collection of Sutras in their abbreviated form, consisting altogether of 2,500 verses. Moreover, he obtained an expanded volume (Vaipulya) of the Parinirvana Sutra, containing about 5,000 verses.

Moreover, he procured a copy of the Abhidharma according to the school of the Mahasanghikas. On this account Fa Hian abode in this place for the space of three years engaged in learning to read the Sanskrit books, and to converse in that language, and in copying the Precepts. When To-ching arrived in mid-India and saw the customary behaviour of the Sramans, and the strict decorum observed by the assembly of priests, and their religious deportment, even in the midst of worldly influences, then, sorrowfully reflecting on the meagre character of the Precepts known to the different assemblies of priests in the border land of China, he bound himself by a vow and said, "From the present time for ever till I obtain the condition of Buddha, may I never again be born in a frontier country." And in accordance with this expression of his wish, he took up his permanent abode in this place, and did not return. And so Fa Hian, desiring with his whole heart to spread the knowledge of the Precepts throughout the land of Han (China), returned alone.

11

At Tamralipti, Stays for Two Years, Reaches Sri Lanka

Following down the river Ganges in an easterly direction for eighteen yojanas distance, we find the great kingdom of Tchen-po (Champa) on its southern shore. In the place where Buddha once dwelt and where he moved to and fro for exercise, also where the four previous Buddhas sat down; in all these plaees towers have been erected, and there are still priests resident in them. From this, continuing to go eastwards nearly fifty yojanas, we arrive at the kingdom of Tamralipti. Here it is the river empties itself into the sea. There are twenty-four Sangharamas in this country, all of them have resident priests, and the Law of Buddha is generally respected.

Fa Hian remained here for two years, writing out copies of the Sacred books, and taking impressions of the figures used in worship. He then shipped himself on board a great merchant vessel. Putting to sea, they proceeded in a south-westerly direction, and, catching the first fair wind of the winter season they sailed for fourteen days and nights and arrived at the country of the Lions (Sinhala, Sri Lanka). Men of Tamralipti say that the distance between the two is about 700 yojanas.

This kingdom of Lion is situated on a great island. From east to west it is fifty yojanas, and from north to south thirty yojanas. On every side of it are small islands, perhaps amounting to 100 in number. They are distant from one another 10 or 20 Ii, and as much as 200 Ii. All of them depend on the great island. Most of them produce precious stones and pearls. The Mani gem is also found in one district, embracing a surface perhaps of 10 Ii. The king sends a guard to protect the place. If any gems are found, the king claims three out of every ten.

Buddhism in Sri Lanka

This kingdom had originally no human inhabitants, but only demons and dragons dwelt in it. Merchants of different countries however resorted here to trade. At the time of traffic, the demons did not appear in person, but only exposed their valuable commodities, with the value affixed to them. Then the merchantmen, according to the prices marked, purchased the goods and took them away. But in consequence of these visits, and the sojourn of the merchants in the country, men of other countries also hearing of the delightful character of the place, flocked there in great numbers, and so a great populous community was formed.

This country enjoys an equable climate, without any extremes of temperature either in winter or summer. The plants and trees are always verdant. The fields are sown just according to men's inclination; there are no fixed seasons for doing so. Buddha came to this country in the first instance from a desire to convert a malevolent dragon. By his spiritual power he planted one foot to the north of the royal city, and one on the top of a mountain, the distance between the two being 15 yojanas. Over the impression on the hill, to the north of the royal city, is erected a great tower, in height 470 feet. It is adorned with gold and silver, and every precious substance combines to make it perfect. By the side of this tower, moreover, is erected a Sangharama, which is called Abhayagiri, the mountain without fear, containing 5,000 priests. They have also built here a Hall of Buddha, which is covered with gold and silver engraved work, conjoined with all the precious substances. In the midst of this hall is a jasper figure of Buddha, in height about 22 feet. The entire body glitters and sparkles with the seven precious substances, while the various characteristic marks are so gloriously portrayed, that no words can describe the effect. In the right hand it holds a pearl of inestimable value.

Fa Hian had now been absent from China for many years; the manners and customs of the people with whom he had intercourse were entirely strange to him. The towns, people, mountains, valleys, and plants and trees which met his eyes, were unlike those of old times. Moreover, his fellow travellers were now separated from him—some had remained behind and some were dead—to think upon the past was all that was left to him, and so his heart was continually saddened. All at once, as he was standing by the side of this jasper figure, he beheld a merchant present to it, as a religious offering, a white taffeta fan, of Chinese manufacture. Unperceived Fa Hian gave way to his sorrowful feelings, and the tears flowing down filled his eyes.

A former king of this country sent an embassy to mid-India, to procure a slip of the Pei-to tree. This they planted by the side of the Hall of Buddha. When it was about 220 feet high, the tree began to lean towards the south-east. The king, fearing it would fall, placed eight or nine props round the tree to support it. Just in the place where the tree was thus supported, it put forth a branch, which pierced through the props, and, descending to the earth, took root. This branch is about 20 inches round. The props, although pierced through the centre, still surround the tree, which stands now without their support, yet men have not removed them.

Under the tree is erected a chapel, in the middle of which is a figure of Buddha in a sitting posture. Both the clergy and laity pay reverence to this figure with little intermission. Within the capital, moreover, is erected the chapel of the Tooth of Buddha, in the construction of which all the seven precious substances have been employed. The king purifies himself according to the strictest Brahminical rules, while those men within the city who reverence this relic from a principle of belief, also compose their passions according to strict rule.

This kingdom, from the time when this chapel was erected, has suffered neither from want, famine, calamity, or revolution. The treasury of this congregation of priests contains numerous gems and a Mani jewel of inestimable value. Their king once entered the treasury, and, going round it for the purpose of inspection, he saw there this Mani gem. On beholding it, a covetous feeling sprang up in his heart, and he desired to take it away with him. For three days this thought affected him, but then he came to his right mind. He directly repaired to the assembly of the priests, and, bowing down his head, he repented of his former wicked purpose, and, addressing them, said, "Would that you would make a rule from this time forth and for ever, on no account to allow the king to enter your treasury to look at the jewels, except if he is a member of the fraternity and of forty years of age—after that time he may be permitted to enter."

There are many noblemen and rich householders within the city. The houses of the Sa-pho (Sabaean) merchants are very beautifully adorned. The streets and passages are all smooth and level. At the head of the four principal streets there are Preaching Halls; on the 8th, 14th, and 15th day of the month, they prepare a lofty throne within each of these buildings, and the religious members of the community of the four classes all congregate to hear the preaching of the Law. The men of this country say, that there are, in the country, altogether fifty or sixty thousand priests, all of whom live in community and take their meals in common. Besides these, the king supplies five or six thousand persons within the city with food. These persons, when they require, take their alms-bowls and go to the appointed place, and, according to the measure of the bowls, fill them and return.

They always bring out the tooth of Buddha in the middle of the third month. Ten days beforehand, the king magnificently caparisons a great elephant, and commissions a man of eloquence and ability to clothe himself in royal apparel and, riding on the elephant, to sound a drum and proclaim as follows:—"Bodhisattva, during three asankhya kalpas, underwent every kind of austerity, he spared himself no personal sufferings, he left his country, wife, and child; moreover, he tore out his eyes to bestow them on another, he mangled his flesh to deliver a dove from the hawk, he sacrificed his head in alms, he gave his body to a famishing tiger, he grudged not his marrow or brain. Thus he endured every sort of agony for the sake of all around. Moreover, when he became perfect Buddha, he lived in the world forty-nine years preaching the Law, and teaching and converting men. He gave rest to the wretched: he saved the lost. Having passed through countless births, he then entered nirvana. Since that event is 1497 years. The eyes of the world were then put out, and all flesh deeply grieved. After ten days the tooth of this same Buddha will be brought forth and taken to the Abhayagiri vihara. Let all ecclesiastical and lay persons within the kingdom, who wish to lay up a store of merit, prepare and smooth the road, adorn the streets and highways, let them scatter every kind of flower, and offer incense in religious reverence to the Relic."

This proclamation being finished, the king next causes to be placed on both sides of the road representations of the 500 bodily forms which Bodhisattva assumed, during his successive births. For instance, his birth as Su-jin-no; his appearance as a bright flash of light; his birth as the king of the elephants, and as an antelope. These figures are all beautifully painted in diverse colours, and have a very lifelike appearance. At length the tooth of Buddha is brought forth and conducted along the principal road. As they proceed on the way, religious offerings are made to it. When they arrive at the Abhayagiri vihara, they place it in the Hall of Buddha, where the clergy and laity all assemble in vast crowds and burn incense, and light lamps, and perform every kind of religious ceremony, both night and day, without ceasing.

After ninety complete days they again return it to the vihara within the city. This chapel is thrown open on the chief holidays for the purpose of religious worship, as the Law of Buddha directs. Forty li to the east of the Abhaya vihara is a mountain, on which is built a chapel called Po-ti (Bodhi); there are about 2,000 priests in it. Amongst them is a very distinguished Sraman called Ta-mo-kiu-ti (Dharmakoti or Dharmagupta). The people of this country greatly respect and reverence him. He resides in a cell, where he has lived for about forty years. By the constant practice of benevolence he has been able to tame the serpents and mice, so that they stay together in one habitat, and are not mutually injurious one to the other.

Witnessing Cermonies

Seven li to the south of the capital is a chapel called Maha vihara, in which there are 3,000 priests. There was amongst them one very eminent Sraman, who observed the precepts perfectly. The men of the country generally gave him credit for being an Arhat. At the time of his approaching death, the king, having come to enquire after him, followed the custom of the Law, and assembled the priests to ask whether this Bhikshu had attained Reason (i.e., had arrived at the condition of a Bodhisattva). They then, according to their true belief, answered him, "He is an Arhat."

After his death, the king immediately examined the Sacred Books, with a view to perform the funeral obsequies according to the rules for such as are Arhats. Accordingly, about 4 or 5 li to the east of the vihara, they erected a very great pyre of wood, about 34 feet square, and of the same height. Near the top they placed tiers of sandalwood, aloe, and all kinds of scented wood. On the four sides they constructed steps by which to ascend it. Then, taking some clean and very white camlet cloth, they bound it around and above the pyre. They then constructed a funeral carriage, just like the hearses used in my country except that there are no dragon-ear handles to it.

Then, at the time of the cremation, the king, accompanied by every class of his people, assembled in great numbers, came to the spot provided with flowers and incense for religious offerings. The multitude followed the hearse till it arrived at the place of the funeral ceremony. The king then in his own person offered religious worship with flowers and incense. This being over, the hearse was placed on the pyre, and oil of cinnamon poured over it in all directions. Then they set light to the whole. At the time of kindling the fire, the whole assembly occupied their minds with solemn thoughts. Then removing their upper garments, and taking their winglike fans, which they use as sun-shades, and approaching as near as they can to the pyre, they flung them into the midst of the fire, in order to assist the cremation.

When all was over, they diligently searched for the bones and collected them together, in order to raise a tower over them. Fa Hian did not arrive in time to see this celebrated person alive, but only to witness his funeral obsequies. At this time, the king, being an earnest believer in the Law of Buddha, desired to build a new vihara for this congregation of priests. First of all he provided for them a sumptuous entertainment; after which, he selected a pair of strong working oxen, and ornamented their horns with gold, silver, and precious things. Then providing himself with a beautifully gilded plough, the king himself ploughed round the four sides of the allotted space; after which, ceding all personal right over the land, houses, or people, within the area thus enclosed, he presented the whole to the priests.

Then he caused to be engraved on a metal plate the following inscription:—"From this time and for all generations hereafter, let this property be handed down from one body of priests to the other, and let no one dare to alienate it, or change the character of the grant." When Fa Hian was residing in this country he heard a religious brother from India, seated on a high throne, reciting a sacred book and saying. "The Patra (alms-bowl) of Buddha originally was preserved in the city of Vaisali but now it is in the borders of Gandhara. In somewhat like a hundred years—Fa Hian, at the time of the recital, heard the exact number of years, but he has now forgotten it—it will again be transported to the country of the Western Yu-chi.

After about a hundred years more it will be transported to the country of Khoten. After a similar period it will be transported to Koutche. In about a hundred years more it will once more come back and be taken to the land of Han; after the same period it will return to the land of Lions;

after the same period it will return to mid-India; after which it will be taken up into the Tusita heaven. Then Maitreya Bodhisattva will exclaim with a sigh, 'The alms-dish of Sakya Muni Buddha has come.' Then immediately all the Devas will pay religious worship to it with flowers and incense for seven days. After this it will return to Jambudwipa, and a sea dragon, taking it, will carry it within his palace, awaiting till Maitreya is about to arrive at complete wisdom, at which time the bowl, again dividing itself into four as it was at first, will reascend the Pin-na Mountain. After Maitreya has arrived at Supreme Wisdom, the four heavenly kings will once more come and respectfully salute him as Buddha, after the same manner as they have done to the former Buddhas.

The thousand Buddhas of this Bhadrakalpa will all of them use this same alms-dish; when the bowl has disappeared, then the Law of Buddha will gradually perish; after which the years of man's life will begin to contract until it be no more than five years in duration. At the time of its being ten years in length, rice and butter will disappear from the world, and men will become extremely wicked. The sticks they grasp will then transform themselves into sharp clubs, or knives and clubs, with which they will attack one another, and wound and kill each other.

In the midst of this, men who have acquired religious merit, will escape and seek refuge in the mountains; and when the wicked have finished the work of mutual destruction, they will emerge from their hiding places, and coming forth again, will converse together and say: 'Men of old lived to a very advanced age, but now, because wicked men have indulged without restraint in every transgression of the Law, our years have dwindled down to their present short span, even to the space of ten years—now, therefore, let us all practise every kind of good deed, encouraging within ourselves a kind and loving spirit; let us enter on a course of virtue and righteousness.

Thus, as each one practises faith and justice, their years will begin to increase in double ratio till they reach 80,000 years of life. At the time when Maitreya is born, when he first begins to declare his doctrine and turn the Wheel of the Law, his earliest converts will be the followers of the bequeathed law of Sakya Buddha, who have forsaken their families, and sought refuge in the three sacred names, and observed the five great commandments, and attended to their religious duties in making continued offerings to the three precious objects of worship. His second and third body of converts shall be those who, by their previous converts have put themselves in a condition for salvation.

Fa Hian, on hearing this discourse, wished to copy it down, on which the man said, "This is no sacred book, but only what I have learnt by memory, and repeat verbally."

12

The Return Journey

Fa Hian resided in this country for two years. Continuing his search for the sacred books, he obtained a copy of the Vinaya Pitaka according to the school of the Mahisasikas. He also obtained a copy of the Great Agama (Dirghagama), and of the Miscellaneous Agama (Sanyuktagama), and also a volume of miscellaneous collections from the Pitakas (Samyukta Pitaka). All these were hitherto entirely unknown in the land of Han. Having obtained these works in the original language (Fa), he forthwith shipped himself on board a great merchant vessel, which carried about two hundred men. Astern of the great ship was a smaller one, as a provision in case of the large vessel being injured or wrecked during the voyage.

Having got a fair wind they sailed eastward for two days, when suddenly a tempest sprung up, and the ship sprang a leak. The merchants then desired to haul up the smaller vessel, but the crew of that ship, fearing that a crowd of men would rush into her and sink her, cut the towing cable and fell it off. The merchantmen were greatly terrified, expecting their death momentarily. Then dreading lest the leak should gain upon them, they forthwith took their goods and merchandise and cast them overboard. Fa Hian also flung overboard his water-pitcher (koundika) and his washing basin, and also other portions of his property. He was only afraid lest the merchants should fling into the sea his sacred books and images. And so with earnestness of heart he invoked Avalokiteswara, and paid reverence to the Buddhist saints of the land of Han, speaking thus: " I, indeed, have wandered far and wide in search of the Law. Oh! would that by your spiritual power you would turn back the flowing of the water and stop the leak and cause us to reach some resting place."

Nevertheless, the hurricane blew for thirteen days and nights, when they arrived at the shore of a small island and, on the tide going out, they found the place of the leak; having forthwith stopped it up, they again put to sea on their onward voyage. In this ocean there are many pirates, who, coming on you suddenly, destroy everything. The sea itself is boundless in extent—it is impossible to know east or west, except by observing the sun, moon, or stars in their motions. If it is dark, rainy weather, the only plan is to steer by the wind without guide. During the darkness of night, one only sees the great waves beating one against the other and shining like fire, while shoals of sea monsters of every description surround the ship.

The merchantmen were now much perplexed, not knowing towards what land they were steering. The sea was bottomless and no soundings could be found, so that there was not even a rock for anchorage. At length, the weather clearing up, they got their right bearings, and once more shaped a correct course and proceeded onwards. But if during the bad weather they had happened to have struck on a hidden rock, then there would have been no way to have escaped alive.

Thus they voyaged for ninety days and more, when they arrived at a country called Yo-po-ti (Java). In this country heretics and Brahmins flourish, and the Law of Buddha is not much known. Stopping here the best portion of five months, Fa Hian again embarked on board another merchant vessel, having also a crew of 200 men or so. They took with them fifty days' provisions, and set sail on the 15th day of the fourth month. Fa Hian was very comfortable on board this ship. They shaped a course north-east for Kwang Chow (Canton province in China).

After a month and some days, at the stroke of two in the middle watch of the night, a black squall suddenly came on, accompanied with pelting rain. The merchantmen and passengers were all terrified. Fa Hian at this time also, with great earnestness of mind, again entreated Avalokiteswara and all the priesthood of China to exert their Divine power in his favour, and bring them daylight. When the day broke, all the Brahmins, consulting together, said: "It is because we have got this Sraman on board with us that we have no luck, and have incurred this great mischief—come let us land this Bhikshu on the first island we meet with, and let us not, for the sake of one man, all of us perish."

The religious patron (Danapati) of Fa Hian then said: 'If you land this Bhikshu, you shall also land me with him; and if not, you had better kill me; for if you really put this Sraman on shore as you threaten, then, when I arrive in China, I will go straight to the king and tell him what you have done. And the king of that country is a firm believer in the Law of Buddha, and greatly honours the Bhikshus and priests." The merchantmen on this hesitated, and in the end did not dare to land him.

The weather continuing very dark, the pilots began to look at one another in mutual distrust. Nearly seventy days had now elapsed. The rice for food, and the water for conjee, was nearly all done. They had to use salt water for cooking, while they gave out to every man about two pints of fresh water. And now, when this was just exhausted, the merchants held a conversation and said: "The proper time for the voyage to Kwang Chow is about fifty days, but now we have exceeded that time these many days—shall we then undertake the navigation ourselves?" On this, they put the ship on a north-east course to look for land..

After twelve days continuous sailing, they arrived at the southern coast of Lau Shan which borders on the prefecture of Chang Kwang. They then obtained good freshwater and vegetables; and so, after passing through so many dangers, and such a succession of anxious days, they suddenly arrived at this shore. On seeing the Le-ho vegetable (a sort of reed), they were confident that this was, indeed, the land of Han at which they had arrived. But not seeing any men or traces of life, they scarcely knew what to take for granted. Some said they had not yet arrived at Kwang Chow, others maintained they had passed it. In their uncertainty, therefore, they put off in a little boat, and entered a creek to look for someone to ask what place it was they had arrived at.

Just at this moment, two men who had been hunting were returning home; on this the merchants requested Fa Hian to act as interpreter and make inquiries of them. Fa Hian having first tried to inspire them with confidence, then asked them, "What men are you?" They replied, "We are disciples of Buddha." Then he asked, "What do you find in these mountains here, that you should have gone hunting in them?" They prevaricated and said, "Tomorrow is the 15th day of the 7th month, and we were anxious to catch something to sacrifice to Buddha." Again he asked, "What country is this?" They replied, "This is Tsing Chow, on the borders of the prefecture of Chang Kwang, dependent on the Leou family."

Having heard this, the merchants were very glad, and, immediately begging that their goods might be landed, they deputed men to go to Chang Kwang. The Prince Lai Ying, who was a faithful follower of the Law of Buddha, hearing that there was a Sraman on board with sacred books and images, took ship and embarked and came on board to see Fa Hian. Then, immediately engaging men from the nearest shore, he dispatched the books and sacred figures to be landed and taken forthwith to the seat of his government.

After this the merchants returned towards Yang Chow. Meanwhile, Leou of Tsing Chow entertained Fa Hian for the whole winter and summer. The summer period of rest being over, Fa Hian dismissed all the scholars of religion who had been with him. He had been anxious for a long time to get hack to Tehang'an. But as the engagements he had entered into were pressing ones, he directed his course first towards the southern capital, where the different scholars edited the sacred books he had brought back.

After Fa Hian left Tehang'an, he was five years in arriving at mid-India. He resided there during six years, and was three years more before he arrived at Tsing Chow. He had successively passed through thirty different countries. In all the countries of India, after passing the Sandy Desert of Gobi, the dignified carriage of the priesthood and the surprising influence of religion amongst the people cannot be adequately described. But, because our learned scholars had not heard of these things, he was induced, regardless of all personal considerations, to cross the seas, and to encounter every conceivable danger in returning home. Having been preserved therefore by Divine power by the influences of the Three Honourable Ones, and brought through all dangers safely, he was further induced to commit to writing these records of his travels, desiring that the virtuous of all ages may be informed of them together, as well as himself.

In this year Kea-yin, being the twelfth of the reign of I Hi of the Tsin dynasty, when the star Sheau was just emerging from the summer mansion, Fa Hian, the pilgrim, arrived home. He was detained all the winter in answering the multitude of questions put to him. Whoever enquired of him respecting his travels he always answered obligingly and exactly according to truth. Of these answers, the summary is found in this book. But **when they pressed**

him to write a full record of all that happened to him from first to last, then he said, "If I were to recall all which has occurred to me, then persons of unstable minds would be excited to strive how they might enter on similar dangers and encounter corresponding risks, reckless of their personal safety. For they would argue in this way, 'Here is a man who has escaped all and come back safe and sound;' and so these foolish persons would set about jeopardizing their lives in lands impossible to explore, and to pass through which, not one in ten thousand could hope for."

On hearing these remarks, they all said, with a sigh of assent, "This man, in order to preserve the knowledge of old things and new, has himself penetrated to the eastern source of the great doctrine, and is yet alive. He has sought out the Law, and now exhibits it to us. Equally with us, then, shall all those who hereafter attain this knowledge, give him boundless thanks. And those also who assist to diffuse this knowledge, where it has not prevailed, shall acquire incalculable merit; and the chief merit of a sage is this—to neglect those things which are generally esteemed, and esteem those things which are generally neglected."

Huen Tsang: Harsha Vardhan's Favourite

1

Early Life

The infant name of the Master of the Law (Fa-sse) was Huen Tsang; his ordinary family name was Chiu; he was a native of Chin-Liu. He descended from Chang-Kong, who during the Han dynasty was lord of Tai-K'iu. His great-grandfather, whose name was Kin, was prefect of Shang-Tang, under the after-Wei dynasty. His grandfather Kong, by his distinguished scholarship, obtained employment in the public service. During the Tsi dynasty he was appointed president of the Imperial College, having, as endowment, the revenues of the town of Chow-nan; he thus founded the fortunes of his descendants; he also was born in the district of Kowshi. His father Hwui was distinguished for his superior abilities, the elegance of his manners and his moderation. At an early age the father began to recite the Sacred Books; in figure he was eight feet in height, with finely lined eyebrows, and bright eyes. He wore his dress large, and his girdle was full, loving to be recognised as a scholar. Born in those times, and a man of a remote district, he was simple in his manners and contented, and sought neither honour nor preferment.

Anticipating the decay and fall of the Sui dynasty, he buried himself in the study of his books. Many offers of provincial and district offices were pressed on him, which he persistently refused; he declined all magisterial duties on the plea of ill-health; so he remained in retirement, much to the admiration of his acquaintances.

He had four sons, of whom the Master of the Law was the fourth. Even when a child he was grave as a prince, and of exceptional ability. When he was eight years old his father sitting near his table was reading aloud the Hiau classic on filial piety, and coming to the passage when Tsang-tseu rose before his master, suddenly the boy arranged his dress and got up. His father asking him why he did so, he replied: "Tsang-tseu hearing the command of his master, rose up from his seat; surely then Huen Tsang dare not sit at ease while listening to the loving instruction of his father." His father was much pleased by this reply, and perceived that his child would become a distinguished person.

From this age he took to reading the Sacred Books, and was charmed with the writings of the ancient sages. A book without elegance and propriety he would not look at; he would have no intercourse with those whose ways were opposed to the teaching of the holy and wise. He did not mix with those of his own age, nor spend his time at the market-gates. Although cymbals and drums, accompanied by singing, resounded through the public streets, and the girls and boys congregated in crowds to assist in the games, singing and shouting the while, he would not quit his home. Moreover, when he was still young he applied himself with diligence to the duties of piety and gentleness at home.

His second brother Chang-tsi had previously become a disciple of Buddha, and dwelt in the convent of Tsingtu at Loyang the Eastern capital. Observing that the Master was deeply given to the study of religious doctrine, he therefore took him to his convent, seat of sacred wisdom and taught him the method and practice of the Sacred Books of Buddhism.

At this time there was an unexpected Royal mandate for the election at Loyang of fourteen priests, to be supported free of charge. There were several hundred applicants. The Master, owing to his youth, could not be a candidate, but he took his stand close by the hall gate. At this time the high-commissioner, Ch'ing-Shen-Kwo, having an aptitude for recognising talent in those whom he met, observing Huen Tsang, addressed him and said: "My friend, who are you?" Replying he said: "I am so-and-so." Again he asked: "Do you wish to be elected?" He replied, "Yes! certainly; but not, being sufficiently advanced in years, I am excluded." Again he asked: "And what is your motive in becoming a disciple?" He replied: "My only thought in taking this step is to spread abroad the light of the religion of Tathagata, which we possess." Shen-Kwo was deeply gratified with the sentiment, and as the outward appearance of the youth was prepossessing, he selected him and took him to the officers and said: "To repeat one's instruction is easy, but true self-possession and nerve are not so common; if you elect this youth, he will without doubt become an eminent member of the religion of Sakya. Only I fear that neither I nor your Excellencies will live to see the day when the soaring clouds shall distil the sweet dew of Buddha's doctrine. But nevertheless, the illustrious character of this honourable youth will not be eclipsed, as I regard the matter."

And so the words of the noble Ch'ing prevailed. Having been admitted as a recluse, he dwelt with his brother.

At this time there was in the convent a Master of the Law, called King, who recited and preached upon the Sutra of the Nirvana. Huen Tsang having got the book, studied it with such zeal that he could neither sleep nor eat. Moreover, he studied under the direction of Yen, Doctor of the Law, the Sastra of the Great Vehicle Mahayana; and thus every day his love for such studies increased. By hearing a book only once, he understood it thoroughly, and after a second reading he needed no further instructions, but remembered it throughout. All the assembly of priests were astonished, and when at their direction he mounted the pulpit, he expounded with precision and clearness the deep principles of religion to the bottom. The Masters and honourable body of priests listened with attention; he thus laid the foundation of his renown. At this time he was thirteen years old.

After this the Sui dynasty lost the empire, and the whole kingdom was in confusion. The capital became a rendezvous for robbers, and the district between the rivers Ho and Lo a resort of wild beasts. The magistrates were killed and the body of priests either perished or took to flight. The streets were filled with bleached bones, and the burnt ruins of buildings. Since the rebellion of Wang-tong, and dreadful riots of Liu-shih, when massacre and ruin prevailed everywhere, no such calamity had happened to the empire. The Master, although he was young, yet understood thoroughly the nature of these vicissitudes; and so he affectionately addressed his brother and said: "Though this were our native city, yet how could we, during the present state of things, avoid death? Now I understand that the Prince of Tang has repulsed the people of Tsin-Yang, and established himself at Chang'an. The empire relies on him as on father and mother; let my brother go there with me!"

The brother agreeing with this advice, they went both together. It was now the first year of Wu-Teh (618 A.D.).

Ordained as a Monk

And now the Master addressed his brother and said: "There is no religious business being attended to, and we cannot be idle, let us pass into the country of Shuh (Sz'chuen) and pursue our studies."

His brother having consented, they traversed together the valley of Tseu-wu and entered Han-chuen, and there they met the two Doctors Kong and King, the principal priests of their convent. At the sight of these persons they were moved to tears with joy, and they abode with them a month and some days, receiving instruction; after this they went on together to the town of Shing-tu. As there were many priests assembled in this town they founded there a religious place of assembly. Thus they listened once more to Sai-tsin explaining the Shi-lun (Mahayana Samparigraha Sastra) and the Pi-tan (Abhidharma Sastra), while the Master Chin expounded the works of Kia-yen (Katyayana). Studying thus without loss of a moment, and with great earnestness, after two or three years, they had thoroughly mastered the teaching of the different schools.

At this time the Empire was visited with famine and riot; in Shuh alone there was abundance and peace; priests from every quarter therefore flocked there, and hundreds of men ever assembled under the pulpit of the Preaching Hall. The Master by his profound wisdom and eminent talent in discussion, surpassed them all; so that throughout Wu and Shuh and Khing and Tsuh there was no one but had heard of him, and desired to witness his skill, as those of old respected the names of Li and Kwoh.

The Master for the sake of being with his brother took up his abode in the Hung-hwui temple of Shing-tu.

When the Master had completed his twentieth year, that is, in the fifth year of the period Wu-teh, he was fully ordained in Shing-tu. During the rain-retreat he studied the Vinaya according to tbe rule of the five divisions and seven sections; after mastering this at one time, he then turned his attention to the Sutras and Sastras, and having investigated these he once more thought of going to the Capital, to inquire from the most celebrated masters concerning some difficulties he had met with in his studies. However, being restrained from effecting his purpose by his brother's influence, he secretly embarked with some merchants, and passing down the river through the three gorges he arrived at Hang-chow, where he retired into the temple called Tien-hwang. The clergy and laity of that place had for a long time known of him by report, and now they came together and prayed him to explain the Sacred Books. The Master on their account preached on the Shi-lun and the Abhidharma.

At this time the king of Han-yang, by his highly virtuous character and his affectionate kindness, held his country in constraint and obedience. Hearing of the arrival of the Master, be was exceedingly rejoiced, and went in person to salute him. On the day when he stated the theme of the religious discussion, the king and his officers and a great number of lay and religious people came together to see him and hear him. And now they pressed forward in vast bodies to raise a discussion. The Master answered them in turn and gave them the desired explanations. They soon confessed themselves to be surpassed in argument—while the more learned were grieved to think that they were not able to gain the victory.

The king then spoke of him in admiration without bounds and offered him abundant presents, which he declined to accept. After the conferences he proceeded again northwards, seeking the most renowned priests. Arriving at Siang-chow, he began to place his difficulties before Hiu, a Master of the Law, and ask for explanations of his doubts.

From this he came to Chiu-chow, and there he visited Shin, a Master of the Law, and studied the Shing-shih-lun (Satyasiddha-vyakarana Sastra). After this he entered Chang'an and took up his abode in the Ta-hioh (Mahabodhi) Temple. There he studied with Yoh, a Master of the Law, the Kiu-she (Kosha) Sastra.

At this time there were at Chang'an two great teachers, Shang and Pin; they had thoroughly explained the Two Vehicles, and investigated the Three Systems; they were the leaders of the religious people in the Capital. Both clergy and laity resorted to them; the entire district resounded with their praises, and their reputation spread beyond the sea; moreover their disciples were as numerous as the clouds. Although they had mastered all the Sutras, they loved to discourse principally on the Ski-la-lun. The Master had already distinguished himself in the land of Wu and Shuh; from the time he arrived at Chang'an, he persistently inquired of these teachers, and in a moment perceived the meaning of the deepest truths that they could explain. They were filled with admiration and overwhelmed him with praise. "Master," they said, "you can be well styled in the religion of Sakya, 'a courier who traverses a thousand li in a day.' You are called to make the sun of wisdom shine again; as for us, worn out by age, we fear that we shall not see the day!"

2

Decides to Visit India

The Master of the Law having visited the celebrated Masters all round, devoured their words and examined their principles, and so **he found that each followed implicitly the teaching of his own school; but on verifying their doctrine he saw that the holy books differed much, so that he knew not which to follow. He then resolved to travel to the Western world in order to ask about doubtful passages.** He also took the treatise called Shi-tsih-ti-iun (Sapta-dala-bhumi Sastra) to explain his various doubts; this treatise is now called Yu-kia-sse-ti-lun. (Yogacharya-bhumi Sastra). "Moreover," he said, "Fa Huen and Chi-yen, the first men of their age, were both able to search after the Law for the guidance and profit of the people; should I not aim to preserve their noble example so that their blameless character may not be lost to posterity? The duty of a great teacher should be to follow in their steps."

On this he agreed to go in company with others and present a petition; but there was an imperial rescript forbidding the project of going abroad. On this the others gave up the plan; the Master of the Law alone did not abandon his purpose, and resolved to travel alone. Then he entered a sacred building and made known his undertaking, and requested permission to carry it out, humbly praying all the Holy Ones by their mysterious influences to cause his journey and his return to be without damage.

At the birth of the Master his mother had dreamt that she saw him going to the West clothed in a white robe—on which she said: "You are my son, where then are you going?" In reply he said, "I am going to seek for the Law." This was the first indication, then, of his foreign travels.

In the third year and the eighth month of the period Cheng Kwan (630 A.D.), he was prepared to make a start. Desiring some happy omen, he dreamt at night that he saw in the middle of the great sea the Mount Sumeru, perfected with the four precious substances—its appearance supremely bright and majestic. He thought he purposed to scale the Mount, but the boisterous waves arose aloft and swelled mightily. Moreover, there was neither ship nor raft; nevertheless, he had no shadow of fear, but with fixed purpose he entered the waves. Suddenly he saw a lotus of stone burst as it were exultingly from the deep, trying to put his foot on it, it retired; while he paused to behold it, it followed his feet and then disappeared;—in a moment he found himself at the foot of the Mount, but he could not climb its craggy and scarped sides; as he tried to leap upwards with all his strength, there arose in a moment a mighty whirlwind which raised him aloft to the summit of the Mount. Looking around him on the four sides from the top he beheld nought but an uninterrupted horizon; ravished with joy he awoke.

Starts Journey, Age 26

On this he forthwith started on his journey. He was then twenty-six years of age. At this time there was a Tsin-Chow priest called Hiau-Ta who lived in the capital and studied the Nirvana Sutra. His study being finished he was returning to his home—they both went together therefore so far as Tsin-Chow. Having stopped there one night, he met with an associate from Lan-Chow; going on with him he came to Lan-Chow and stopped there one night. Here he met with some mounted men who were returning to Liang-Chow, after escorting an officer. Going with them, he came to that place, and stopped there a month and some days. Now Liang-Chow is the place of rendezvous for people dwelling to the west of the river; moreover, merchants belonging to the borders of Si-Fan (Tibet) and countries to the left of the T'sung-Ling Mountains, all come and go to this place without hindrance.

On the day of opening of the Religious Conference, tbese men all came together to the place and offered jewels and precious things, as they bowed down and uttered the praises of the Master. And on their return to their several countries, they loudly applauded the Master of the Law to their rulers, saying that he was about to go westwards to seek the Law in the country of the Brahmins.

They offered him in charity abundant gifts, gold and silver money, and white horses without number. The Master accepting one half, caused the lamps of the different convents to be lit, and as for the rest of the money, he distributed it among the various religious establishments. At this time the administration of the country was newly arranged, and the frontiers did not extend far. There were severe restrictions placed on the people, who were forbidden to go abroad into foreign parts. Just then the governor of Liang-Chow was called Li-ta-liang. Obedient to the royal mandate he strictly adhered to the rules of prohibition. And now there came a man who addressed Liang thus:— "There is a priest here from Chang'an who is intending to go to the western regions—I do not know his plans." Liang, full of anxiety, called the Master to his presence and asked him the object of his arrival. The Master replied, "I wish to go to the West to seek for the Law." Liang, hearing this, urged him to return to the capital.

There was then at Liang-chow a Master called Hwui-wei, the most renowned of all priests of the region west of the river, for his spiritual perception and vast abilities. He greatly admired the profound reasoning of the Master, and hearing of his intention to go in search of the Law, he was very greatly rejoiced. Secretly sending two of his disciples, one called Hwui-lin, the other Taou-ching, he bade them conduct the Master in secret towards the West.

From this time he dare not be seen in public—during the daytime he hid himself, at night he went on. In process of time he came to Kwa-chow; the governor To-Kiu having heard of his coming was greatly pleased, and provided him with all necessary provisions in plenty. The Master inquiring as to the western roads, he was told in reply that north from this point fifty li or more there was the river Hu-lu, the lower part of which is wide, the upper course narrow. Its stream is very impetuous and suddenly becomes deep, so that no boat can pass over it. On the upper part is fixed the Yuh-men barrier, so that one must pass by this; thus it is the key to the western frontiers. North-west beyond the barrier there are five signal towers in which officers, charged to watch, dwell—they are one hundred li apart. In the space between them there is neither water nor herb. Beyond the five towers stretches the desert called Mo-Kia-Yen, on the frontiers of the kingdom of I-gu.

On hearing these palticulars he was filled with anxiety and distress. His horse was dead, and he did not know what steps to take; he remained there a month or so, sad and silent. Before his departure there came certain spies from Liang-chow, who said: "There is a priest called Huen Tsang who is purposing to enter on the Si-Fan territory. All the governors of provinces and districts are ordered to detain him." The governor of the province, Li-chang, was a man of a religious turn and he suspected in his heart that the Master was the person named; accordingly he secretly brought the mandate and showing it to Huen Tsang he said: "Is not the Master the person here named?" The Master hesitated and made no reply, on which Chang said: "The Master ought to speak the truth, and your disciple will make some plan for you to escape." The Master then replied truthfully. Chang, hearing it, was filled with admiration and surprise: and then he said, "Since the Master is indeed capable of such a project, I will for his sake destroy the document," and forthwith he tore it up before him. "And now, Sir," he said, "you must depart in all haste."

From this time his anxieties and fears greatly increased. Of the two novices who accompanied him, one, called Taou-ching, returned at once to Tun-hwang; the other, called Hwui-Lin, alone remained, but because the Master knew that he had not strength for so distant a journey, he let him also return. He now procured a horse by exchange.

That night there was a foreign priest in the temple who had a dream. His name was Dharma, and in his dream he saw the Master sitting on a lotus flower and going towards the West. Dharma was lost in surprise, and on the morrow he told his dream to the Master, whose heart was rejoiced thereat, taking it as a sign of his being able to go.

And now suddenly a foreign person came into the temple to worship Buddha, after doing which he saluted the Master by turning round him three times. The Master then asked him his family and personal name, on which he said, "My family name is Shi, my personal name is Pan-to." The foreigner then asked to be allowed to take on him the five Rules, and having done so he was greatly rejoiced, and asked permission to come back; after a little while he returned with cakes and fruit. The Master spoke to him about his purpose to go westwards. The foreigner readily acquiesced, and said he would conduct the Master beyond the five signal towers.

On the morrow at sundown he proceeded towards the bush, where shortly afterwards the foreigner with an old greybeard, likewise a foreign person, riding on a lean horse of a red colour, came to meet him. "This venerable greybeard is intimately acquainted with the western roads, and has gone to and come back from I-gu more than thirty times; I have therefore brought him to go with you, hoping it may give you assurance."

The Master then recalled to himself the following circumstance: when he was at Chang'an forming his purpose of visiting the western world, one day there was a diviner named Ho-wang-ta, who by reciting spells and prognosticating, could tell a great deal about the matters in which one was engaged. The Master requested him to prognosticate about his journey. Ta said, " Sir! you may go; the appearance of your person as you go is that of one riding an old red horse, thin and skinny; the saddle is varnished, and in front it is bound with iron."

Now having observed that the horse which the old foreigner was riding was lean and of a red colour, and that the varnished saddle was bound with iron, agreeing with the words of the diviner, he made up his mind that this was the fulfilment of the augury, and accordingly he exchanged his horse.

And now having packed his baggage, he went on through the night with the young foreigner. In the third watch they came to the river, and saw the guard-house called the Yuh-Men a good way off. At ten li from the barrier the upper stream is not more than ten feet wide; on each side there is a scrub composed of the Wu-tung tree; the foreigner, cutting down some wood, made a bridge and spread over it branches, filling it up with sand. Thus they led over the horses and went on.

The Master having crossed the river was filled with joy. Being fatigued, he dismounted and sought some repose. The foreign guide also, separated about fifty paces or so from the Master, spread his mat on the ground and they both slept. After a while the guide took his knife in his hand, and rising up, approached towards the Master; when about ten paces off, he turned round. Not knowing what his intention was, and being in doubt about the matter, the Master rose from his mat and repeated some Scripture, and called on Kwan-yin Bodhisattva. The foreigner having seen this went back, and slept.

At the first dawn of day the Master called to him and bade him fetch water. Having washed and taken some little food, he purposed to go onwards. The guide said: "Your disciple is leading you forward on a way full of danger and very remote; there is no water or grass; only beyond the fifth tower there is water. It will oe necessary to go there at night-time and get the water and pass on. But if at anyone place we are perceived, we are dead men! Is it not better to return and be at rest?" The Master having positively refused to return, they both went forward. Now the guide, with his knife drawn and his bow strung, begged the Master to go on in front; but the Master would not consent to the proposal. The foreigner going by himself, after a few li stopped and said: "Your disciple can go no further—he has great family concerns to attend to, and he is not willing to transgress the laws of his country." The Master, knowing his purpose, let him go back.

The young foreigner replied: "It is impossible for the Master to carry out his plan; how can you avoid being seized and brought back?" The Master answered: "Though they cause my body to be cut up as small as the very dust, I will never return; and I here take an oath to this." So the matter rested; and they parted.

Travels Alone

And now, alone and deserted, he traversed the sandy waste; his only means of observing the way being the heaps of bones and the horse-dung, and so on; thus slowly and cautiously advancing, he suddenly saw a body of troops, amounting to several hundreds, covering the sandy plain;

sometimes they advanced and sometimes they halted. The soldiers were clad in fur and felt. And now the appearance of camels and horses, and the glittering of standards and lances met his view; then suddenly fresh forms and figures changing into a thousand shapes appeared, sometimes at an immense distance and then close at hand, and then they dissolved into nothing.

The Master when he first beheld the sight thought they were robbers, but when he saw them come near and vanish, he knew that they were the hallucinations of demons. Again, he heard in the void sounds of voices crying out: "Do not fear! do not fear!" On this he composed himself, and having pushed on eighty li or so, he saw the first watch-tower. Fearing lest the lookouts should see him, he concealed himself in a hollow of sand until night; then going on west of the tower, he saw the water; and going down, he drank and washed his hands. Then as he was filling his water-vessel with water an arrow whistled past him and just grazed his knee, and in a moment another arrow. Knowing then that he was discovered, be cried with a loud voice: "I am a priest come from the capital, do not shoot me!" Then he led his horse towards the tower, while the men on guard opening the gate, came out; after looking at him they saw that he was indeed a priest, and so they entered in together to see the commander of the guard-house, whose name was Wang-siang. Wang, having ordered the fire to be well lit up for the purpose of inspecting the Master, said: "This is no priest of our country of Ho-si, he is indeed one from the capital;" then he asked him about his object in travelling.

The Master replied: "Captain! have you not heard men of Liang-chow talk about a priest named Huen Tsang, who was about to proceed to the country of the Brahmins to seek for the Law?" He answered: "I have heard that Huen Tsang has returned already to the east. Why have you come here? The Master then took him to his horse, and showed him various places on which were written his name and familiar title. On this the other was convinced. He then said: "Sir, the western road is dangerous and long, you cannot succeed in your plan. But I have no fault to find with you. I myself am a man of Tun-hwang and I will conduct you there. There is a Master there called Chang-kiau, he reveres men of virtue and honours the priesthood; he will be rejoiced to see you: I ask your consent to this."

The Master replied: "If you must needs detain me here let me be punished with death! Huen Tsang will never return one step to the east, nor give up his first intention!"

Siang, hearing these words, filled with emotion, said: "I am indeed fortunate in having met with you! How can I but rejoice? But now, sir, you are fatigued and worn; take some sleep before the day dawns. I will then myself conduct you, and show you the proper route." He then spread out a mat for him to rest upon.

When the morning came, the Master of the Law having taken some food, Siang sent a man to fill bis water-vessel, and providing him with some cakes made of flour, he himself conducted him for ten li or so, and then he said:—"From this point, sir, the road goes straight on to the fourth watch-tower; the man there is a good-hearted person; moreover, he is a near relation of mine. His family name is Wang, his private name is Pi-lung. When you come to see him you can say that I have sent you to him." Then, with tearful salutations, they parted.

Having gone on till night he came to tbe fourth watch-tower, and fearing lest he should be detained, he purposed to get some water quietly, and to go on. Coming to the water, and scarcely there, there came an arrow flying towards him; turning round he called out as before, and went forward to the tower. Then the men coming down, he entered the building. The officer of the tower having spoken to him, he answered:—"I propose going to India, and my way is in this direction. Wang-siang, the officer of the first tower, has commissioned me to meet you." Hearing this he was much pleased, and detained him for the night; moreover, he gave him a great leather bottle for water, and fodder for his horse.

Then conducting him by his side he said:—"You had better not, sir, go towards the fifth tower, for the men there are rude aud violent, and some mishap may befall you. About 100 li from this is the Ye-ma spring, where you can replenish your supply of water."

Having gone on from this he forthwith entered on the Mo-kia-Yen (Taklamakan) desert, which is about 800 li in extent. The old name for it is Sha-ho. There are no birds overhead, and no beasts below; there is neither water nor herb to be found. On occasions, according to the sun's shadow, he would, with the utmost devotion, invoke the name of Kwan-shai-yin Bodhisattva, and also recite the Pan-jo-sin Sutra (Prajna-paramita-hridaya Sutra).

At first when the Master was dwelling in Shuh he saw a diseased man whose body was covered with ulcers, his garments tattered and filthy. Pitying the man he took him to his convent, and gave him clothing and food; the sick man, moved by a feeling of deep gratitude, gave to the Master this little Sutra-book, and on this account he was in the habit of reciting it continually. Arriving at the Sha-ho as he passed through it, he encountered all sorts of demon shapes and strange goblins, which seemed to surround him behind and before. Although he invoked the name of Kwan-Yin, he could not drive them all away; but when he recited this Sutra, at the sound of the words they all disappeared in a moment.

After going a hundred li or so, he lost his way, and searching for the fountain called Ye-ma he could not find it, to get water from. Then when he was going to drink from the pipe of his water-vessel, because of its weight it slipped from his hands, and the water was wasted; thus, a supply enough for 1000 li was lost in a moment. Then again, because of the winding character of the road, he did not know which way to follow it. At length, purposing to return eastward to the fourth watch-tower, after going ten li, he thought thus within himself, **"I made a vow at the first that if I did not succeed in reaching India I would never return a step to the East;** what then am I now doing here? It is better to die in the attempt to go to the West, than to live by returning to the East." Then turning his bridle he invoked Kwan-Yin, and proceeded in the north-west direction.

At this time as he looked in the four directions, the view was boundless; there were no traces either of man or horse, and in the night the demons and goblins raised fire-lights as many as the stars; in the day-time the driving wind blew the sand before it as in the season of rain. But notwithstanding all this his heart was unaffected by fear; but he suffered from want of water, and was so parched with thirst that he could no longer go forward. **Thus for four nights and five days not a drop of water had he to wet his throat or mouth; his stomach was racked with a burning heat, and he was well-nigh thoroughly exhausted.** And now not being able to advance he lay down to rest on the sands, invoking Kwan-Yin without intermission, although worn out with suffering.

Thus praying with earnest heart and without cessation the while, till the middle of the fifth night, when suddenly a cool wind fanned his body, cold and refreshing as a bath of icy water. His eyes forthwith recovered their power of sight and his horse had strength to get up. His body being thus refreshed, he lay still and fell asleep for a little while. While he slept thus he had a dream, and in his sleep he thought he saw a mighty spiritual being, several chang in height, holding in his hand a halberd used for signalling, who spake thus: "Why are you still sleeping and not pressing on with all your might?"

The Master, rousing himself from slumber, pushed on for ten li, when his horse suddenly started off another way and could not be brought back or turned. Having gone some li in the new direction, he saw all at once several acres of green grass; getting off his horse, he let him graze; when leaving the grass, purposing to rcsume his journey, about ten paces off he came to a pool of water, sweet, and bright as a mirror; dismounting again, he drank without stint, and so his body and vital powers were restored once more, and both man and horse obtained refreshment and ease. Now we may conclude that this water and grass were not natural supplies, but undoubtedly were produced through the loving pity of Bodhisattva, and it is a proof of his guileless character and spiritual power.

Having bivouacked near the grass and fountain of water for a day, on the day following he filled his water vessel and cut some grass, and proceeded onward. After two days more they got out of the desert and arrived at I-gu. The myriads of dangers and difficulties through which he passed cannot be recounted in detail.

Having arrived at I-gu, he stopped in a temple where there were three Chinese priests; one was an old man whose vestment was without any girdle, and whose feet were bare. Coming forth, he embraced the Master, with many cries and piteous exclamations which he could not restrain; but at length he said, "How could I have hoped at this time, ever to have seen again a man of my own country?" The Master likewise, as he saw him, was moved to tears. The foreign priests outside, and the foreign kings also, came to pay their respects to Huen Tsang. The king invited him to his own house and provided him with abundance of entertainment.

At this time the king of Kau-chang, Khio-wen-t'ai, had previously sent some messengers to I-gu, and on this day as they were about to return they met the Master. Accordingly, when they had got back they told the king of his arrival. The king hearing it, immediately sent messengers to order the king of I-gu to send the Master to him. Moreover, the king selected several tens of superior horses and sent his officers and chief ministers to escort him to his presence. After the usual delay of ten days, the king's messengers came and explained the king's plan, and then they earnestly besought him to comply with the arrangement. The Master had purposed in his mind to take the road leading past the Feou-tu (Stupa) of the Khan, but now, notwithstanding his respectful refusal of the king of Kau-chang's request, he could not escape from it—and so was obliged to go.

Crossing the southern desert, after six days they came to the borders of Kau-chang, to the town of Pih-li. When the Master entered the city, the king, surrounded by his attendants in front and rear, bearing lighted torches, came forth in person to meet him. The Master having entered the inner hall, took his seat beneath a precious canopy in a pavilion of two stages. After salutation the king said in a most agreeable manner, "From the time that I knew of your honour's name, my happiness has prevented me from sleeping or eating; after calculating the distance of the road, I was sure you would arrive to-night, and therefore my wife and children with myself have taken no sleep, but reading the Sacred Books, have awaited your arrival with respect." A moment after, the queen, with several tens of servant-women, came in to pay her respects.

Then in the morning before the Master had arisen, the king in person, with the queen also, and her followers, waiting below, came to the door to salute him. After this he ordered food to be provided according to the rules of religion. Moreover, by the side of the palace there was an oratory to which the king himself conducted the Master and installed him there. Moreover, he commissioned certain eunuchs to wait on him and guard him.

In this convent there was a certain Master of the Law called Tun who formerly studied at Chang'an and was well versed in the details of religion. The king, who highly esteemed him, commissioned him to go visit the Master. After a short interview he left, on which the king again ordered a Master of the Law called Kwo-tong-wang, about eighty years of age, to take up his residence with the Master, with a view to persuade him to remain where he was and not to go to the western regions. The Master was unwilling to assent, and after ten days' delay he wished to be allowed to go on his way. The king said: "I have already commissioned the Master Tong to confer with you and request you to remain here."

The Master replied, "To request me to remain here is surely an act of goodness on the part of the king, but truly my heart cannot consent."

The king replied: "Let me persuade you, sir, to remain with me here. I will provide for your wants to the end of my life, and I will undertake that all the people of my realm shall become your disciples, if, as I hope, you on your part will instruct them. The priests and their followers, although not numerous, still amount to several thousands. I will cause them to take the Sacred Book in hand which you select and to attend with the rest to your instructions."

The Master, in declining the invitation, said: "How can I, a poor and solitary priest, sufficiently acknowledge the king's generosity. But I undertook this journey not with a view to receive religious offerings. At the risk of my life I have set out for the West, to inquire after interpretations not yet known. My purpose is that the sweet dew of the expanded Law shall not only water Kapila, but that the mysterious words may also spread through the regions of the East. I pray your majesty to change your mind, and do not overpower me with an excessive friendship."

Then the king, colouring with anger and stretching out his hand beyond the sleeve, said in loud words and a menacing manner: "I have a different way of deciding this question, sir! If, sir, you still think you can go when you like, I will detain you here by force and send you back to your own country."

The Master answered: "You have only power over my body, your majesty cannot touch my will or my spirit."

The Master, seeing that he would be detained by force in opposition to his original design, declared with an oath that he would eat nothing in order to affect the king's heart. So he sat in a grave posture, and during three days he neither ate nor drank; on the fourth day the king seeing that the Master was becoming fainter and fainter, overcome with shame and sorrow, he bowed down to the ground before him and said: "The Master has free permission to go to the West! I pray you take a slight morning meal!"

The Master still fearing his insincerity, required him to repeat his words with his hand pointing to the sun. The king answered: "If it needs be so, let us both go into the presence of Buddha, and bind ourselves mutually together!" Accordingly, they went both together into the sacred precinct and paid adoration to Buddha. With them was the royal mother, and the empress Ohang.

Then he invited him to remain one month and to expound the Sutra called Jin-wang-pan-jo, in order that during the interval the king might prepare travelling garments for the Master. The Master giving his full consent, the empress was greatly rejoiced and desired to be connected with the Master in close relationship during successive ages. Then the Master consented to eat; from this we can see the firmness of his will and determination.

And now on a day following the king prepared a large pavilion for the purpose of beginning the religious conferences; the pavilion could seat three hundred persons or so; the empress sat on the right of the king; the masters and chief nobles all took different seats, to attend the preaching.

Every day at the time of preaching, the king himself conducted the Master, preceding him with a brazier containing incense. When ascending the pulpit the king, humbly bowing, placed his foot-stool and begged him to mount and be seated. Day by day this was done. After the sermon he begged the Master to arrange for four Sramaneras to wait upon him and to make thirty priests' vestments; and considering that the western regions are very cold, he had various articles of clothing made suitable for such a climate, such as face-coverings, gloves, leather boots, and so on. Moreover, he gave him a hundred gold ounces, and three myriads of silver pieces, with five hundred rolls of satin and taffeta, enough for the outward and home journey of the Master during twenty years. He gave him also thirty horses and twenty-four servants. Moreover, he commissioned Hun-Sin, one of the imperial censors belonging to his court, to conduct him to the Khan Yeh-hu. Again he composed twenty-four official documents to be presented at Kiu-chi and twenty-four different countries; each letter had a large roll of satin, accompanying it as a credential. Lastly, he loaded two conveyances with five hundred pieces of satin and taffeta, and fruit of luscious taste, as a present for the Khan Yeh-hu. Accompanying this present was a letter to the following purport: "The Master, a friend of your humble servant, desires to search for the Law in the country of the Brahmins; I beseech the Khan to be kind to him, as he has ever been kind to me, his humble servant."

On the day of his departure the king, with the religious community and the great ministers and people, escorted him to without the city on his way to the West; then the king and the people embraced him with tears, and their cries and groans resounded on every side.

After this he journeyed westward, and after passing through the towns of Wu-pwan and To-tsin, he entered the country of O-ki-ni (Yenki).

3

Journey upto Kanauj

From this, going westward, he came to the kingdom of O-ki-ni; here is the fountain of A-fu the Master. The fountain is situated to the south of the road on a sandy hillock. The hillock is several chang in height, and the water comes from the hill half way up.

The tradition says: There was formerly a band of merchantmen, several hundred is number, who found their supply of water exhausted on their mid-journey. Arriving at this point exhausted and worn out, they knew not what to do. At this time there was a priest in their company, who had brought no provisions for the journey, but relied on the alms of the rest for his support. The others, considering the case, said: "This priest serves Buddha; on this account we, as a company, give him our offerings. Although he has travelled ten thousand li, he has had no provision of his own, and now, whilst we are full of anxiety, he is unmoved by any care; we ought to ask him about it."

The priest, in reply to their question, said: "You, sirs, who are anxious to get a supply of water, ought each one of you to adore Buddha, and receive the three refuges and take on you the five moral obligations. Then I will, for your sake, ascend yonder hill and cause a supply of water to proceed from it."

The entire company, having arrived at such a condition of distress, agreed to his order, and received the rules of moral obligation; after which the priest instructed them thus: "After I have gone up the hill you cry out 'A-fu-sse! cause water to flow down for our use, enough to sustain us.' " With these words he left them. After a little while the company called out and requested, as he had instructed them. In a moment the water began to descend in supplies sufficient for their necessity.

The whole congregation were filled with joy and gratitude; but as the Master did not return they went in a body up the hill to see what had happened, and found that he was dead. And now having wept and lamented, they burnt his body according to the rules of the western world; on the place where they found him they collected stones and made a tower, which still exists. Moreover, the water has not ceased to flow, but, according to the number of the travellers who pass by this place, it flows down for their use, in small or large supply. If there is no one there, the fountain dries up; it is a mere secretion.

The Master, with the rest, passed the night near the fountain. At sunrise he went on and crossed the "Silver Mountain." This mountain is very high and extensive. It is from this place that the silver is dug which supplies the western countries with their silver currency. On the west of the mountain he encountered a band of robbers; after giving them what they demanded, they departed.

After a while they came to the place of the site of the royal city, and passed the night by the side of a stream. At this time some foreign merchants in their company, to the number of several tens, coveting an early sale of their merchandise, privately went forward in the middle of the night. Scarcely had they gone ten li when they met a band of robbers who murdered everyone of them. And so, when the Master and the others came to the place, they found their dead bodies there, but all their riches gone; they passed on, deeply affected with the sight, and shortly afterwards they saw the royal city before them.

The king of O-ki-ni with his ministers coming forth to meet the Master, conducted him, and invited him to enter the palace as his guest. The Master, stopping one night, went forwards and crossed a great river. To the west he traversed a level valley, and after going several hundred li he arrived at the borders of the kingdom of K'iu-chi. As he approached the capital, the king, accompanled by his ministers and a celebrated priest called Mo-cha-kiu-to (Mokskagupta) came forth to meet him; other priests, to the number of several thousands, had remained at the eastern gate of the city, outside which they had erected a wide floating pavilion pointed like a tent, and having brought the images of Buddha in procession, with sounds of music, had placed them there.

The Master having arrived, the priests rising to meet him, addressed him in affectionate language, and then each one returned to his seat. They then caused a priest to offer to the Master a bouquet of flowers freshly gathered. The Master having accepted it, advanced before the image of Buddha, scattering the flowers and offering worship. After this Mokshagupta took his seat beside him. The two being seated, the priests again formed a procession with flowers in their hands, after which they offered grape juice as they passed. Having thus accepted flowers and grape juice in the first temple, he next received the same in the other temples, and thus going the round, the day began to decline, and the priests and their attendants gradually dispersed.

There were several decades of men belonging to Kau-chang who had become monks in K'iu-chi; they dwelt apart in one particular temple; this temple was to the south-east of the city. As the Master came from their native country, they were the first to invite him to stop the night with them. Because he accepted this invitation the king and the priests returned each to his own abode. The next day the king invited him to pass over to his palace to receive every kind of religious offerings and the three pure aliments. The Master would not accept them, at which the king was very vexed; the Master replied, "This is the license granted by the 'gradual' system of the Law; but the Great Vehicle in which Huen Tsang has been instructed, does not admit of it. I will accept the other reserved food."

Having finished his repast, he proceeded in a north-west direction from the city to the temple called O-she li-ni where the priest Mokshagupta resided. Gupta by his rare ability and intelligence had acquired the respect of all the different schools of religion. He had travelled in India for twenty years and more, learning the Sacred Books. Although he had gone through all the Sutras, yet he excelled in the knowledge of the Shing-ming (Sabdavidya Sutra). The king and the people of the kingdom were all affected by the utmost respect for him, and had named him Tuli-po, without equal. When he saw the Master come to his abode, he received him with the politeness due to a guest, not knowing as yet his advanced acquaintance with religon.

Addressing the Master he said: "In this land we have the Tsa-sin (Samyuktabhidharma), the Kiu-she (Kosha), the Pi-sha (Vibhasha) and other Sutras; you can gain sufficient knowledge by studying these here, without troubling yourself to voyage to the West, encountering all sorts of dangers."

The Master replied: "And have you here the Yoga Sastra or not?"

He answered: "What need you ask about such an heretical book as that? The true disciple of Buddha does not study such a work!"

The Master was at first filled with reverence for the person but hearing this reply he regarded him as dirt, and answering, said: "In our country too we have long had the Vibhasha and Kosha; but I have been sorry to observe their logic superficial and their language weak; they do not speak of the highest perfection. On this account I have come so far as this, desiring to be instructed in the Yoga Sastra belonging to the Great Vehicle. And the Yoga, what is it but the revelation of Maitreya, the Bodhisattva next to become Buddha, and to call such a book heretical, how is it you are not afraid of the bottomless pit?"

The other replied: "You have not yet understood the Vibhasha and the other Sutras, how can you say they do not contain the deep principles of religion?"

The Master replied: "Do you, sir, at present understand them?" He answered, "I have a complete knowledge of them."

The Master then cited the beginning of the Kosha, and asked him to continue. Forthwith he began to blunder, and as he came at last to a dead stop, he changed colour, and said with perturbation: "You may question me on some other portion of the work."

Then he referred to another passage, but neither could he recite this, but said: "The Sastra has no such passage as the one you name." Now at this time the king's uncle, called Chi-Yueh, had become a monk and was well acquainted with Sutras and Sastras; he was on this occasion seated by the side of Huen Tsang. Forthwith, he testified to the correctness of the quotation, in these words: "This passage is really taken from the Sastra;" and then, taking the original, he read it out. Mokshagupta on this was exceedingly abashed and said: "I am getting old and forgetful." He was questioned also regarding the other Sutras, but could give no correct explanation.

And now, as the snow passes of Mount Ling were not yet open, the Master could not advance, but was obliged to remain, for sixty days or so, detained by this circumstance. Going west from this two days journey, he encountered about 2000 Tuh-Kiuch (Turkish) robbers on horseback; they were in the act of dividing among themselves the booty they had got from a caravan, and when they could not agree, they began to fight among themselves and so were dispersed.

Then going forward 600 li they crossed a small desert and arrived at the kingdom of Poh-luh-kia (Balakh) and stopped there one night. Then proceeding north-west and going 300 li, they crossed a desert and came to the Ling Mountain, which forms the northern angle of the T'sung Ling range. This mountain is steep and dangerous, and reaches to the clouds. From the creation the perpetual snow which has collected here in piles, has been changed into glaciers which melt neither in winter nor summer; the hard-frozen and cold sheets of water rise mingling with the clouds; looking at them the eye is blinded with the glare. When desirous of food or sleep there is no dry place to be found for a halt; the only way is to hang the pot for cooking, and to spread the mat on the ice for sleeping.

After seven days they began to get out of the mountain; **twelve or fourteen of the company were starved and frozen to death, while the number of the oxen and horses that perished was still greater.** After leaving the mountains they arrived at the lake called Tsing. The circuit of this lake is 1400 or 1500 li, longer from east to west, narrower from north to south. Looking at the watery expanse, the wind suddenly arising swells the waves to a height of several chang.

Following the borders of the sea for about 500 li in a north-west direction, the Master came to the city of Suyeh. Here he encountered the Khan of the Turks called Yeh-hu, who was then engaged on a hunting expedition. He was surrounded by about 2000 offcers, who were all clothed in brocade stuff, with their hair braided. On the right and left he was attended by independent troops all clothed in furs and fine spun hair garments; they carried lances and bows, and standards, and were mounted on camels and horses. The eye could not estimate their numbers.

When they saw each other, the Khan, full of joy, said: "Stay here for a while; after two or three days I will come back." He then directed one of his chief officers, Ta-mo-chi, to conduct him towards a large tent and to arrange things for his comfort. After three days in this residence the Khan returned, and taking the Master by the hand he conducted him within.

The Turks worship Fire; they do not use wooden seats, because wood contains fire, and so even in worship they never seat themselves, but only spread padded mats on the ground and so go through with it. But for the sake of the Master they brought an iron warming-pan covered with a thick padding, and requested him to be seated thereon. A short time afterwards they introduced the Chinese mission and the legates from Kau-chang with their letters of introduction and presents.

The Khan with his ministers drank to the envoys, while he caused the juice of the grape to be offered to the Master. After this they drank one with the other, challenging one another in succession, filling their cups and emptying them in succession, ever more and more animated, during which time the sounds of all kind of music—Kin, Mae, Li, etc., music of the north, south, east and west—resounded in confused clang. In a little while there were other articles of food brought forward, such as boiled quarters of mutton and veal, which were heaped up before the guests: but for the Master they prepared distinct entertainment, consisting of the pure articles of food such as rice-cakes, cream, sugar-candy, honey-sticks, raisins, etc.

When the feast was over, they sent round the grapewine again, and then asked the Master to expound the doctrines of religion. Then he, with a view to admonish them, spoke upon the subject of the ten precepts (Dasa Silam), love of preserving life, and the Paramitas, and works that lead to final deliverance. Raising his hands, the king humbly prostrated himself to the ground, and joyously accepted the teaching of the Master.

The Khan then ordered inquiry to be made in his army for anyone who could speak the Chinese language and that of other countries. So they found a young man who had lived for many years at Chang'an, and thoroughly understood the Chinese language. He was appointed, under the title of Mo-to-ta-kwan, to prepare letters of commendation for the different countries and to accompany the Master to the kingdom of Kapisa. Moreover, the Khan gave to Huen Tsang a complete set of vestments in red satin, and fifty pieces of silk; and then with his officers in person he conducted him to a distance of ten li, or so.

From this, going west 400 li or so, he arrived at Ping-yu. This is also called "The Thousand Springs." The district is several hundred li square. From Ping-yu, advancing westward 150 li, we come to the town of Ta-lo-sse (Taras). Again going south-west 200 li, we come to the town of Peh-shwui; again going south-west 200 li, we come to Kong-yu city; again going south 50 li, we come to the kingdom of Nu-chih-kien; again going west 200 li, we come to the kingdom of Che-shi, the stone country. This country, on the west, borders on the river Yeh-yeh (or, She-She). Again going west 1000 li or so, we come to the kingdom of Su-tu-li-sse-na. To the east this kingdom borders on the Yeh-yeh river. This river comes from the northern plateau of the Ts'ung-Ling mountains and flows to the north-west. Again going north-west, we enter on a great desert without water or grass. We advance guided by observing the bones left on the way. After 500 li or so we arrive at the country of Sa-mo-kien the happy country. The king and people do not believe in the law of Buddha, their religion consists in sacrificing to fire. There are here two religious foundations, but no priests dwell in them. If stranger-priests seek shelter therein, the barbarians follow them with burning fire and will not permit them to remain there.

The Master on his first arrival was treated disdainfully by the king, but after the first night's rest, he discoursed for the king's sake on the destiny of men and Devas; he lauded the meritorious qualities of Buddha; he set forth, by way of exhortation, the character of religious merit. The king was rejoiced, and requested permission to take the moral precepts as a disciple, and from that time showed him the highest respect. The two young disciples went to the temple to worship, on which the barbarians again pursued them with burning fire—the two Sramaneras going back told the king of it. The king hearing it ordered them to arrest the fire-carriers; having done so, **he assembled the people and ordered the hands of the culprits to be cut off. The Master, wishing to exhort them to a virtuous life, would not consent to their bodies being mutilated and so saved them.** The king having beaten them severely, expelled them from the city.

From this circumstance the higher and lower sort of people regarded him respectfully, and as a body sought to be instructed in the faith. Accordingly, having summoned a large assembly, he received many of them into the priesthood and established them in the convents. It was thus that he transformed their heretical hearts, and corrected their evil customs. And so it was wherever he went.

Again going about 300 li to the west, he arrived at K'iuh-shwang-ni-kial (Kashania). Again going west 200 li or so, we come to the kingdom of Ho-Han, The eastern-rest country. Again going west 400 li, we come to the country of Pu-ho, the middle-rest country. Again going west 100 li or so, we come to the Fa-ti country, the western-rest country. Again going west 500 li, we come to the kingdom of Ho-li-sih-mi-kia, Khwarezm. This country, on the east borders on the Po-tsu river (Oxus). Again going south-west 300 li or so, we come to the country of Kie-shwang-na (Kesh). Again going south-west 200 li, we enter the mountains.

From this, having gone several hundred li, we cross the Oxus, and arrive at the kingdom of Hwo (Kunduz). This was the residence of the eldest son of the Khan Yeh-hu, called Ta-tu-sheh. It was he who had married the sister of the king of Kau-chang.

Moreover, the king of Kau-chang had sent letters to this place in recommendation of the Master; on his arrival, the princess Ho-kia-tun was dead, and Ta-tu-sheh was sick. When he heard that the Master of the Law had come from Kau-chang with letters for himself and his wife, he was overpowered with grief thereat, and calling the Master, said: "Your humble servant at view of you has received sight! Would that you could remain here a little while, and rest. If I should recover my health, I will personally conduct you to the country of the Brahmins."

There was then a Sramana called Ta-mo-sang-kia (Dharmasinha), residing in this country. He had travelled for instruction to India; beyond the T'sung-ling mountains on the western side they called him Fa-tsiang (i,e. Artisan of the Law, or Law-maker). The priests of Su-leh (Kashgar) and Yu-tin (Khotan) dare not discuss with him. The Master wishing to know his profound or shallow knowledge, sent messengers to him, to ask how many Sutras or Sastras he was able to explain. The disciples who were surrounding him, when they heard the message were piqued, while Dharmasinha answered with a smile: "I can explain any of them you like." The Master, knowing that he did not understand the Great Vehicle, turned his questions to the Vibhasha and other Sutras belonging to the Little Vehicle. These questions, not easy to solve, made him allow his inferiority. The disciples were filled with shame. From this time whenever they met, the Sramana was full of expressions of pleasure, and ceased not to praise the Master, acknowledging that he was by no means his equal.

At this time there were in this place many tens of priests of Baktra, who had come to express sympathy with the new Sheh on the death of his predecessor; when the Master met them, he expressed his intention, and to this they replied: "You ought to go with us at once—the road is open now, but if you delay here longer the change of place will be difficult." The Master on these words forthwith took leave of the Sheh, and taking up his carriage, departed with those priests. Having arrived at this place, Balkh, observing the city and its suburbs, he noticed the apparently barren character of the city and its neighbourhood.

There were about a hundred Sangharamas and three thousand priests, or so, all belonging to the Little Vehicle. Outside the city on the south-west quarter there is the Navasangharama, which is remarkable for its imposing structure and unusual ornaments. Inside the Sangharama, in the hall of Buddha, there is the water-pot of Buddha, able to contain about two pecks. There is also here a tooth of Buddha, about one inch long, and eight or nine-tenths in breadth, of a yellow-white colour; this relic always irradiates a bright miraculous light.

There is also here the sweeping brush of Buddha, made of Kasa grass; it is about three feet long, and perhaps seven inches round; the handle is ornamented with various precious substances. These three things are brought out every feast day, and the priests and laymen draw near to worship them.

To the north of the Sangharama there is a Stupa about 200 feet high. To the south-west of the Sangharama there is a Vihara of an old date. All the priests who have attained to the four degrees of holiness—the fruition of the four paths—during successive ages, dwelling here, after their Nirvana, have had erected to their memory towers, the foundations of which, to the number of several hundreds, are close together in this vicinity. Fifty li to the north-west of the capital, we come to the town of Ti-wei; forty li to the north of this town there is the town of Po-li. There are two stupas in this town, three chang in height; in former days when Buddha first arrived at Supreme Enlightenment he accepted some honey and meal at the hands of two merchants, who were in that place; when they had heard from him the fine moral precepts and the ten rules (Sikshapadas), they asked to be allowed to present their religious offerings. Tathagata gave to them, for the purpose, some pieces of his nails and portions of his hair, and ordered them to construct a tower, and furnished them with a model. The two merchantmen, taking the relics, returned to their own country or, and built these two sacred spiritual towers. About seventy li to the west of the city there is a stupa more than two chang high; they were built in the days of Kasyapa Buddha long ago.

In the New Sangharama there was a priest of the kingdom of Tcheka who had studied the three Pitakas belonging to the Little Vehicle; his name was Prajnakara. Hearing that the Master had come from a distance to search for religious books, he was exceedingly glad to meet him. The Master, in the course of his statement respecting his doubts and difficulties about the Kosha and Vibhasha and other books, asked him for some explanations, and was answered in each case with extreme clearness. He remained here a month and studied the Vibhsha Sastra. In this Sangharama, moreover, there were two other priests versed in the Tripitaka according to the Little Vehicle; their names were Ta-mo-pi-li (Dharmapriya) and Ta-mo-ki-li (Dharmakara); they were exceedingly honoured by the others. Seeing the sacred features of the Master and the marks of intelligence which distinguished him, they paid him marked respect.

There were at this time to the south-west of Baktra the countries named Jui-mo-to (Jumadha) and Hu-shi-kien (Juzgana). Their kings, hearing that the Master had come from a distant country, both sent their chief ministers to salute him, and to request him to pass through their countries and receive religious offerings; but he declined to go. The messengers having returned and again come back several times, in consequence of his continual refusals, at last he complied with the request. The kings, being overjoyed, offered him gold and precious stones, and abundance of drink and food; the Master declined all such gifts, and returned.

Going south from Balkh in company with Prajnakara, the Master, they entered the kingdom of Kie-chi (Gaz).

To the south-east of this kingdom they entered the great Snowy Mountains, and going 600 li and more they left the boundaries of the Tu-ho-lo (Tukhara) country, and entered the kingdom of Fan-yen-na (Bamiyan). This country from east to west is about 2000 li in extent. It is situated in the middle of the Snowy Mountains; the muddy roads and dangers of the passes and tracks are double those of the frozen desert.

At Bamiyan, the chlef town possesses something like ten religious foundations, with several thousand priests; these belong to the Little Vehicle, according to the Lokottaravada school.

The king of Bamiyan went forth to escort him, and invited him within his palace to receive his religious offerings; after a day or two he went forth to make his observations. **There were there two priests belonging to the Mahasanghika school, whose names were Aryadasa and Aryasena, both of them deeply versed in the Law. When they met the Master they were full of admiration, that so remote a country as China should possess such a distinguished priest.** They conducted him from place to place to pay his reverence, or to inspect, and did not cease in their attention and services to him.

North-east of the capital, an the declivity of a hill, there is a standing stone figure about 150 feet high. To the east of the figure there is a Sangharama, to the east of which is a standing figure of Sakya, made af calamine stone, in height one hundred feet. Within the Sangharama there is a figure of Buddha represented as when he was asleep on entering nirvana, about 1000 feet in length. All these figures are of an imposing character and extremely good execution.

Going south-east from this, 200 li or so, crossing the great Snowy Mountains, we came to a small valley where there is a Sangharama, in which there is a teeth of Buddha, and also a tooth of a Pratyeka Buddha, who lived at the beginning of the present Kalpa. This tooth is five inches long, and four inches broad, or a little less.

Thus passed fifteen days, and then, leaving Bamiyan, on the second day he encountered a snowstorm, which caused him to miss his road. Coming to a small sand hillock, he met some hunters, who showed him the way. Crossing the Black Ridge (Koh Baba) he arrived at the borders of Kapisa.

This kingdom is about 4000 li in circuit. On the north it is bounded by the Snowy Mountains. The king is selected from the Kshatriya caste. He is a clever, shrewd man, and has brought under his control some ten kingdoms. When Huen-Tsang was about to arrive at the capital, the king and all the priests went forth from the city to escort him. There are some hundred or so religious foundations, the residents in which had sharp words together, each convent wishing to induce the Master to stop there.

There was a temple belonging to the Little Vehicle, which was named Sha-lo-kia. The story goes that the temple was built some time ago, when the son of the Han emperor was held as an hostage. The priests of this temple said: "Our temple was originally founded by a son of the Han emperor, and now, as you come from that country, you ought first to stop with us."

The Master seeing them thus, was deeply impressed; and as his companion, Hwui-Sing (Prajnakara), Master of the Law, belonged to this school of the Little Vehicle, to which these priests were attached, he did not desire to live in a temple belonging to the Great Vehicle; accordingly, they went to stop at the temple made for the hostage.

Moreover, at this time there was treasured here by the hostage, under the foot of the image of the Great-Spirit King (Vaisravana) on the south side of the eastern gate of the Hall of Buddha, a countless quantity of jewels and gems, as a means for the after repairs of the building. The priests, in gratitude for such favours, had in various places painted on the walls the figure of the hostage prince. At the time of the conclusion of the rest, during the rains, this congregation holds an assembly for preaching and reciting the Scriptures, as a means for perpetuating his religious merit; this custom has been handed down from generation to generation, and is still observed.

Recently there was a wicked king who, fired by a covetous disposition, desired to carry off the priests' treasure. Accordingly, he sent men to dig underneath the foot of the Spirit-King. Then the earth greatly quaked, and the figure of the parrot which was on the top of his head, seeing them digging, flapped his wings, and screamed violently. The king and his troops were all seized with terror and fell to the earth; after this, they returned home. There is in the temple a stupa. The encircling rings of this building having tumbled down, the priests wished to take the treasure and to repair it. On making the attempt, the earth again trembled and roared, so that no one dared to go near. When the Master arrived, the whole assembly came together, and, as a body, requested the Master to assist them, setting forth and relating the previous circumstances.

He ordered the men to dig into the ground; they did so calmly and without molestation. At the depth of seven or eight feet, they came to a great copper vessel, which contained several hundred catties of gold, and several scores of pearls. The great congregation were filled with joy, and without exception paid their services to the Master. The Master kept the rain-rest in this temple.

The king of this country thinks little of the polite arts, he entirely trusts to the teaching of the Great Vehicle. As he was fond of the sight of religious conferences and discussions, he asked the Master and Prajnakara of the three Pitakas, to a religions assembly to be held in a temple of the Great Vehicle. In that temple there was a Doctor of the three Pitakas called Manojnaghosha (Mo-nu-jo-kiu-sha), and also a Sa-po-to, A-li-ye-fa-mo (Aryavarma of the Sarvastivadin school) and also a priest of the Mi-sha-seh school (Mahisasaka) named Ku-na-po-to (Gunabhadra); these priests were reputed the chief in that convent. Their acquirements, however, were not universal, but confined to one or other points in the Great of Little Vehicle as the case might be, and although clear on that point, yet narrowed in its extent. But the Master had thoroughly examined the teachings of all the schools, and answered the questions put to him by all comers, according to the several systems of doctrine, so that all present were constrained to acknowledge his superiority. Thus for five days the discussion continued, then the assembly dispersed.

Enters India

The Master proceeded eastward, and having advanced some 600 li, passing the Black Ridge, he entered the borders of India, and came to the country of Lan-po (Lamghan). This country is about 1000 li in circuit. There are ten Sangharamas, the priests are all devoted to the Great Vehicle. Having stopped three days, he proceeded southward, and came to a little hill on which was a stupa. This is where Buddha stopped in former days when he came here from the south. All places to the north of this are called Mi-hu-ku (Mleccha) lands. Tathagata, when he desired to instruct and convert these people, in so doing, used to pass through the air coming and going, and would not tread on the earth, as the earth trembled and shook under his footsteps.

From this, going south twenty li or so, and descending the mountain ridge, after crossing a river, he came to the country of Na-kie-lo-ho (Nagarahara). Two li to the south-east of the capital of the country is a stupa 300 feet or so in height; it was built by king Asoka. It was here that Sakya Bodhisattva, in the second Asankhya of years from the present time, met Jen-tang-Fo (Dipankara Buddha). He spread his deer-skin robe and unloosed his hair, to preserve the Buddha from the mud, and in consequence received a predictive assurance that he would become a Buddha. Although there have passed Kalpa destructions since that period, the traces of this event remain intact. The Master when he arrived at this spot, paid his devotions and religiously circumambulated the building.

About ten li to the south-west is a stupa; this is the place where Buddha when he was Dipankara bought the flowers. Again, to the south-east, after crossing a sandy peak, we come to the town of Buddha's skull bone (Hidda). In this town is a double-storeyed tower and in the upper storey is a small stupa, made of the seven precious substances, which contains the bone of the top of the head of Tathagata. This bone is one foot and two inches round. The marks of the hair orifices are quite distinct. The colour of the bone is a yellowish white; it is enclosed in a jewelled box. If anyone wishes to know the indications of his guilt, or, his religious merit, he mixes some powdered incense into a paste, which he spreads upon a piece of silken stuff, and then presses it on the top of the bone; according to the resulting indications the good fortune or ill fortune of the man is determined.

The Master, in taking an impression, obtained the figure of the Bodhi tree; of the two Sramaneras who also took impressions, the first obtained a figure of Buddha, the other a figure of a lotus. There is also here a tower of the skull bone shaped like a lotus leaf. Also the eyeball of Buddha, as large as an Amra fruit, and so bright that its rays dart forth from the box to some distance outside. Again, there is the Sanghati robe of Buddha, made of a very fine silky cotton stuff.

Again, there is the staff of Buddha, the rings whereof are made of tin, and the hand of sandalwood. All these the Master of the Law adored with reverence; after which, in consequence of this opportunity of paying his heartfelt respect, he presented at different shrines fifty gold pieces, one thousand silver pieces, four silken banners, two pieces of brocaded satin, and two sets of religious vestments, then having scattered flowers, and again prostrated himself in worship, he went forth.

And now he heard that to the south-west of the city of Dipankara, about twenty li or so, there was the cave where dwelt the Nagaraja Gopala. Tathagata in former days having tamed this Naga, left to him as a bequest his shadow to remain in the cavern. The Master wished to go there to worship, but he was told that the roads were deserted and dangerous, and, moreover, that they were frequented by robbers, and that for the last two or three years those who had gone for the purpose of seeing the shadow had not succeeded in their purpose, and so there were few now who went.

On this he went alone, and arriving at the town of Dipankara, he entered a monastery, and inquired some particulars as to the road, but found no one who would go with him as a guide. After a while he met with a little boy who said: "The farmhouse of the convent is not far from this place, I will guide you so far." The Master then went with the boy and arrived at the farmhouse, where he passed the night. He then found an old man who knew the place, and so with him as a guide they set out together.

After going a few li they were met by five robbers who came upon them sword in hand. The Master immediately removed his loose cloak, so as to let his religious vestments appear. The robbers said: "Where is the Master going?" In reply he said: "I am wishful to worship the shadow of Buddha." The robbers said: "Have you not heard that this road is infested with brigands?" He answered: "Robbers are human beings. I am now going to adore Buddha; though the road be filled with savage beasts, I have no fear; how much less should I fear you, who are my human protectors?" The robbers were touched to the heart by these words and allowed him to go to perform his act of worship, and so they arrived at the cave.

The cave lies to the eastward of a stony water-course; the door through the wall of the cave faces the west. Looking into the cave all is wrapped in gloom and no object is visible. The old man spoke to the Master thus: "You must enter and pass straight on to the eastern wall; when you touch that, stop, and then go backwards fifty paces and no more; then face the eastern wall and look; the shadow is in that place." The Master entered the cave and paced forward, it may be fifty strides, and touched the eastern wall, and then according to the directions he went backwards and stood still. Then animated by the most sincere desire, he paid his worship with a hundred and more prostrations; but he saw nothing. He reproached himself for his shortcomings, and with lamentable cries he expressed his deep sorrow. Then again with his utmost heart he paid his worship and recited the Shing-kwan and other sutras; he also repeated the verses of the Buddhas, making one prostration after each verse of praise.

After about one hundred prostrations, he saw on the eastern wall a great light about the size of a Patra; which disappeared in a moment. Again paid his adorations, and then there appeared a great light round as a basin, which again as quickly disappeared. Then, filled with additional ardour and desire, he vowed within himself that if he did not see the shadow of the Lord of the world, then he would never leave the place. Then he performed two hundred more acts of worship, and then, while the whole cave was brightened up with light, the shadow of Tathagata of a shining white colour appeared on the wall, as when the opening clouds suddenly reveal the golden Mount and its excellent indications. Bright were the divine lineaments of his face, and as the Master gazed in awe and holy reverence, he knew not how to compare the spectacle; the body of Buddha and his kashaya robe were of a yellowish red colour, and from his knees upward the distinguishing marks of his person were exceedingly glorious; but below, the lotus throne on which he sat was slightly obscured. On the left and right of the shadow and somewhat behind, were visible the shadows of Bodhisattvas and the holy priests surrounding them.

Having gazed on the vision, he summoned six men, from some distance outside the gate, to get some fire, and bring it in for burning incense. But as soon as the fire was brought in, the shadow of Buddha disappeared. Then he quickly ordered them to put the fire out, and, on his earnest request, the shadow again appeared. Among the six men, five of the number were able to see the shadow, but one of them could see nothing. Thus the appearance lasted for the short space of half a mealtime, during which having uttered his praises in worship and scattered flowers and incense, the light then suddenly disappeared.

As they were returning together those five brigands, laying aside their arms, received the moral precepts and departed. After this the Master rejoined his companions, and passing over the mountains in a south-easterly direction, 500 li or so, they came to the country of Gandhara. This kingdom on the eastern side borders on the Sin-tu river; the capital is called Po-lu-sha-po-lo (Purushapur, Peshawar). In this country many sages and saints from old days composed Sastras, as for instance, Na-lo-yen-ti'en (Narayana Deva), Wu-cho-Pu-sa (Asanga Bodhisattva), Shi-tsin-pu-sa (Vasubandhu Bodhisattva), Fa-k'iu (Dharmatrata), Ju-i (Manohita), Hi-tsun-che (the Venerable Parsvika), and others, all of whom came from this kingdom.

To the north-east of the capital there is erected a precious tower of the Patra of Buddha. This Patra afterwards removed itself through various countries, and at present is found in the country of Po-lai-na-se (Benaras).

Eight or nine li to the south-east beyond the capital is a Pi-po-lo tree, about 100 feet high. The four past Buddhas have all sat underneath this tree, and now there are the figures of these four Tathagatas placed here. The 996 Buddhas yet to come will also sit here. By the side of this tree there is a stupa; this was built by Kanishka-raja; it is 400 feet high, the foundation part is a li and a half in circuit, and 150 feet high. Above the stupa is raised a series of imperishable diamond wheels or, metal rings, twenty-five in number. In the stupa there are Sariras (relics) of Buddha to the amount of ten pecks.

A hundred paces or so to the south-west of the great stupa there is a figure, carved out of white stone, eighteen feet high; it stands with its face to the north. Very many spiritual portents are exhibited here. Frequently, there are persons who see the statue at night going round the great stupa. A hundred li or so to the north-east of the Sangharama of Kanishka, we cross a great river and come to the town of Po-sih-kie-lo-fa-ti (Pushkalavati). To the east of the town there is a stupa built by Asoka. Here the four past Buddhas have preached the Law.

Four or five li to the north of the town is a Sangharama, within which is a stupa, about 200 feet high, erected by Asoka; it was here that Sakya Buddha when formerly living as a Bodhisattva, delighted in performing deeds of charity. For a thousand births he was born as king of this country, and here, during these births, he plucked out his eyes and gave them in charity. Of all these acts there are innumerable holy traces. The Master visited these sacred spots in succession, and offered worship.

From this place he arrived at the town of U-to-kia-han-cha (Utakhanda). Travelling northwards from this town and passing over mountains and valleys, after going 600 li or so, he entered the country of U-chang-na (Udyana). On either side of the river Su-po-sa-tu (Subhavastu) there were formerly 1400 Sangharamas, with some 18,000 priests; but now all is desert and depopulated. The priests who observe the rules and follow the traditions of religion, belong to five schools, the Dharmagupta, the Mahisasaka, the Kasyapiya, the Sarvastivada, and the Mahasanghika. The king mostly lives in the town of Mung-kie-li (Mankalai) which is well populated and prosperous. To the east of the town four or five li, is a great stupa celebrated for its miraculous capabilities.

To the north-east of the town 250 li, entering on a great mountain region, we come to the fountain of the Naga Apo-lo-lo, which in fact is the upper source of the river Suvastu. It flows to the south-west. Thirty li or so south-west of the Naga fountain on the north side of the river on the top of a large flat stone, there is a trace of Buddha's foot. This trace appears long or short, according to the merit or prayers of the men who inspect it. In former days when Buddha subdued the naga Apalala, he came to this spot and left this trace as a fortunate indication.

Following down the stream thirty li or so, we come to the stone of Tathagata on which he washed his robe. The marks of the flowery tracery of the kashaya garment are plainly seen. To the south of the town 400 li or so, we come to Mount Hi-lo. Here Tathagata in former days, hearing a half-gatha, in gratitude to the Yaksha, threw his body down from a tree for his use.

Fifty li to the west of the town of Mankalai, after crossiug a great river, we came to a stupa called Lu-hi-ta-ka (Rohitaka, i.e., red); it is about ten chang high (100 feet), and was built by Asoka. Here Tathagata in former days being born as Maitribala raja, cut his body with a knife in charity to five Yakshas. To the north-east of the city thirty li or so, we come to a stone stupa called "The Miraculous" (Adbhuta). It is about thirty feet high. To the west of the stupa, after crossing a great river and going three or four li, we come to a Vihara, in which is a figure of Avalokitesvara

Bodhisattva, which is possessed of exceedingly august spiritual qualities.

In this valley is a large Sangharama, by the side of which is a carved wooden statue of Maitreya Bodhisattva, of a golden colour and very majestic in appearance. It is about 100 feet in height, and was made by the Arhat Madhyantika of Maitreya's body; after going there three times, the meritorious work was Finished.

Going south from the town of U-to-kia-han-cha, we cross the Sin-tu river, which is here three or four li in width. Crossing the river we come to the country of Ta-oh'a-shi-lo (Takshasila). To the north of this town, about twelve or thirteen li, there is a stupa which was built by King Asoka. It constantly emits a sacred light from its surface. In olden times when Tathagata was practising the duties of a Bodhisattva, he cut off his head in this place. He was then king of a great country, and his name was Chandraprabha. By so doing he aimed to acquire the supreme wisdom of Bodhi. By the side of the stupa is a Sangharama; in olden days Ku-mo-lo-to (Kumaralabdha) a master of the Sautrantika school, composed in this place various sastras.

From this, going about 700 li in a south-easterly direction, we pass through the kingdom of Sang-ho-po-lo (Sirhapura). After leaving the northern borders of Takshasila, and crossing the Sindhu river about 200 li to the south-east, we go through a great rocky pass. This is the spot where in olden times the Mahasattva as a Prince royal, gave up his body to feed the seven cubs of the starving Wu-t'u (tiger cat). The land here was originally dyed with the blood of the Royal Prince, and now it remains of the same colour, and the shrubs and trees partake of this hue.

Again going from this in a south-easterly direction 500 li or so across the mountains, we come to the country of Wu-la-shi (Urasa). Still going to the south-east, climbing precipitous passes and crossing iron bridges for 1000 li or so, we arrive at the country of Kashmir. The capital of this country on the west borders on the Great River. There are 100 religious foundations in it, and about 5000 priests. Moreover, there are four stupas of wonderful height and great magnificence: these were built by Asoka. Each of them has about one measure of the sariras of Tathagata. When the Master first arrived at the borders of this kingdom, he entered it by the stone gates, the western entrance of the kingdom. The king sent his mother and younger brother with chariots and horses to escort him. Having entered the stone gates, he visited successively the Sangharamas and offered his adorations; then coming to a temple he passed the night there. The name of the temple was U-sse-kia-lo (Hushkara). Thus they continued for several days, after which the Master gradually approached the capital; when distant from about it one li he reached the preaching-hall (Dharmasala). Then the king, with his assembled ministers and all the priests belonging to the capital, advanced to the preaching-hall, and escorted him onwards, being altogether something like a thousand men, with standards and parasols, with incense and flowers filling the roads. They stopped at Che-ye-in-to-lo (Jayendra) convent.

On the morrow the king besought him to enter his palace and receive his religious offerings; he also ordered several tens of the most distinguished priests to attend on this occasion. The repast ended, the king invited them to open the conference, and requested the Master to discuss difficult parts of the doctrine. Observing his readiness, and finding that having come from far, fired by a desire to learn, he had no original texts from whence to read—the king gave him twenty men to copy the Sacred Books and Sastras.

This country was formerly a Naga's lake. Fifty years aftar the Nirvana of Buddha, Madhyantika, a disciple of Ananda, converted the dragon-king. Quitting his lake he founded 500 Sangharamas, and invited sages and saints to come and dwell there, and receive the religious offerings of the Nagas. After this, Kanishka, king of Gandhara, in the four hundredth year from the nirvana of Tathagata, at the request of Parsvika, convoked an assembly of saintly men, who were conversant with the esoteric doctrine of the three Pitakas, and had investigated the exoteric doctrine of the five vidyas.

Thus 499 men came together, and these, with the venerable Vasumitra, composed 500. The saints and sages then assembled, and recited connectedly the three pitakas. First they composed, in ten myriad stanzas, the Upadesha-sastra, to explain the Sutra Pitaka. Next in ten myriad stanzas they composed the Vinaya-vibasha-sastra, to explain the Vinaya. Next they composed in ten myriad verses, the Abhidharma-vibasha-sastra. Altogether they composed thirty myriad of verses consisting of ninety-six myriad words. The king ordered these Sastras to be engraved on sheets of copper, which he enclosed in a stone chest, sealed and inscribed. Then he built a great stupa and placed the chest within it, commanding the Yaksha spirits to protect and defend it.

Thus having halted here, first and last, for two years, and having studied the Sutras and Sastras, and paid reverence to the sacred traces, the Master took his leave. Proceeding in a south-westerly direction, he crossed mountains and streams, and going 700 li, he came to the kingdom of Pun-nu-tso (Punach).

Thence going east 400 li or so, he came to Ho-lo-she-pu-lo (Rajapur). From this, going south-east down the mountains and crossing the river, after 700 li or so, he came to the kingdom of Tseh-kia (Takka).

Going from the country of Rajapuri, after two days they crossed the Chandrabhaga river, and came to the town of Che-ye-pu-lo (Jayapura), where they lodged for the night in a temple belonging to the heretics. This temple was outside the western gate of the town, and at this time contained about twenty disciples. The day after the morrow, they reached the town of Che-kia-lo (Sakala). In this town is a Sangharama with about a hundred priests. In the old days Vasubandhu Bodhisattva here composed the treatise Shing-i-tai-lun. By the side of the convent is a stupa, about 200 feet high.

Robbers Attack

Leaving this place he arrived at a great forest of Po-lo-che (Palasas), trees just to the eastward of the town of Na-lo-sang-ho (Narasimha). In the forest he encountered a band of fifty robbers. These men, having taken the clothes and goods of the Master and his companions, without leaving anything, then pursued them, sword in hand, till they reached a dried-up marsh, ready to slay them all. This marsh was covered with a tangled mass of prickly, matted creepers. The Master and the Sramaneras who accompanied him, looking eagerly through the interstices of the wood, saw on the southern side of the marsh a water-course wide and deep enough to contain several men. Having privately told the Master of this, he and they together passed through it, and coming out on the south-east side, they ran as quickly as they could for two or three li, when they met a Brahmin at work ploughing the land.

When they told this man about the robbers he was very much frightened, and immediately unyoked his oxen, and went with the Master to the village. Here he assembled the people by blowing the conch and beating of drums. When he had got about eighty men, each taking what weapon he could, they went in haste to the place where the robbers were. The robbers seeing the crowd of men, quickly dispersed and entered the forest.

And now while the men were weeping and lamenting, the Master alone was smiling. On this his companions asked him, and said: "The robbers have thoroughly despoiled us of our travelling robes and goods; and we have only just escaped with our lives. Being beggared thus, our difficulties and dangers are at their extremest point. When we reflect and think of the circumstances that occurred in the forest, we cannot but experience the greatest sorrow. How is it that the Master alone does not share in our sorrow, but is able to keep a smile on his face?" Answering, he said: "The greatest gift which living creatures possess, is life. If life is safe, what need we care about the rest?"

On the morrow he arrived at the eastern frontiers of the kingdom of Tcheka (Takka) and entered a great city (probably Lahore). On the west of the city on the north side of the road, there is a great forest of An-lo (Amra) trees; in this forest dwelt a Brahmin of 700 years (sic) who in appearance was but about thirty years old. His form and complexion were perfect. His understanding was of a divine character; his reasoning powers, superabundant. He had thoroughly investigated the chung and pih sastras (the Pranyamula and Satasastra); he was eminent in the study of the Vedas, and other books. He had two followers, each of whom was aged 100 years or more. When he had an interview with the Master he was overjoyed in affording him hospitality; and when he heard of the adventure with the robbers he sent one of his servants to tell the people of the town, who were Buddhists, to prepare food for the Master. In this town there were several thousand dwellings; a few of the people were believers in Buddha, but most of them were sacrificing heretics.

A messenger, therefore, from the Brahmin, came to the neighbouring city, and announced as follows: "The priest from China has come to our neighbourhood, and robbers have spoiled him of his clothes and effects; now then let all who hear me understand that this is an opportunity for adding to the amount of their religious merit."

In consequence of this address, all hostile religious feeling was laid aside, and some 300 persons of distinction came together and brought a length of cotton stuff and provisions for eating and drinking, which they respectfully presented to him.

The Master, after repeating certain forms of prayer, proceeded to declare the doctrine of rewards and punishments, as a consequence of present conduct. In consequence of this the men arrived at a knowledge of truth and gave up their erroneous doctrine and returned to right reason. Here he remained for one month studying the Sutras, the Peh-lun (Satasastra), the Kwang-peh-lun (Sata-sastra Vaipulyam).

From this place going 500 li to the east, he arrived at the kingdom of Chi-na-po-tai (Chinapati), and took up his quarters in the convent called Tu-she-sa-na. Here there was a renowned priest named Pi-ni-to-poh-la-po (Vinitaprabha). He was of a good reputation and had mastered the three pitakas. He had himself composed a commentary on the Panchaskanda Sastra, and on the Vidyamatrasiddhi-Tridasasastra. On this account the Master remained there fourteen months. He studied the Abhidharma Sastra, the Abhidharma-prakarana-sasana Sastra, the Nyayadvara-taraka Sastra, and others.

To the south-east of the capital, after going 50 li or so, we arrive at the Tamasavana Sangharama; in this convent there are some 300 priests, who belong to the Sarvastivadina school.

From this, going north-east 140 or 150 li, we come to the kingdom of Jalandhara. On entering this country the pilgrim went to the Nagaradhana convent, where there was an eminent priest called Chandravarma, who was thoroughly acquainted with the Tripitaka. On this account he rested here four months, studying the Prakarana-pada-vibhasa Sastra. From this, going north-east after traversing precipitous mountain passes and going 700 li or so, he arrived at the kingdom of Kuluta. From Kuluta, going about 700 li south across a mountain range and over a river, we arrive at the kingdom of She-to-tu-lu (Satadru). Going south-west from this kingdom about 800 li, we come to the kingdom of Po-li-ye-ta-lo (Paryatra).

Reaches Mathura

From this, going east about 500 li, we come to the kingdom of Mo-t'u-lo (Mathura). There are stupas containing relics of the bodies of Sakya Tathagata and his holy disciples still existing in this place: of Sariputra, of Maudgalyayana, of Purnamaitreyani-putra, of Upali, of Ananda, of Rahula, and of Manjusri. Every year, on religious festival days, priests and disciples assemble at these several stupas, according to their school, and offer religious worship and offerings. The followers of the Abhidharma offer to Sariputra; the Quietists—those who practise meditation—offer to Maudgalyayana; the students of the Sutras offer to Purnamaitreyaniputra; the followers of the Vinaya offer to Upali; the Bhikshunis offer to Ananda; the Sramaneras offer to Rahula; the followers of the Great Vehicle offer to the Bodhisattvas.

Five or six li to the east of the city there is a mountain Sangharama which was founded by the venerable Upagupta; there are herein relics of his nails and hair. Going north-east from this about 500 li, we come to Sa-ta-ni-shi-fa-lo (Sthanesvara). Still going east about 400 li we come to Lu-le-na (Srughna?). On the east this kingdom borders on the river Ganges, on the north it abuts on a great mountain range, through its centre flows the river Yamuna.

Going about 800 li to the east of this river we come to the source of the river Ganges. This head-stream is about three or four li in width; it flows south-east, and where it enters the sea it is about ten li in width. Its waters are sweet and soft to the taste, and the stream carries with it sands of extreme fineness. The ordinary books of the country speak of it as the "Blessed River;" those who bathe in it are cleansed from sin; those who drink its waters, or even rinse their mouth therefrom, escape from all dangers and calamities, and when they die forthwith are born in heaven, and enjoy happiness. There was a renowned priest in this kingdom named Jayagupta, who had well studied the Tripitaka. The Master therefore remained here one winter and half the spring season, and heard him explain the Vibhasa according to the school of the Sautrantikas.

After this he crossed to the eastern bank of the river and came to the kingdom of Matipura. The king of this country is of the caste of Sudras. There are some ten Sangharamas and about eight hundred priests here. They study the Little Vehicle, according to the school of the Sarvastivadins. To the south of the capital four or five li, there is a little Sangharama with about fifty priests in it; it was here that Gunaprabha of old composed the Pin-chin and other Sastras, amounting to about one hundred in all.

Three or four li to the south of the Sangharama of Gunaprabha, there is a Sangharama with about two hundred priests, who also study the Little Vehicle. It was here the Doctor of Sastras called Sanghabhadra ended the years of his life. After Sanghabhadra's death they erected to his memory a stupa in an Amra grove, that still remains; by the side of this grove there is a stupa which contains the relics of Vimalamitra, a Doctor of Sastras.

In this kingdom there was an eminent priest called Mitrasena, ninety years of age. He was a disciple of Gunaprabha and deeply versed in the Tripitakas. The Master stopped with him half the spring and the summer following, studying the Tattvasatya Sastra, the Abhidharma-jnana-prasthana Sastra, and others.

Proceeding northward from this 300 li or so, we come to the country of Po-lo-hi-mo-pu-lo (Brahmapura); again south-east of this, going 400 li or so, we come to the kingdom of Hi-chi-ta-lo (Ahikshatra). Again, going south 200 li or so, we cross the Ganges, and then going south-west we arrive at the country of Pi-lo-na-na. (Virasana).

Again, going east 200 li or so, we come to the country of Kie-pi-tha (Kapitha).

About twenty li to the east of the city there is a Sangharama, within the court of which there are three ladders composed of precious substances; they are placed side by side in a direction from south to north and face the east. It was down one of these that Buddha of old descended from the Trayastrimshas heaven, and returned to Jambudvipa after preaching for the sake of his queen-mother Maya. The middle ladder is of gold, the one on the left of crystal, the one on the right of silver.

At this time 100,000 devas and the great Bodhisattvas followed him in his descent. Several centuries ago these ladders existed in their integrity, but at the present time they have disappeared. Kings who came afterwards, from a principle of affection and respect, have reconstructed the foundations of these ladders with stone and brick, ornamented with various gems, to a height of about seventy feet, and over this they have erected a vihara, in which is placed a figure of Buddha in stone.

From this, going north-west 200 li, we come to Kie-jo-kio-she-kwo (Kanauj). This kingdom is four thousand li in circuit; the capital borders on the Ganges on the West; it is about twenty li in length, and five or six li across. There are about 100 Sangaramas and 10,000 priests. The priests study the Great and Small Vehicles promis-cuously.

In Harsha's Kingdom

The king is a Bais Rajput. His name is Harsha-vardhana; his father's name was Prabhakara-vardhana; his senior brother was called Rajya-vardhana. Harsha-vardhana, the present king, is virtuous and patriotic; all people celebrate his praises in songs.

At the time when Rajya-vardhana was on the throne the king of Karna-survarna, in Eastern India, whose name was Sasanka-raja, hating the superior military talents of this king, made a plot and murdered him. Then the great minister Bhani and the subordinate officers, afflicted to see the people without a ruler, agreed to place on the throne his younger brother Siladitya Harsha-vardhana. He was soon able to avenge the injuries received by his brother, and to make himself master of India. His renown was spread abroad everywhere, and all his subjects reverenced his virtues. The empire having gained rest, then the people were at peace.

On this he put an end to warlike expeditions, and began to store up in the magazines, the lances and swords. He gave himself up to religious duties; he prohibited the slaughter of any living creature. He himself set the example, and ordered all his people to abstain from flesh meat, and he founded Sangharamas wherever there were sacred traces of religion.

Yearly during three or seven days—or, perhaps, during thee seven-days, i.e, three weeks—he provided food for the whole body of priests. Every fifth year he convoked a grand assembly of deliverance (Maha-moksha-parishad), and distributed the stores of his treasuries in charity. To describe all his conduct would be but to tell again the deeds of Sudana, the hero of Wissantara Jataka. To the north-west of the city is a stupa about 200 feet high. Six or seven li to the south-east, south of the river Ganges, is a stupa also about 200 feet high. Both were built by Asoka-raja, in places where Buddha had formerly preached the Law.

When the Master entered the kingdom, he went to the temple called Bhadra Vihara. He stopped there three months, and under the direction of Viryasena, a doctor of the three Pitakas, he read the Vibhasha of Buddhadasa, which is called Varmavibhasha-vyakarana.

4

Visiting Buddha Places

From this, going 600 li or so to the south-east and crossing the Ganges, on the south of the river we come to the kingdom of O-yu-to (Ayodhya). There are here about one hundred temples with several thousand priests, who study both the Small and the Great Vehicle.

In the capital city is an old Sangharama. Here the Bodhisattva Vasubandhu composed his treatises on the Great and Little Vehicle, and preached for the good of the community. North-west of the city four or five li, and by the side of the river, is a great Sangharama, in which is a stupa about 200 feet high. This was built by Asoka raja on the spot where Buddha in old days delivered the Law for three months.

To the south-west of the city five or six li, is an old Sangharama; this is the place where Asanga Bodhisattva explained the Law. The Bodhisattva, during the night, ascended to the Tusita heaven, and received from Maitreya Bodhisattva the Yoga Sastra, the Alamkara-Mahayana Sastra, and the Madhyanta-vibhanga Sastra. The next day he descended from the heaven, and declared the Law for the sake of the community.

Asanga, who is also called Wu-cho, was a man of Gandhara. He was born in the middle of the thousand years following the nirvana of Buddha, and became a disciple in the school of the Mahisasakas. Afterwards he joined the school of the Great Vehicle. His brother, Vasubandhu, became a disciple in the school of the Sarvastivadins, but afterwards joined the Great Vehicle. Asanga possessed vast ability in composition, and wrote many sastras, in explanation of, and comment on, the Great Vehicle. He was the principal composer of sastras in India. For example, he wrote the Mahayana-samparigraha Sastra, the Prakaranaryavacha-sastra-karika, the Abhidharma Sastra, the Vidyamatra Sastra, the Kosha Sastra, and others.

Caught to be Sacrificed

The Master left the kingdom of Ayodhya, having paid reverence to the sacred traces, and following the course of the river Ganges, proceeded eastward, being on board a vessel with about eighty other fellow-passengers. He wished to reach the kingdom of 'O-ye-mu-khi (Hayamukha). After going about a hundred li, both banks of the river were shrouded by the thick foliage of an Asoka forest, and amid these trees on either bank were concealed some ten pirate boats. Then these boats, propelled by oars, all at once burst forth into the midstream. Some of those in the ship, terrified at the sight, cast themselves into the river, while the pirates, taking the ship in tow, brought it to the bank. They then ordered the men to take off their clothes, and searched them in quest of jewels and precious stones.

Now these pirates pay worship to Durga a spirit of heaven, and every year during the autumn, they look out for a man of good form and comely features, whom they kill, and offer his flesh and blood in sacrifice to their divinity, to procure good fortune. Seeing that the Master of the Law was suitable for their purpose, both in respect of his distinguished bearing and his bodily strength and appearance, they exchanged joyful glances, and said, "We were letting the season for sacrificing to our god pass by, because we could not find a suitable person for it, but now this Sraman is of noble form and pleasing features—let us kill him as a sacrifice, and we shall gain certain good fortune."

The Master replied, "If this poor and defiled body of mine is indeed suitable for the purpose of the sacrifice you propose, I, in truth, dare not grudge the offering, but as my intention in coming from a distance was to pay reverence to the image of Bodhi and the Gridhrakuta mountain, and to inquire as to the character of the sacred books and the Law, and as this purpose has not yet been accomplished, if you, my noble benefactors kill this body of mine, I fear it will bring you misfortune."

Moreover, his fellow-passengers all, with one voice, asked them to spare him, and some even prayed to be allowed to die in his stead; but the pirates would not consent. Then the captain of the gang despatched some men with water to arrange the ground, and to erect in the midst of the flowering grove an altar besmeared with mud. He then commanded two of the company to take their drawn knives and to bind the Master upon the altar. And now, **when they were about to use their knives for the purpose of sacrificing him, the Master showed no sign of fear** in his face, insomuch that all the pirates were moved to astonishment.

Then the Master, with an undivided mind bent on the courts of Tusita heaven, thought on the Bodhisattva Maitreya, and earnestly prayed to be born in that place, that he might pay reverence and his religious offerings to the Bodhisattva, and receive from him the Yogachariya-bhumi Sastra, and listen to the sound of the excellent Law. Then having perfected himself throughout in wisdom, "let me return and be born here below, that I may instruct and convert these men, and cause them to practise themselves in doing good and to give up their evil deeds, and thus by diffusing, far and wide, the benefits of religion, to give rest to all the world."

And now, while his fellow-passengers gave way to cries and tears, suddenly a black tempest arose from the four quarters of heaven, smiting down the trees; clouds of sand flew on every side; and the lashing waves of the river tossed the boats to and fro. The robbers and their company, greatly terrified, asked the companions of the Master, "Whence comes this Sraman?—what is his name and title?" and so on. They, answering, said: "He comes from the country of China—he is the renowned person who is in search of the Law; if you, my masters, kill him, your guilt will be immeasurable; look now and see the winds and waves—these are but indications of the anger of the spirits of heaven; haste then to repent!"

The pirates then, filled with fear, urged each other to repentance and confession of their fault; then with bowed heads they made profound obeisance. And now one of the robbers accidentally touched the Master with his hand, he opened his eyes and said to the robber, "Has the hour come?" The robber answered: "We dare not hurt the Master! we pray you accept our repentance!" The Master then accepted their reverence and confession of faults, and then preached to them about the future punishment in Avichi of those who gave themselves up to murder, robbery, and impious sacrifices, and other evil deeds.

The robbers then bowed their heads and confessed their faults. They each encouraged one another to deeds of amendment, and collecting their various instruments of robbery together, they cast them into the river, and whatever clothes or private property they had taken, they restored these to their rightful owners, and then they took on themselves the five obligations of a lay-believer. Then the winds and the floods subsided, and the pirates were all overcome with joy, and bowed their heads in adoration.

Reaches Prayag

From this, going south-east 700 li or so, after crossing to the south side of the Ganges, on the north of the river Jumna, we come to the country of Prayag. To the south-west of the town, in a grove of Champaka flowers, there is a stupa built by Asoka. This is the spot where in old days Buddha overcame the heretics. By the side of it is a Sangharama. Here Deva Bodhisattva composed the enlarged Sata-sastra and vanquished the heretics of the Little Vehicle. To the east of the capital is the spot where the two rivers join, and to the west of this point is a level plain about fourteen or fifteen li in circuit. The ground is perfectly level and straight. From ancient days till now, royal and noble personages endowed with virtue and love, in the distribution of their charitable offerings, have all resorted to this spot for the purpose; and hence, the name of the Field of Great Beneficence has been given to it. At the present time Siladitya Harsha-vardhana, following this custom, has distributed here the accumulated wealth of five years, during a period of seventy-five days.

From this, in a south-west direction, we enter a great forest, in which we frequently encounter evil beasts and wild elephants. After going 500 li or so, we arrive at Kiau-shang-mi (Kausambi). There are about ten Sangharamas here with some 300 priests. Within the city is an old and ruined palace in which is a large vihara about sixty feet high, in which is a sandalwood figure of Buddha, surmounted by a stone canopy, made by king Udayana. South of this is a ruined dwelling, the old house of the nobleman Gosira. Not far south of the city is an old Sangharama, which was built on the garden-site of this nobleman. In it is a stupa, about 200 feet high, which was raised by Asoka. Again, south-east of this, is a double-storeyed tower, where Vasubandhu composed the Vidyamatra-siddhiSastra.

Again, to the east is an Amra grove, in which are some old foundation stones. This is where Asanga Bodhisattva composed the Prakaranaryavacha-sastra-karika. Going about 500 li from this, we come to the kingdom of Pi-so-kia (Visakha). It has about twenty Sangharamas and some 3000 priests, belonging to the Sammatiya school of the Little Vehicle. There is a tree here about seventy feet high. Here in former days Buddha, having cleaned his teeth, flung the fragments of the wood on the ground. Immediately they took root, and the umbrageous tree which grew up remains there till now. The followers of heretical views often came to destroy it, but as often as they cut it down, it grew up again as flourishing and verdant as at first.

Going north-east from this 500 li or so, we arrive at the kingdom of Shi-lo-fu-shi-ti (Sravasti). It is about 6000 li in circuit and has several hundred Sangharamas and several thousand priests, all of whom belong to the Sammatiya school. The capital of this country was where king Prasenajita dwelt when Buddha was alive. Within the city there are the old ruins of the king's palace. Not far east from this is a stupa erected on some old foundations; this was the spot where stood a great preaching hall erected by king Prasenajita for Buddha's use.

Next we see a tower; this was where stood the vihara of Prajapati Bhikshuni, the elder maternal aunt of Buddha. East of this again is a tower; this marks the spot of the ruined house of Sudatta. By the side of the house, is a great stupa; this is where the robber Angulimala gave up his evil design. Five or six li to the south of the city is the grove of Jeta, the same as "the garden of the friend of the orphans and desolate." There was formerly a Sangharama here, but now it has been overturned and destroyed. On the right and left side of the eastern gate there have been built stone pillars about seventy feet high. These were placed there by Asoka. All the rooms are completely destroyed except one little stone chamber in which there is a golden figure. This figure was made by king Prasenajita when Buddha in old days ascended to the Trayastrimsha heaven to preach for his mother's sake.

To the east of the convent about 100 paces is a great chasm; this is where Devadatta went down alive into hell after trying to poison Buddha. To the south of this, again, is a great ditch; this is the place where the Bhikshu Kukil went down alive into hell after slandering Buddha. To the south of this, about 800 paces, is the place where the Brahmin woman Chancha went down alive into hell after slandering Buddha. All these chasms are bottomless pits. To the eastward of the Sangharama about seventy paces is a vihara-Sangharama, lofty and large, in which is a sitting figure of Buddha facing the east. This is the place where in olden times Buddha disputed with all the heretics. East from this three or four li, is a stupa; this is the place where Sariputra discussed with the heretics.

KAPILAVASTU

From this, going south-east about 800 li, we come to the kingdom of Kapilavastu. This country is about 4000 li in circuit; the capital, as well as some 1000 villages, are all waste and ruined. The inner city is fifteen li round; it is completely encircled and is exceedingly strong. Within the city are some old foundations belonging to the chief palace of Suddhodana raja. Over these ruins a vihara has been built in which is a figure of the king. To the north of this, again, are some old foundations; these belong to the sleeping hall of Queen Maya. Over this site is built a vihara, in which is a figure of the queen. By the side of this is a vihara; this is where Sakya Bodhisattva descended as a spirit, into the womb of his mother. In it is placed a picture of Bodhisattva descending to be born. To the north-east of this is a stupa; this is the spot where the Rishi Asita took the horoscope of the prince royal.

On the left and right of the city is the place where the royal prince contended in athletic sports with the Sakyas. Again there is the place where the royal prince left the city on horseback, i.e., when he gave up his secular life. And there are the places where he turned back in his chariot, having first seen outside the four gates, the old man, the sick man, the dead man, and the Sraman, who had given up the world from disgust. To the east of the old city is a brick stupa about 100 feet high. After the nirvana of Tathagata the old king of this country, having obtained a share of the relics (Sariras), returned home and built this stupa. It constantly emits rays of glory. Close by the side of this stupa is a Sangh-arama of which a Sramanera is the sub-director (Karmadana).

Going about 100 li to the eastward of the Sramanera convent through a great forest, we find a stupa built by Asoka. It was here that the prince royal, having passed through the city, and reaching this spot, took off his ornaments and clothes and the hair jewel of his sacred tiara, and gave them to Chandaka. Both here and where he cut off his hair there are commemorative towers.

Having left the forest we come to the kingdom of Ku-shi-na-k'ie-lo (Kushinagar). This place is altogether desert and waste. Within the city at the north-east angle is a stupa built by Asoka on the site of the old house of Chunda. In the house is a well which was dug when he was about to make his religious offering. The water of this well is still sweet and clear.

Three or four li to the north-west of the town we cross the O-shi-to-fa-tai (Ajitavati) river. Not far from the bank of the river we come to a Sala grove. This tree resembles the Ho, only its bark is a greenish-blue, and its leaves white, and very shining and lustrous. **There are four trees in pairs, of equal height; this is the place where Buddha died.** There is a great vihara here, built of bricks, within which is a figure of the nirvana of Tathagata; his head is towards the north, and his appearance is as if he were asleep. By the side of the vihara is a stupa about 200 feet high, constructed by Asoka raja. There is, moreover, a stone column standing here, which records the circumstances of the nirvana of Buddha, but does not state the year or the month. The current tradition relates that Buddha lived in the world eighty years, and that he entered nirvana on the 15th day of the latter half of the month Vaisakha, which corresponds with the 15th day of the second month with us. The school of the Sarvastivadins again say that Buddha entered nirvana during the second half of the month Kartika. This would correspond with the 8th day of the ninth month with us. Some say that 1200 years have passed since the nirvana; others, 1500 years; others, more than 900 years, but not yet the full period of 1000 years.

Benares

Again, passing 500 li or so through a great forest, we come to the kingdom of Po-lo-ni-sse (Benaras). This kingdom is about 4000 li in circuit. The capital borders, on the west, on the river Ganges; it is about ten li in length, and five or six li in breadth. There are about thirty Sangharamas, and 2000 priests who study the teaching of the Sarvastivadins, belonging to the Little Vehicle.

Crossing the Po-lo-ni-sse (Varuna) river and going north-east ten li or so, we come to the Sangharama of the "Stag-desert" (Deer Park). The lofty turrets of the convent mingle with the clouds, and the long galleries unite at the four corners of the building. There are about 1500 priests here, who study the Little Vehicle according to the Sammatiya school. Within the great court is a vihara 100 feet high; there are stone steps, and brick niches arranged in regular order round the storeys of the building, in each niche is a gilded figure of Buddha. Within the great hall is a figure of Buddha in calamine stone, of the actual size of Tathagata's body; he is represented as turning the Wheel of the Law.

To the south-east of the vihara is a stone stupa, erected by Asoka, about 100 feet high; in front of it is a stone column about 70 feet high. This is the place where Buddha first began to preach. To the west of the Sangharama is the washing tank of Tathagata, and where he cleansed his begging dish and washed his clothes. These tanks are protected by Nagas, so that no one may defile the water.

VAISALI

From this, following the course of the Ganges for about 300 li eastwards, we arrive at the kingdom of Chen-chu (Ghazipur). From this, going north-east and crossing the Ganges, after 140 or 150 li, we come to the kingdom of Vaisali. This kingdom is about 5000 li in circuit; the soil is loamy and richly watered; it produces many Amra and Mocha fruit-trees. The capital town is waste and in ruins; its old foundations are sixty or seventy li in circuit; the inhabitants are very few in number.

Five or six li to the north-west of the royal precincts is a Sangharama, by the side of which is a stupa; this is the place where in old times Buddha recited the Vimala-kirti Sutra. Again, three or four li to the north-east of this is a stupa; this is the site of the ruined house of Vimala-kirti; this house is the scene of many strange spiritual porents. By the side of this is the old dwelling of Ratnakara and of the Lady Amradarika (Amrapali). Next, about three or four li to the north, there is a stupa; this is where Buddha stopped when about to proceed to the kingdom of Kusinara to attain nirvana, surrounded by Devas and men. To the west, again, is the place where Buddha turned round to behold Vaisali for the very last time. Again, to the south, is the place where the Lady Amradarika gave the garden in charity to Buddha. Again, there is the place where Buddha consented to attain nirvana, in accordance with the request of Mara raja.

Leaving the southern borders of Vaisali and following the Ganges river for 100 li or so, we came to the town of Svetapura, where the Master obtained the Sutra called Bodhisattva-pitaka. Again, going south and crossing the Ganges river, we come to the kingdom of Magadha. This kingdom is about 5000 li in circuit. The population is learned and highly virtuous. There are about fifty Sangharamas and ten thousand priests, mostly attached to the Great Vehicle.

Pataliputra

To the south of the river there is an old town about seventy li in circuit. Although it is waste and desolate, the parapets of the walls still remain. In old days, when men's lives were of immeasurable length, then this town was called Kusumapura; because the king's palace had so many flowers, it was so called. Afterwards, when men's lives dwindled down to a few thousand years, then it was called Pataliputrapura after the Patali tree the trumpet flower tree.

One hundred years after the nirvana there was a king called Asoka, the great grandson of Bimbisara; he transferred his court from Rajagriha to this place. Since then many generations have passed, and now nothing but the old foundations remain, and of several hundred convents only two or three survive. To the north of the old palace, bordering on the river Ganges, is a little town; this town has about 1000 houses; to the north of the palace there is a stone pillar several tens of feet high; this is the place where Asoka made the hell place of torture. The Master remained in the little city seven days, and paid worship to the sacred traces.

Again, there is a vihara in which is a stone on which Tathagata walked; on the stone is an impression of the feet of Buddha; in length a foot and eight inches, in breadth six inches. Under either foot is the sign of the 1000-spoked wheel, and on each of the ten toes is the mark of the swastika, with figures of flowers, vases, fishes, etc., all of which sparkle with light. These are the traces left on a great square stone upon which Buddha stood, when, after leaving Vaisali, he reached this spot, being about to attain nirvana; he was on the southern side of the river, and addressed Ananda thus, as he stood: "This is the very last time that I shall gaze at a distance upon the Vajrasana and Rajagriha," and the traces of his feet on this stone remained. To the south-east of the old city are the ruins of the Kukkutarama convent, which was built by Asoka. It was here he convoked the 1000 priests and supplied them with the four kinds of religious offerings. The Master paid reverence to all these sacred traces during seven days, visiting them severally.

At Bodhi Tree

From this, again, proceeding southwards 100 li or so, we come to the Bodhi tree. The tree is protected by high and very solid brick wall; the wall stretching east and west is long, but narrower from north to south. The principal gate faces the east looking towards the river Ni-len-shan (Nairanjana). The southern gate borders on a great flower-tank. The west a mountain side protects. The north gate leads into the great Sangharama. Within this on every side are the sacred traces of religion, viharas, stupas, and so on, all of which kings and great ministers and rich nobles have constructed from a principle of reverence, and for the perpetual memory of their religion.

In the centre of the whole enclosure is the Diamond throne, which was perfected at the beginning of the Bhadra

Kalpa, and rose up from the ground when the world was formed. It is the very central point of the universe, and goes down to the golden wheel, from whence it rises upwards to the earth's surface. It is perfected of diamond, and is about 100 paces round. In using the word diamond we mean that it is firm and indestructible, and able to resist all things. If it were not for its support the earth could not remain.

After the nirvana of Buddha the kings of the different countries agreed to define the limits of this sacred enclosure towards the north and south from the point of the two images of Kwan-tsze-tsai Bodhisattva, which are seated looking towards the east. According to tradition, when these images of the Bodhisattva become invisible, then the Law of Buddha will perish. The southern image has already been swallowed up as far as the breast. The Bodhi tree is the same as the Pippala tree (Ficus religiosa).

While Buddha was in the world the height of the tree was several hundred feet; but as wicked kings have continually cut it down and destroyed it, the tree is now only about fifty feet high. As Buddha, while sitting beneath this tree, reached perfect wisdom, Anuttara Bodhi, it is therefore called the Bodhi Tree. The bark is of a yellowish white colour, and its leaves of a shining green; it retains its leaves through the autumn and winter; only, when the day of Buddha's nirvana comes, the leaves all fall off, but when the day has passed, they all grow again. Every year on this day the kings of the countries, the ministers and magistrates, assemble beneath the tree, and pour milk on its roots and light lamps and scatter flowers, then collecting the leaves, they retire.

The Master when he came to worship the Bodhi Tree and the figure of Tathagata at the time of his reaching perfect wisdom, made afterwards by the interposition of Maitreya Bodhisattva, gazed on these objects with the most sincere devotion, he cast himself down with his face to the ground in worship, and with much grief and many tears in his self-affliction, he sighed, and said: "At the time when Buddha perfected himself in wisdom, I know not in what condition I was, in the troublous whirl of birth and death; but now, in this latter time of image worship having come to this spot and reflecting on the depth and weight of the body of my evil deeds, I am grieved at heart, and my eyes filled with tears."

At this time there happened to come to the spot, from different quarters, a body of priests who had just broken up from their religious retreat, numbering several thousand men; these persons, when they beheld the Master were all moved to pity and sorrow. For a yojana around this spot the space is full of sacred traces. The Master therefore remained here for eight or nine days to pay his worship at each spot successively.

NALANDA

On the tenth day he went to the Nalanda temple; the congregation there had selected four of their number, of distinguished position, to go and meet him; journeying in their company about seven yojanas he reached the farm-house belonging to the temple. It was in the village, where this house stands, that the honourable Maudgalyayana was born.

After this he went to the college of Baladitya-raja and took up his residence in the dwelling of Buddhabhadra, having four storeys, who entertained him for seven days. After this he went to reside in a dwelling to the north of the abode of Dharmapala Bodhisattva, where he was provided with every sort of charitable offering. Each day he received 120 Jambiras, 20 Pin-long-tseu (puga, areca nut), 20 Tau-k'au (nutmegs), an ounce of Camphor, and a ching (peck) of Mahasali rice. This rice is as large as the black bean, and when cooked, is aromatic and shining, like no other rice at all. It grows only in Magadha, and nowhere else. It is offered only to the king or to religious persons of great distinction; and hence the name kung-ta-jin-mai (i.e., rice offered to the great householder).

Every month he was presented with three measures of oil, and daily a supply of butter and other things according to his need. An Upasaka and a Brahmin, relieved from all religious duties, accompanied him with a riding elephant. In the Nalanda convent the abbot entertains a myriad priests after this fashion, for besides the Master there were men from every quarter; and where in all their wanderings have they met with such courteous treatment as this?

The Nalanda monastery is the same as the "charity without intermission" monastery. The place was originally the garden of the lord Shreshtin Amra (or, Amara). Five hundred merchants bought it for ten lacs of gold pieces, and presented it to Buddha. Here Buddha preached the law for three months, and most of the merchants obtained the fruit of Arhatship, in consequence. After the nirvana of Buddha an old king of this country called Sakraditya, from a principle of loving obedience to Buddha, built this convent. After his decease his son Buddhagupta-raja seized the throne, and continued the vast undertaking; he built, towards the south, another Sangharama. Then his son Tathagata-raja built a Sangharama to the eastward.

Next, his son or, direct descendant Baladitya built a Sangharama to the north-east. Afterwards the king, seeing some priests who mime from the country of China to receive his religious offerings, was filled with gladness, and he gave up his royal estate and became a recluse. His son Vajra succeeded and built another Sangharama to the north. After him a king of mid-India built by the side of this another Sangharama. Thus six kings in connected succession added to these structures.

Moreover, the whole establishment is surrounded by a brick wall, which encloses the entire convent from without. One gate opens into the great college, from which are separated eight other halls, standing in the middle of the Sangharama. The richly adorned towers, and the fairy-like turrets, like pointed hill-tops, are congregated together. All the outside courts, in which are the priests' chambers, are of four stages. The stages have dragon-projections and coloured eaves, the pearl-red pillars, carved and ornamented, the richly adorned balustrades, and the roofs covered with tiles that reflect the light in a thousand shades, these things add to the beauty of the scene.

The Sangharamas of India are counted by myriads, but this is the most remarkable for grandeur and height. The priests, belonging to the convent, or strangers residing therein always reach to the number of 10,000, who all study the Great Vehicle, and also the works belonging to the eighteen and not only so, but even ordinary works, such as the Vedas and other books, the Hetuvidya, Sabdavidya, the Chikitsavidya, the works on Magic (Atharvaveda), the Samkhya; besides these they thoroughly investigate the miscellaneous works. There are 1000 men who can explain twenty collections of Sutras and Sastras; 500 who can explain thirty collections, and perhaps ten men, including the Master of the Law, who can explain fifty collections. Silabhadra alone has studied and understood the whole number. His eminent virtue and advanced age have caused him to be regarded as the chief member of the community. Within the temple they arrange every day about 100 pulpits for preaching, and the students attend these discourses without any fail, even for a minute, an inch shadow on the dial.

The king of the country respects and honours the priests, and has remitted the revenues of about 100 villages for the endowment of the convent. Two hundred householders in these villages, day by day, contribute several hundred piculs (picul = 133 lbs) of ordinary rice, and several hundred catties (catty = 160 lbs) in weight of butter and milk. Hence the students here, being so abundantly supplied, do not require to ask for the four requisites—clothes, food, bedding, medicines. This is the source of the perfection of their studies, to which they have arrived.

RAJAGRIHA

The Master having resided in the Nalanda temple for some time, then proceeded towards Rajagriha. The old city of Rajagriha is that which is called Kiu-she-kie-la-po-lo (Kusagarapura). This city is in the centre of Magadha, and in old times many rulers and kings lived in it. This land, moreover, produces some excellent scented grass (Kusa), and hence the name given to the city. On the four sides it is entirely shut in by lofty and steep mountains, as if they had been cut out like a wall. On the west side the approach is through a narrow passage, but passing in from the north, is a large gate. The land is extended from north to south, and narrow from east to west; it is about 150 li in circuit. Within it is another little town, the foundation walls being about thirty li round. On every side are forests of the Kanaka tree, which flower all the year round, the petals being of a golden colour.

Outside the north face of the royal precinct there is a stupa; this is the spot where Devadatta in conjunction with Ajatasatru let loose the treasure-protecting drunken elephant wishing to destroy Buddha. North-east of this is a stupa; this is the spot where Sariputra heard the Bhikshu Asvajita explain the Law, and in consequence attained the fruit of Arhatship. Not far to the north of this is a large and deep ditch; this is the place where Srigupta, obeying the words of the heretics, desired to destroy Buddha by fire concealed in the ditch, and by poisoned food.

Again, to the north-east of the great ditch, in a corner of the mountain city, is a stupa; this is the place where the great physician, Jivaka, built a preaching hall for Buddha. By the side of it is the old house of Jivaka, still visible.

GRIDHRAKUTA

Going north-east of the palace-city Kusagarapura fourteen or fifteen li, we come to the mountain called Ki-li-to-lo-kiu-to (Gridhrakuta). This mountain is a connected succession of ridges, the northern peak, rising grandly above the rest, stands up boldly by itself, and is in shape like a vulture; it also has the form of a high tower; hence its name Tower, or Peak of the Vulture. The springs are clear, the rocks singular in shape, and the trees covered with rich verdure. When Tathagata was in the world be used frequently to live here, and it was here he declared the Fa-hwa (Saddharma Pundarika), the Ra-pan-jo (Mahaprajna), and other sutras innumerable.

Going through the north gate of the mountain city one li or so, we come to the bamboo garden of Kalanda, where there is still a brick house. Here Buddha in old time often dwelt, and here he laid down the binding rules of the Vinaya. The owner of this garden was called Karanda; he had before given this garden in charity to different heretics, but after he had seen Buddha and heard the deep truths of his Law, he was sorry that he had not given the garden in charity to Tathagata.

To the east of the garden is a stupa, which was built by Ajatasatru. After the nirvana of Tathagata the different kings received a portion of his relics; Ajatasatru raja, having got his share, coming back, built a tower for the purpose of paying them religious worship. Asoka-raja, exciting his heart to religion, desired to build in every place sacred edifices, and so he opened this tower and took the relics; but he let a small portion of them remain, which, even down to the present time, on occasions, emit a brilliant light.

Going south-west from the bamboo garden five or six li, by the side of a mountain, there is another garden, of the same sort, in which is a great house (Saptaparni cave). This is where the honourable Maha Kasyapa with 999 Arhats after the nirvana of Buddha, collected together the three Pitakas. At the time of the collection there were an innumerable number of holy persons assembled together, like clouds. Kasyapa, addressing them, said: "Among those present may remain who have a personal knowledge of the three vidyas, and who possess the six supernatural powers, and have completely mastered the entire treasure of the Law of Buddha, without flaw or omission. Of the rest let each return to his place of residence. There remained, in consequence, 999 men who were Arhats, in the selected place of study.

Twenty li to the west of this place is a stupa built by Asoka-raja; this is the spot where the assembly of the Great Congregation (Mahasanghikas) was held. The many thousand priests both of those who had reached complete wisdom, and those of inferior condition, who were not admitted to the assembly of Kasyapa, all collected here, and said among themselves: "During Tathagata's lifetime, we had all one master, but now the Lord is dead, they have excluded us by their vote; why should not we also make a collection of the Dharma-pitaka, in return for the goodness of Buddha?" So they made another collection of the Sutra-pitaka, and the Vinaya-pitaka, and the Abhidharma-pitaka, and the Miscellaneous-pitaka, and the Dharani-pitaka, five pitakas in all. As in this assembly there were both ordinary persons and holy men present; it is called the convocation of the Mahasanghikas.

North-east of this three or four li we come to the town of Rajagriha; the outside walls have been destroyed, within the city there are still lofty buildings. It is about twenty li round, and has one gate. Within the palace-city towards the south-west corner there is a stupa; this is the site of the ruinous house of Jyotishka (Chang-che) the nobleman. By the side of it is the place where Rahula was received as a disciple. To the north-west of the Nalanda convent there is a great vihara in height about 200 feet, which was built by Baladitya raja. It is highly decorated and of an imposing character. In it there is an image of Buddha the same as the image under the Bodhi Tree. To the north-east of the vihara is a stupa, the site where Buddha formerly preached the law for seven days.

Again to the east about 200 paces is a copper image of Buddha about eighty feet high, housed over by a pavilion in six stages. This was the work of Purnavarma-raja in old days. Again going eastward several li there is a stupa which denotes the place where Bimbisara, with many myriads of people, went to meet and first saw Buddha, who having arrived at supreme wisdom, was directing his way towards the city of Rajagriha. Again going east thirty li or so we come to the Indrasilaguha Mountain. In front of a Sangharama on the eastern cliffs is a stupa called Hamsa.

Thus the Master having visited the sacred traces all round, and paid his reverence to them, returned to the Nalanda monastery, and requested Silabhadra, Master of the Law, to explain the Yoga Sastra, in the presence of many thousand auditors.

The Master while he stopped in the convent, heard the explanation of the Yoga Sastra, three times; the Nyaya-Anusara Sastra, once; the Hin-hiang-tui-fa-ming, once; the Hetuvidya Sastra and the Sabda-vidya and the Tsah-liang sastras, twice; the Pranyamula Sastra-tika, and the Sata Sastra, thrice. This done, he also devoted himself to the study of the Brahmin books and the work called Vyakarana on Indian letters, whose origin is from the most remote date, and whose author is unknown.

At the beginning of the Kalpa of perfection Vaivarta kalpa, Brahma first declared this book; it then comprised 100 myriads of slokas; afterwards, at the beginning of the Vaivarta-siddha Kalpa, that is, the kalpa, or period, of establishment, Ti-shih (Sakra) reduced them to ten myriad slokas. After this a Brahmin of the town Salatura in Gandhara of North India, whose name was Panini Rishi, reduced them to 8000 slokas. This is the work at present used in India.

Again, there is a Vyakarana work (mnemonic treatise) of a short kind having 1000 slokas; again, there is one of 300 slokas on the roots of letters; again, there are treatises on the two separate kinds of letter-groupings, one named Mandaka in 3000 slokas, the other called Unadi in 2500 slokas. These distinguish letter-groupings from letter-roots. Again, there is the treatise called Ashta-dhatu (Dhatu-vritti?) in 800 slokas; in this work there is a brief conjunction of letter-bases and letter-groupings. These are all the Vyakarana treatises.

The Master thoroughly investigated the language words and phrases, and by talking with those men on the subject of the "pure writings," he advanced excellently in his knowledge. Thus he penetrated, and examined completely all the collection of Buddhist books, and also studied the sacred books of the Brahmins during five years.

In the middle of an open space is a vihara in which is a sandalwood figure of the Bodhisattva Avalokitesvara; its appearance is divine and truly worshipful. There are many tens of men who for seven or fourteen days continue without food or drink, putting up their prayers and entreaties in the presence of this figure. Those whose minds are most sincere, forthwith behold the Bodhisattva with all its characteristic marks, glorious and resplendent, come forth from the sandalwood figure, and graciously speak with those men concerning the subject of their prayers. There are very many men who have thus beheld the Bodhisattva, and on this account the worshippers have increased in number.

The Master wishing to go to put up his request, bought every kind of flower, and stringing them into garlands, he went to the place of the image. Having in the greatest sincerity paid his worship and offered his praises—he fell down on his hands and knees towards the image and put up these three vows:

1st. Would that I, having finished my studies, may return in peace and quiet to my own country without accident; if so, may the flowers alight on the hands of the venerable one!

2nd. Would that, in return for the merit and wisdom I am aiming to acquire, I may be born in the Tusita courts, and be permitted there to worship Maitreya Bodhisattva; if so, may the flowers hang on both the arms of the venerable one!

3rd. The holy writings say that there is a portion of creatures born in the world, who are without "the nature of Buddha." Huen Tsang in his ignorance knows not what is his case. But if he has the nature of Buddha, and so by preparatory conduct may at last reach perfection as a Buddha, then let the flowers hang suspended from the neck of the venerable one!

Having thus spoken he flung the garlands from the distance, and they each alighted according to his vow. Having thus accomplished what he sought, he was overpowered with joy, and those who were worshipping by his side, and the guardians of the vihara, having seen what had occurred, clapped their hands and stamped their feet, as they said: "It is a miracle! hereafter, if you arrive at Perfect Wisdom, remember the history of this day, and first come to save us."

Going on gradually from this spot he came to the country of Hiranya. There are ten monasteries and about 4000 priests in this kingdom; the priests mostly study the Little Vehicle, and belong to the school of the Sarvastivadins. To the south of the capital is a stupa; here Buddha in old days preached for three months for the good of Devas and men. By the side of it are traces where the past Buddhas walked to and fro. On the western borders of this country, south of the river Ganges, is a little solitary hill. Here Buddha in old days rested in retreat for three months, and subdued the Yaksha Vakula.

From this place, following the southern bank of the Ganges in an eastward direction 300 li or so, we come to the kingdom of Champa. There are here some ten Sangharamas, with about 300 priests, who practise the Little Vehicle. Many tens of yojanas from the southern frontiers of this country, there are great mountain forests, thick and wild, embracing a space of 200 li and more. Here are many hundred wild elephants who roam in herds. Hence the elephant army of Hiranya and Champa is very numerous. Every now and again they send elephant masters to go round and catch them. In these countries they keep them for drawing carriages or, riding. Wolves, the rhinoceros, and black leopards are abundant, so men dare not go there.

From this, going eastward 400 li or so, we come to the kingdom of Ki-shu-ho-kie-lo (Kajugira). Here also he examined and reverenced the sacred traces. There are six or seven Sangharamas with about 300 priests. Going east from this and crossing the Ganges, after about 600 li we come to Pu-na-fa-tan-na, (Pundra-vardhana). Here again he paid reverence to the sacred traces. There are about twelve Sangharamas here and 3000 priests, belonging to the Small and Great Vehicle.

Twenty li or so to the west of the capital is the Po-chi-sha Sangharama. The towers and balconies are lofty and grand. There are about 700 priests. By the side of it is a stupa, built by Asoka. Here Tathagata formerly dwelt for three months preaching the Law. Going south-east from this 900 li or so, we come to the country of Kie-lo-na-su-fa-lar-na (Karnasuvarna). There are about ten Sangharamas here and 300 priests; they study the Little Vehicle belonging to the Sammatiya school. Besides these there are two Sangharamas where they do not use either butter or milk—this is the traditional teaching of Devadatta. By the side of the capital is the Sangharama called Ki-to-mo-chi (red mud: the Si-yu-ki gives Lo-to-wei-chi, Raktaviti).

Going from this south-east we come to the country of Samatata, whose frontiers border on the great sea. The climate is in consequence soft and agreeable. There are about twenty Sangharamas here, with 3000 priests. They affect the teaching of the Sthavira school. Again going from this a short distance is a Sangharama in which is a green-jade figure of Buddha, about eight feet high; its characteristic marks are beautiful and imposing. It exhales constantly of itself a delicious perfume, which fills the temple court like that of opening flowers wafted from far.

Going from this north-east along the borders of the sea, across mountains and valleys we come to the country of Oki-li-t'sa-ta-lo (Srikshetra); still going south-east, in a bay of the sea, is the country of Kamalanka (Pegu); east of this is the country of Dvarapati (Sandoway); east of this is the country of Isanapura; east of this is the country of Mahachampa (Siam); west of this is the country of Yen-mo-Io (Yamaraja). These six kingdoms are bordered by mountains and the deep sea. Although Huen Tsang did not enter their territory, he was yet able to gain knowledge of the customs and manners of the people. Going from this country of Samatata in a westerly direction about 900 li, we come to the kingdom of Tamralipti, which lies along a bay of the sea. There are some ten Sangharamas here, and a congregation of about 1000 priests.

At this time the Master heard that in the middle of the ocean there was a country called Simhala; it was distinguished for its learned doctors belonging to the Sthavira school, and also for those able to explain the Yoga Sastra. After a voyage of 700 yojanas, it was possible to reach that country.

On hearing about this he inquired of a priest of South India, who, in consultation, told him, as follows: 'Those who go to the Simhala country ought not to go by the sea route, during which they will have to encounter the dangers of bad winds, the Yakshas, and rolling waves; you ought rather to go from the south-east point of South India, from which it is a three days' voyage. For although in travelling you may have to scale mountains and pass through valleys, yet you are safe. Moreover, you will thus be able to visit Orissa and other countries, and observe the sacred traces.

The Master immediately set out in a south-westerly direction towards Orissa (Uda). There are here about 100 Sangharamas, and 10,000 priests or so. They study the Great Vehicle. The south-eastern frontiers of the country border on the great sea. There is a town caned Ohi-li-ta-lo (Charitra). This is a rendezvous for merchants who embark on the sea, and for others from distant places who travel here and there. At a distance of 20,000 li south, is the country of Simhala.

From this, going south-west and passing through a vast forest about 1200 li, we come to the country of Kong-u-t'o (Konyodha, Ganjam?). From this, going south-west 1400 or 1500 li through a wild forest, we come to the Kie-ling-kia country (Kalinga). There are about ten Sangharamas here, occupied by some 500 priests, who study the Law according to the Sthavira school. Going north-west from this about 1800 li, we come to Southern Kosala. The king is of the Kshatriya caste. He deeply reverences the Law of Buddha, and is well affected towards learning and the arts. There are 100 Sangharamas here, and 10,000 priests.

Not far to the south is an old Sangharama. By the side of it is a stupa built by Asoka. In old days Tathagata exhibited great spiritual changes in this place and overcame the heretics. Afterwards Nagarjuna Bodhisattva dwelt here. At that time the king of the country was named Sadvaha (So-to-p'o-lo); he highly esteemed Nagarjuna, and abundantly supplied all his wants. From this, tending southwards, he passed through a great forest, and going some 900 li south-east, he came to the kingdom of Andhra. By the side of the capital is a large Sangharama with richly ornamented beams, extensive courts, and its whole appearance venerable and majestic. Before it is a stone stupa several hundred feet high which was constructed by the Arhat Achala.

Going about 1000 li to the south of this we come to the kingdom of Dhanakataka. To the east of the capital resting against a mountain is a Sangharama called Purvasila. To the west of the capital resting against a mountain is a Sangharama called Avarasila. The Master, while in this country, met with two priests, the first named Subhuti, the second Surya; both of them eminent for explaining the Tripitaka according to the Mahasanghika school. The Master on this account remained there several months studying the Mulabhidharma and other sastras, according to the Mahasanghika school.

Going south from this through a great forest some 1500 or 1600 li, we come to the kingdom of Dravida; the chief capital of this kingdom is named Kanchipura; this was the birthplace of Dharmapala Bodhisattva. He was the son of a great minister of this kingdom. The city of Kanchipura is situated on the mouth of the southern sea of India, looking towards the kingdom of Simhala, distant from it three days' voyage.

In the interval before the Master of the Law left this kingdom, the king of Simhala died; the country was at that time suffering from famine and in a state of disorder, there were two eminent priests there called Bodhimeghesvara and Abhayadanshtra. These two with 300 other priests, coming to India, arrived at Kanchipura. They said: "The king of our country is dead; and the people are suffering from famine, without any resource for help. We heard that Jambudvipa possessed abundance of food and was at peace and settled. This, too, is the place of Buddha's birth, and full of sacred traces of his presence; for this reason we have come."

To the south of this kingdom bordering on the sea is Malayagiri, with its precipices and ravines, towering upwards and lying deep. Here is found the white sandal-scented tree, the Chandan tree. Again there is the Karpura scented tree. It is like the trine in its trunk, but leaves are different, as also its blossoms and fruit. Border of the sea is a city, and from the city, going south-east 3000 li or so, we come to the country of Simhala. The circuit of this country is about 7000 li, and its capital about forty li round.

It is thickly populated and produces an abundance of grain. The people are black, small of stature, and very impulsive—such is their character.

From Dravida he went north-west in company with about seventy priests from Simhala, and visited the sacred traces for the purpose of reverent observation. After going about 2000 li, we come to Kin-na-po-lo [Kongkanapura]. There are about 100 Sangharamas here, and 10,000 priests belonging both to the Great and Little Vehicle. By the side of the royal palace precincts is a large Sangharama with about 300 resident priests, all of them greatly reverenced for their literary talents. In this vihara is a precious head-dress of the Prince Siddhartha about two feet high; it is preserved in a richly adorned casket.

From this, going north-west, we pass through a great forest which is infested with savage animals and desert; after 2400 or 2500 li, we come to the kingdom of Maharashtra. The people of this country despise death, and highly esteem right conduct. The king is of the Kshattriya caste. He is fond of military affairs, and boasts of his arms. There are about 100 Sangharamas here, and 5000 priests, who belong to the Great and Little Vehicle promiscuously. There are also followers of the heretics who worship the Devas, and cover themselves with ashes.

From this kingdom, going north-west a thousand li or so, crossing the river Ni-mo-to (Narmada), we come to the kingdom of Po-lu-kie-chen-po (Baroch). From this, going north-west about 2000 li, we come to the country of Mo-la-p'o (Malawa). The people of this country in their manner are polished and agreeable. They exceedingly love the fine arts. There are about 100 Sanghramas in this country, with 20,000 priests who study the Small Vehicle and belong to the Sammatiya school. There are also heretics who cover themselves with ashes and worship the host of Devas. Tradition says: Sixty years before this there was a king called Siladitya, of high talent and singular learning.

From this, going north-west three days, we come to the kingdom of K'ie Ch'a. About 1000 li to the north of this we come to the kingdom of Fa-la-pi (Vallabhi). There are about 100 Sangharamas here, and 6000 priests who study the Little Vehicle, according to the Sammatiya school. From this, going north-east 1800 li, we come to the country of Kin-che-lo (Gurjara). Again, going south-east 2800 li or so, we come to the country of U-che-yen-na (Ujjayani).

From this, going west about 2000 li, we come to the country of Lang-kie-lo (Langala), which lies near the Great Sea, towards the country of the western women. From this, going north-west, we come to the country of Po-la-sse (Persia), which is not within the boundaries of India.

Going from this eastwards, we come to the country of Sin-tu (Sindh). This country produces gold, silver, calamine stone (t'au-shih), oxen, sheep, camels, red salt, white salt, black salt, etc. From this, going east 900 li or so, crossing the river to its eastern bank, we come to Mu-lo-san-po-la (Mulas- thnapura or Multan.. The people sacrifice to the gods and worship U-fa-tsun (Aditya?), that is, the Sun-God.

From this, returning again by a south-east route to Magadha, the Master arrived at the Nalanda monastery. There he paid his respects to the priest called Ching-fa-tsong, after which he heard that to the west of this place about three yojanas there was a convent called Tiladaka, where lived a renowned priest called Prajnabhadra, a native of Fo-lo-po-ti (Balapati?), who had embraced the religious life in the school of the Sarvastivadins. This man had distinguished himself by his knowledge of the three Pitakas, and of the Sabdavidya and the Hetuvidya sastras, and others.

The Master of the Law having remained here for two months, closely questioned him about matters on which he had doubts. From this he went again to the hill called Yashtivana, and stopped with a householder who was a native of Suratha and a Kshatriya by caste—his name was Jayasena, a writer of Sastras. The Master remained with him first and last for two years, and studied a treatise on the difficulties of the Vidya-matra-siddhi Sastra, the I-i-li-lun, the Shing-wu-wai-lun, the Puh-chu-ni-pan-shih-i-yin-un-lun, the chwong-yan-king-lun; and he also asked explanations of passages in the Yoga and the Hetuvidya sastras which yet caused him doubt.

When this was done he unexpectedly dreamt in the night and saw all the chambers and courts of the Nalanda monastery deserted and foul; moreover, there were nought but water buffaloes fastened in them, with no priests or followers. The Master of the Law entering through the western gate of the hall of Baladitya raja, beheld on the top of the four-storeyed pavilion a golden-coloured man, of a grave and imposing countenance, while a glorious light shone within the entire abode. His mind was overjoyed, and he wished to ascend to the top, but he found no way to do so; he then besought him to reach down and lift him up, but he replied: "I am Manjusri Bodhisattva; your karma does not yet admit of such a privilege"—and then pointing to the outside of the convent, he said: "Do you see that?" The Master looking in the direction indicated by his finger, saw a fierce fire burning without the convent, and consuming to ashes villages and towns. Then the golden figure said; "You should return soon, for after ten years Siladitya raja will be dead, and India will be laid waste and in rebellion, wicked men will slaughter one another; remember these words of mine." After he had finished, he disappeared.

5

Prepares to Return

A naked Nirgrantha disciple, whose name was Vajra, unexpectedly entered the chamber of the Master. Now the Master had heard of old time that the Nirgranthas are skilled in divining by lots. He asked this man therefore to be seated and opened out his doubts to him, questioning and saying: "Huen Tsang, a priest of China, has been here inquiring and studymg for a year and some months. He now wishes to return home, but does not know whether his way is open to do so, nor whether it is better for his good fortune to stay or to go; he is in doubt, too, about the length or shortness of his life. I pray you, good sir, cast my horoscope and see."

The Nirgrantha then took a piece of white stone and drew a figure on the ground, and after casting the lots, he replied: "It is very good for the Master to stay, all the clergy and laity in the five Indies have a profound respect for him; the time for going and successfully returning, with the respect of all, is also fortunate; but not so good as the other. As for the years of your life, you will have ten years added to your present age. But as for evidence as to the continuation of your present good fortune, there is nothing to be found out."

The Master of the Law again asked him: "My mind's purpose is to return. but having a great number of images and sacred books, I hardly know if I shall succeed in arriving with them."

The Nirgrantha said: "Do not be anxious; Siladitya raja, and Kumara-raja will themselves despatch men as escort; the Master will successfully return without accident."

The Master, in reply, said: "As to these two kings I have never yet seen them, how then can such a kindness befall me?"

The Nirgrantha said: "Kumara-raja has already sent messengers to invite you to go to him, in two or three days they should arrive. After you have seen Kumara you will also see Siladitya."

Having thus spoken he went away.

The Master forthwith making up his mind to return, paid special attention to his books and images. All the priests hearing of it, came to him in a body and begged him to remain, saying: "India is the place of Buddha's birth. The great Saint, although he has passed away, has yet left behind him many traces of his presence; what greater happiness in life than to visit, and adore, and exalt these relics? Why then do you leave these, after having come so far?"

The Master replied: "The king of the Law, i.e., Buddha, in establishing the principles of his doctrine, designed them for universal diffusion; how then can those who have received the benefit thereof, exclude those not yet enlightened. In that country of China the superior magistrates are clothed with dignity, and the Laws are everywhere respected. The prince is regarded as sacred, the ministers are faithful, parents are loving, children are obedient, virtue and justice are highly esteemed, age and uprightness is preferred in honour.

"From the time the bequeathed doctrine of Buddha penetrated to the East, they have highly venerated the

Great Vehicle; in meditation, they are placid as the shining waters; in morals, their renown is like the perfume of opening flowers; in practice, they engage the heart; their earnest vow is to obtain the fullest degree of merit.

"How then can you say that Buddha did not go to this (China) because of its insignificance?"

The priests having perceived that there was no agreement likely, besought him to go with them to Silabhadra, Master of the Law, and set forth his intention to him. Then Silabhadra, Master of the Law, addressing him, said: "Why, sir, have you come to this resolution?"

He replied: "This country is the place of Buddha's birth: it is impossible not to regard it with affection; only Huen Tsang's intention in coming hither was to inquire after the great Law for the benefit of his fellow creatures. I have visited and adored the sacred vestiges of our religion, and heard the profound exposition of the different schools. My mind has been overjoyed, and my visit here, has been of the utmost profit. I desire now to go back and translate and explain to others what I have heard, and for this reason I am unwilling to a delay my return and remain here."

Silabhadra joyfully replied: "These are thoughts worthy of a Bodhisattva; my heart anticipates your own wishes! I will give orders for your conveyance hence; and you, my friends, do not cause any trouble by delaying him."

Having said this, he retired to his room. After two days the messenger sent by Kumara-Raja of eastern India presented a letter to Silabhadra, to this effect: "Your disciple wishes to see the great priest come from China. I pray you, respected sir, to send him and so gratify this imperial thought of mine."

Silabhadra having received the letter, addressed the Master thus: "With regard to that king, his virtuous mind is fast bound and weak; within his territories the law of Buddha has not widely extended; since the time that he heard your honourable name, he has formed a deep attachment for you; perhaps you are destined to be in this period of your existence his good friend. Use your best diligence then and go."

The Master, leaving his teacher, went with the envoy, and arrived there. The king seeing him was greatly rejoiced, and met him with his great officers, and paying him reverence with much ceremony, conducted him within his palace. Every day he arranged music and banquets, with religious offerings of flowers and incense, and requested him to follow the ordinary rules of religious fast days.

Thus passed a month and more, when Siladitya-raja Harshavardhana, returning from his attack on Kongyodha, heard that the Master of the Law was residing with Kumara. Being surprised, he said: "I frequently asked him to come here before this—and he did not come, how is it that he is now living there?" Sending a messenger, therefore, he bade Kumara-raja to send the priest of China to him at once.

The king replied, "He can take my head, but he cannot take the Master of the Law yet." The messenger returning gave this answer, on which the Siladitya-raja was greatly enraged, and calling together his attendants, he said: "Kumara-raja despises me. How comes he to use such coarse language in the matter of a priest?"

Then he sent another messenger who said, in an abrupt manner: "Send the head, that I may have it immediately by my messenger who is to bring it here."

Kumara, deeply alarmed at the folly of his language, immediately ordered his army of elephants, 20,000 in number, to be equipped, and his ships, 30,000 in number. Then embarking with the Master they passed up the Ganges together in order to reach the place where Siladitya-raja was residing. Siladitya seeing him coming was overjoyed, and knowing his respect and love for the Master of the Law, he did not repeat his former threatening words.

About the first watch of the night the king arrived. There were some men who reported that on the river there were several thousand lighted torches, and that they heard the sound of beating drums. As Siladitya-raja marched, he was always accompanied by several hundred persons with golden drums, who beat one stroke for every step taken; they called these the "music-pace-drums" (tsieh-po-ku). Siladitya alone used this method, other kings were not permitted to adopt it.

On his arrival the king bowed down at the feet of the Master of the Law, then scattering flowers before him he regarded him with respect, and uttered his praises in verses innumerable; this done, he addressed the Master thus: "Your disciple invited the Master in former days to come,—why did you not comply with my request?"

Answering, he said: "Huen-Tsang came from far in search of the Law of Buddha, and for the sake of hearing the Yoga-bhumi-sastra. When your order arrived I had not finished examining this sastra, and so did not immediately come to meet the king."

The king said: "Such a man is one sent by heaven to be the Lord of the world."

Again addressing the Master of the Law, he said: "Your disciple must now return; to-morrow I will escort the Master to our palace—I trust he will not suffer from fatigue."

Thus taking leave, he departed.

On the next morning the messenger came, and the Master with Kumara went together to Siladitya's palace, on arriving near which the king with some twenty attendants came forth to meet them. Entering they sat down, when choice viands were set before them, accompanied with music and strewn flowers.

The entertainment being over, the king said: "I have heard that the Master has composed a Sastra with a view to restrain wicked doctrine—where is this work?"

The Master of the Law replied, "It is here," and then he caused the king to take it and look at it.

Having examined it the king was much pleased.

The Master of the Law and the chief servants of the king were directed severally to mount a great elephant, and to follow the king in order; moreover, there were other 300 great elephants appointed for the princes, great ministers, and chief priests of the different countries, on which they rode in double file on each side of the procession course, chanting laudatory verses as they went. The procession began at early dawn from the palace of the king. As they drew nigh the gate of the outer court of the place of assembly, each one was directed to dismount while they conducted the figure of Buddha within the hall. There they placed it on a precious throne, while the king and the Master in succession, presented it with offerings.

After five days had passed, the unbelievers of the Little Vehicle, plotted to take his life. The king hearing of it, issued this proclamation: "The seething of error obscuring the truth, is the experience of ages. The followers of false doctrine, hiding the true, deceive the people; if the world were without superior sages, how could their falsehood be discovered? The Master of the Law of China, whose spiritual power is so vast, and whose power of explanation is so grand and deep, with a view to rebut the errors of the people, has come to sojourn here, to exhibit the character of the great Law, and to rescue the foolish and the deceived. But the followers of delusion and falsehood, not knowing the way of repentance or the forsaking of error, have conceived a murderous purpose against his person; this intention must inspire everyone with resentment. If, then, anyone should hurt or touch the Master of the Law, he shall be forthwith beheaded; and whoever speaks against him, his tongue shall be cut out; but all those who desire to profit by his instruction, relying on my goodwill, need not fear this manifesto."

From this time the followers of error withdrew and disappeared.

Siladitya-raja stowed on the Master of the Law 10,000 pieces of gold, 30,000 pieces of silver, 100 garments of superior cotton, while the princes of the eighteen kingdoms each presented him with rare jewels. But all these the Master of the Law declined to accept.

The Master of the Law, having taken his books and images, on the 19th day, paid his respects to the king with a view to his departure home. The king said: "Your disciple, succeeding to the royal authority, has been lord of India for thirty years and more. I have constantly regretted the small increase to my religious merit, resulting from a want of previous good deeds. In consequence of this I have accumulated every kind of treasure and precious substance in the kingdom of Prayag, and between the banks of the two rivers, I have established a great religious convocation every five years, to attend which all the Sramans and Brahmins of the five Indies are invited, and besides these the poor and the orphans and the destitute; on this occasion during seventy-five days the great distribution of alms called the Moksha is attended to; I have completed five of these assemblies and am now about to celebrate the sixth: why does not the Master delay his departure till then, and so, by witnessing the spectacle, rejoice with us?"

The Master answered, "Bodhisattva by meritorious conduct and by wisdom prepared himself for enlightenment; the wise man having obtained the fruit of his conduct, does not forget the root of his happiness; if your Majesty does not grudge his treasure for the good of others, how can Huen Tsang grudge a short delay in his departure. I ask leave, therefore, to accompany your Majesty on your journey."

The king hearing this was delighted, and on the twenty-first day he went forward, conducting him to the kingdom of Po-lo-ye-kia (Prayag), and proceeded to the great-distribution arena.

Sometime before these preparations the king had summoned by decree, through the five Indies, the Sramans, heretics, Nirgranthas, the poor, the orphans, and the solitary bereaved, to come together to the Arena of Charity, to receive the prepared gifts. Siladitya-raja pitched his tent on the north bank of the Ganges. The king of South India, Tu-lu-po-pa-cha (Dhruva-batta or Dhruvabhata), located himself on the west of the junction of the rivers. Kumara-raja occupied the south side of the river Jumna, by the side of a flowering grove. All the recipients of bounty occupied the ground to the west of the position of Dhruvabatta raja.

On the morrow morning the military followers of Siladitya-raja Harshavardhana, and of Kumara-raja, embarked in ships, and the attendants of Dhruvabatta-raja mounted their elephants, and so, arranged in an imposing order, they proceeded to the place of the appointed assembly. The kings of the eighteen countries joined the cortege according to arrangement.

On the first day of the first period, they installed the image of Buddha within one of the thatched buildings on the field of charity. They then distributed precious articles of the first quality, and clothing of the same character, and offered exquisite meats, while they scattered flowers to the sound of music. At the close of the day they retired to their tents.

The second day they installed the image of Aditya-deva, and distributed precious things and clothing in charity, to half the amount of the previous day.

The third day they installed the image of Isvara-deva, and distributed gifts as on the day before.

On the fourth day they gave gifts to 10,000 of the religious community, arranged in a hundred ranks. Each received 100 pieces of gold, one pearl, one cotton garment, various drinks and meats, flowers and perfumes. After the distribution they retired.

The fifth arrangement was the bestowal of gifts to the Brahmins, which lasted for twenty days.

The sixth turn related to the heretics, which lasted ten days.

The next occasion was the bestowal of alms on those who came from distant spots to ask for charity; this lasted for ten days.

The eighth distribution was to the poor and the orphans and destitutes, which occupied a month.

By this time the accumulation of five years was exhausted. Except the horses, elephants, and military accoutrements which were necessary for maintaining order and protecting the royal estate, nothing remained. Besides these the king freely gave away his gems and goods, his clothing and necklaces, ear-rings, bracelets, chaplets, neck-jewel and bright head-jewel, all these he freely gave without stint.

All being given away, he begged from his sister an ordinary second-hand garment, and having put it on he paid worship to the Buddhas of the ten regions, and as he exulted with joy with his hands closed in adoration, he said: "In amassing all this wealth and treasure I ever feared that it was not safely stored in a strong place; but now having bestowed this treasure in the field of religious merit, I can safely say it is well bestowed. Oh that **I Siladitya may in all my future births ever thus religiously give in charity to mankind my stores of wealth,** and thus complete in myself the ten independent powers (dasabạlas) of a Buddha."

Now the Master of the Law requested the king to let him return home, as he desired. The king replied: "Your humble disciple, in common with yourself, desires to spread far and wide the knowledge of the bequeathed Law of Buddha; why then do you so hastily return home?"

On this he remained yet another ten days.

"I will undertake to found one hundred monasteries on the Master's behalf."

Huen-Tsang, perceiving that the kings' purpose was not to let him go, afflicted with grief, addressed them as follows: "The country of China is very far from this, and has but recently heard of the law of Buddha. Although it has received a general knowledge of the truth, yet it has not accepted it in its entirety. On this account therefore have I come to inform myself how to put an end to differences. And now having completed my aim, I remember how the learned men of my country are longing to fathom to their depth the points I have ascertained. Therefore I dare not delay a moment."

The king replied: "Your humble disciple admires and values the virtue of the Master; and I would ever look up to and serve him; but to stand in the way of the benefit of so many men would truly cause my heart to be filled with fear; I leave the Master to his choice, to go, or to stay; but I know not, if you prefer to go, by what route you propose to return; if you select the Southern Sea route then I will send official attendants to accompany you."

The Master replied: "When I left China and arrived at the western limits of the country, I reached a territory called Kau-chang; the king of this place was an enlightened man and passionately attached to the Law. When he saw me, in my search after the truth, come to his kingdom, he was filled with profound joy, and freely provided me with every necessary, praying me on my return to visit him once more; my heart is unable to forego this duty; I will therefore return by the Northern road."

The king answered, "I pray you, then, let me know what provisions you stand in need of."

The Master replied, "I require nothing."

The king said, "It is impossible to permit you to go thus."

On this the king ordered them to offer him gold coins and other things; Kumara-raja also bestowed on him every sort of valuables. But the Master would take none of them, except from Kumara-raja he accepted a cape called ho-la-li, made of coarse skin lined with soft down, which was designed to protect from rain while on the road.

Thus he took his departure. The king with a large body of attendants accompanied him for several ten lis, and then returned. On their final separation they could none of them restrain their tears and sad lamentations.

As for his books and images, the Master confided them to the military escort of a king of North India called Udhita, to be carried on horseback, but the advance being slow King Siladitya Harshavardhana afterwards attached to the escort of Udhita-raja a great elephant, with 3000 gold pieces and 10,000 silver pieces, for defraying the Master's expenses on the road.

Three days after separation the king, in company with Kumara-raja and Dhruvabatta-raja, took several hundred light horsemen and again came to accompany him for a time and to take final leave, so kindly disposed were the kings to the Master.

Then he commissioned four Ta-kwan, official guides, to accompany the escort: they call such officers Mo-ho-ta-lo (Mahataras?) The king also wrote some letters on fine white cotton stuff and sealed them with red wax, which he ordered the Ta-kwan officers to present in all the countries through which they conducted the Master, to the end that the princes of these countries might provide carriages or modes of conveyance to escort the Master even to the borders of China.

From the country of Prayag he went south-west, through a great desert waste for seven days, when he arrived at the kingdom of Kausambi To the south of the city is the place where the lord Goshira presented a garden to Buddha.

Having adored the sacred traces again, he proceeded with Udhita-raja north-west for one month and some days, passing through various countries. Once more he paid adoration to the sacred traces of the heavenly ladder, and then proceeding north-west three yojanas, he came to the capital of the country of Pi-lo-na-na (Virashana). Here he halted two months, during which time he met with two fellow students, Simhaprabha and Simhachandra, who discoursed with him on the Kosha-samprigraha Sastra, the Vidyi-matra-siddha Sastra, etc. He was met and escorted by all the people with great rejoicings.

Thus travelling on for about twenty days, they reached the country of Takshasila, where the Master again did reverence to the spot where Chandraprabha-raja gave for a thousand times his head in charity.

To the north-east of this country fifty yojanas, is the kingdom of Kashmir. The king of this country sent messengers to invite the Master of the Law to come to him, but on account of the heavily laden elephants, he was unable to go.

After a delay of seven days, he again set forward in a north-westerly direction, and after three days, reached the great river Sindhu. This river is five or six li wide. The books, images, and fellow travellers were embarked on board a boat for the passage across, but the Master of the Law crossed the stream mounted on an elephant.

He had deputed one man to accompany the boat for the purpose of looking after and protecting the books and all the different flower-seeds of India. And now when the boat was in the midstream, all at once the winds and the waters commingling, caused the waves to rise, and the boat, violently tossed, was almost swallowed up. The guardian of the books, filled with terror, fell into the water, but was finally rescued by the passengers; but there were lost fifty manuscript copies of sutras, and the flower seeds of various sorts. With these exceptions, all else they managed to save.

At this time the king of Kapisa, who formerly dwelt in the town of U-to-kia-han-ch'a (Utakhanda), hearing that the Master of the Law had come, himself went to the river-side to pay his respects and escort him. Then he said; "I have heard that the Master has lost many sacred books in the middle of the river. Did you not bring with you here from India flower-seeds and fruit?"

"I did so," he replied.

"That is the sole reason," the king said, "of the storm that damaged the boat. It has been so from days of old till now, whoever attempts to cross the river with seeds of flowers is subject to similar misfortunes,"

The Master then returned to the city with the king, and took up his abode in a temple-convent for fifty days or so. In consequence of losing his copies of the sutras, he despatched certain persons to the country of Udyana, for the purpose of copying out the Tripitaka of the Kasyapiya school.

The king of Kashmir, hearing that the Master was gradually nearing his kingdom, in spite of the distance, came in person to pay his respects, and, after some days, returned. After seven days they reached a great mountain top; this mountain is marked by its sharp pointed peaks and dangerous crags, which mount upwards in different and strange forms. Now and then there is a flat surface, and then a high sharp peak; there is no uniformity. It would be impossible to narrate the difficulties and fatigues to which they were exposed in crossing these heights. From this point they were no longer able to ride on horseback; the Master therefore advanced, supported by his staff:

In this land there are numerous snow-drifts and glaciers. If travellers do not carefully follow the steps of their guide, there is great danger of falling and perishing.

They went on thus from dawn till sunset crossing these frozen peaks. At this time the company consisted only of seven priests, twenty followers, one elephant, ten asses, and four horses.

The Master going north-east he fell in with a band of robbers; the merchants, his companions, were panic-stricken and made for the mountains; the elephants being driven about in the pursuit, were engulfed in the water and perished.

The robbers having passed by, they all proceeded slowly to the eastward, over crags and across mountain gorges, descending the heights and patiently enduring the cold. After 800 li they emerged from the T'sungling mountains and reached the kingdom of U-sha (Och).

Geting east we come to the country of Kustana (Khotan). This district is a great flat covered with sand and stones. The soil, however, is fit for the cultivation of cereals and is very productive. They manufacture carpets from wool, fine haircloth, and silken taffeta; the soil produces much white jade and dark jade. The climate is temperate, and the common people understand politeness and right principles; they esteem learning and are fond of music. They are upright in their conduct and truthful, and in these respects differ from other Tartar tribes (Hu). Their lettes resemble that of India with some slight differences. They greatly esteem the Law of Buddha.

There are 100 monasteries here and about 5000 priests.

The king of Khotan hearing that the Master was entering his territories, went forth in his own person to meet him, and the following day he conducted him on his way. The king, arriving at his capital in advance, left his son to attend the Master.

After various detours, we arrive at the borders of China. Having obtained conveyances the Master then sent back to Khotan the messengers and their horses and camels. They returned therefore, having declined to accept the recompense awarded them for their services.

Having reached Sha-chow, he forwarded a memorial to the emperor. The Emperor was then residing in his palace at Loyang. On receiving the letter he learned that Huen-Tsang was gradually approaching; he then commanded Fong-huan-ling, duke of the kingdom of Liang, of the titular rank Tso-po-she, who had been left as governor of the western capital (Si-gan-fu), to despatch proper officers to go forth and conduct the Master of the Law.

The Master, understanding that the emperor desired to question him as to his fault in leaving the country without permission, wished to avoid any delay in his arrival, and therefore pressed forward on his march with haste, and arrived by way of the canal.

The magistrates not knowing the routine of polite reception and escort, were unable to make the necessary preparations; but the news spreading fast, the people came together of their own accord in vast numbers to behold and pay their homage to the Master. The streets were so crowded that when he wished to disembark, he could not advance for the crush, and so he passed the night on the canal.

6

Last Years

Having disembarked, Huen Tsang was escorted to the western capital (Si-gan-fu), where he arrived in the spring of the year 645 A.D. On the day following, the members of the various monasteries conducted Huen Tsang, with flags and banners, to the convent called Hong-fu (extensive happiness). He here deposited the treasures he had brought from India:

1. One hundred and fifty particles of flesh sariras, of the Tathagata.

2. One golden statue of Buddha according to the pattern of the shadow left in the Dragon cave of the Pragbodhi Mountain in the kingdom of Magadha; also a glittering pedestal 3 ft. 3 in. high. This figure resembles the image of Buddha as he is turning the Wheel of the Law in the deer-park at Benaras.

3. A sandalwood figure of Buddha with a shining pedestal 3 ft. 5 in. high, after the model of the sandalwood figure made according to the likeness drawn by the desire of Udayana, king of Kausambi, when he was longing for the return of Tathagata.

4. A figure of Buddha with a shining pedestal. 2 ft. 9 in. high, after the model of the figure of Tathagata, when he descended on the jewelled ladder from the heavenly palace to the country of Kapitha.

5. A silver figure of Buddha with a translucent pedestal, 4 ft. high, after the model of Buddha delivering the Saddharma Pundarika and other sutras on the Ghridrakuta mountain, in Magadha.
6. A figure of Buddha with a translucent pedestal, 3 ft. 5 in. high, after the model of the figure of his shadow, which he left in the country of Nagarahara, in the place where he subdued the poisonous dragon.
7. A sandalwood figure of Buddha with a translucent pedestal, 1 fit. 3 in. high, after the model of a similar figure representing Buddha as he went round the city of Vaisali on his work of conversion.

He also deposited in this temple the books of the Great Vehicle, which he had brought from the West, including 224 Sutras, 192 Sastras, 15 works of the Sthavira school, including Sutras, Vinaya, and Sastras; the same number belonging to the Sammatiya school; 22 works of the same character belonging to the Mahisasaka school; 67 books of the same character belonging to the Sarvastivadin school; 17 works of the same character belonging to the Kasyapiya school; 42 works of the same character belonging to the Dharmagupta school; 36 copies of the Hetuvidya Sastra; 13 copies of the Sabdavidya Sastra; altogether 520 fasciculi comprising 657 distinct volumes, carried upon twenty horses.

After having visited the chief officers of the western capital, the Emperor being at Loyang, the Master proceeded to that town, and had an interview with the sovereign. He was received with the greatest attention in the I-lwan palace. Being seated, the Emperor asked him why he had gone from home without consulting him. He replied that he had sent three requests for permission to leave the country previous to his departure but having received no answers he was unable to restrain his desire, and accordingly-left without the desired permission.

After a lengthened conversation, Huen Tsang having declined to accept a secular life, retired to the monastery of Hong-fu in Si-gan-fu, and there began his work of translation.

At the conclusion of the year 647 A.D. he had completed the translation of the (1) Bodhisattva-pitaka Sutra, (2) Buddha-bhumi Sutra, (3) Shatmukhi-dharani, and others.

By the end of the year 648 he had completed in all fifty-eight books, including the Si-yu-ki undertaken at the Emperor's express command. In the year 649 the Emperor caused Huen Tsang to take up his residence in the Sse-'en Temple of Great Benevolence. Here he continued the work of translation until his death.

In the year 650 A.D. the Emperor T'ai-Tsung died and was succeeded by Kao-Tsung. From this time the Master of the Law devoted himself with earnest resolution to the work of translation. He rose every morning at dawn of day, and after a slight repast devoted four hours to the explanation of the Sacred Books. And being in charge of the monastery he had regard to the discipline of the resident monks.

Upwards of 100 disciples daily attended his lectures; and notwithstanding his manifold occupations, he showed the same energy in his work as he had exhibited from the first. He discoursed largely on the various systems of the schools and the distinguished Masters of the West, so that the princes and minister who came to listen to his discourses, frequently expressed their admiration and respect for his eminent talent.

In the year 652 A.D. the Master caused the pagoda Feou-to to be constructed at the southern gate of the Hong-fuh temple, in which he finally deposited his sacred books and images for safety. The total height of this structure was 180 ft. It was built after the model of the Indian stupas, and had five stages—surmounted by a cupola.

In the highest storey on the southern side, there was a chamber constructed, in which were preserved copies of the two prefaces composed by the former Emperor and the Prince Royal, to the volumes translated by Huen Tsang.

In the year 654 a deputation from the Mahabodhi Temple in Central India visited the Master and conveyed to him the assurances of the high esteem in which he was held. Huen Tsang replied, acknowledging the honour conferred upon him, and requesting that the books he had lost in crossing the Indus might be replaced by others from India.

During the years 655 A.D. and 656 A.D. the Master continued the task of translating his books; he suffered from an old malady contracted in crossing the mountains of India, but by the help of the physicians sent to him from the court he partly recovered. In the year 658 the Master returned from Loyang to the western capital, the suite of the Emperor, and took up his residence in the newly constructed temple called Si-ming. Here he remained until signs of advancing age caused him some anxiety lest he should be unable to translate the Prajna Paramita work. With the view of entering on this task he requested the Emperor's permission to retire to the Yuh-ja gem flower palace, and there in quietness to prepare for this translation.

In 659 he moved into this palace, and in 660 began the new translation. The Indian copy of the Maha-prajna-paramita Sutra consisted of 200,000 slokas; he purposed to produce an abridged translation, but was warned by a dream not to do so. The Master had procured three copies of this work in India, and he at once proceeded to collate these with a view to correct the text from which he translated. He was now sixty-five years of age, and feeling that his end was near he worked without interruption in order to finish his task before he died.

He completed his labours in the tenth month of the year Lung So (661 A.D.). The entire work of the Mahaprajna-paramita Sutra consists of 600 chapters, in 102 vols.

Having declined to undertake the translation of the Ratnakuta Sutra, he composed himself to await his end. He had now finished the translation of seventy-four distinct works, in 1335 chapters. He had, moreover, made a vast number of pictures, and written out with his own hands copies of various Sutras. When the recital of all these works was finished, he closed his eyes and lay perfectly still. Having now repeated some verses in adoration of Maitreya, he gradually sank until the day of his death, in the tenth month, 13th day, of the year 664.

He was buried in the Western capital, but in the year 669 his remains were removed by order of the Emperor to a space situated to the north of the valley of Fan-chuen, where a tower was constructed to his memory.

●●●